POLICY WITHOUT POLITICIANS

Policy Without Politicians

Bureaucratic Influence in Comparative Perspective

EDWARD C. PAGE

UNIVERSITY PRESS

OXFORD
UNIVERSITY PRESS

Great Clarendon Street, Oxford, OX2 6DP,
United Kingdom

Oxford University Press is a department of the University of Oxford.
It furthers the University's objective of excellence in research, scholarship,
and education by publishing worldwide. Oxford is a registered trade mark of
Oxford University Press in the UK and in certain other countries

© Edward C. Page 2012

The moral rights of the author have been asserted

First Edition published in 2012

Impression: 1

All rights reserved. No part of this publication may be reproduced, stored in
a retrieval system, or transmitted, in any form or by any means, without the
prior permission in writing of Oxford University Press, or as expressly permitted
by law, by licence or under terms agreed with the appropriate reprographics
rights organization. Enquiries concerning reproduction outside the scope of the
above should be sent to the Rights Department, Oxford University Press, at the
address above

You must not circulate this work in any other form
and you must impose this same condition on any acquirer

British Library Cataloguing in Publication Data

Data available

Library of Congress Cataloging in Publication Data

Data available

ISBN 978-0-19-964513-8

Printed in Great Britain by
MPG Books Group, Bodmin and King's Lynn

For Winifred Victoria Page, 1921–2007

Preface

Bureaucracy poses problems for democracy less because it creates powerful bureaucrats and more because political control over it can of necessity only be sporadic and occasional. Cases of outright bureaucratic sabotage, disobedience, or insubordination by top officials tend to be extremely rare in modern democracies, although this does not seem to have inhibited the development a whole sub-branch of the study of administration, the principal–agent approach, from using such bureaucratic recalcitrance as its founding myth. When political leaders with a democratic mandate and political support take decisions, those decisions will almost always stand even if the top officials in the department or agency are unenthusiastic about them, or even oppose them. Bureaucrats might seek to get politicians to change their minds or persuade them to do things differently, but it is generally the politicians' choice to accept or reject that advice.

The degree to which politicians intervene in the activities of the government organizations they head varies substantially. Some political leaders seek actively and frequently to use their executive leadership positions to achieve major policy change in line with party pledges only, others seek to 'micromanage' large parts of their ministries, while others are happier to let their departments or agencies run themselves as far as possible. Moreover, political leaders often have advisers or other staff to help them run their departments or agencies, and management systems that help them monitor what is going on within them. Yet however skilled and enthusiastic they are, and however elaborate their systems of command, supervision, and control, political leaders can generally intervene in the affairs of the bureaucracy for which they are responsible only on a tiny proportion of the total number of transactions that their ministry or agency carries out. There is simply not enough time to devote attention to the full range of activities carried out in most bureaucracies, and devoting attention to one area of activity usually means being forced to take less of an interest in another.

This book looks at bureaucratic involvement in in everyday policy-making, largely away from the main policy debates as they appear in party manifestos, parliament, and the media. It takes items of policy as reflected in secondary legislation (which go under a variety of names such as 'decrees', 'regulations', and 'statutory instruments') to look at this world. Such decrees tend to arouse less politician and public interest than the big laws that are passed by national legislatures. Thus we can more easily test the proposition that bureaucrats can take over when the politician is less interested in a particular policy issue: while the cat is away the mice will play. Observing bureaucrats under such conditions, we are more likely to see them at play.

While the subject of the role of bureaucracy in everyday policy-making might be an important one, and while it might also be neglected, there might be good reasons for this neglect. One reason might be that the topic is itself quite boring. If it is a fair assumption that politicians find it hard to get interested in the kinds of issues raised in everyday policy-making, then an audience for an academic study might experience the same difficulty. The hardest thing about offering an account of the world of everyday policy-making, where many choices and issues revolve around obscure substantive and procedural points that tend to interest few, is to avoid boring people and becoming bored oneself. Few of the individual cases examined in this book were without clear points of interest on their own, but put fifty-two of them side by side and the effect is potentially narcotic. I have done what I can to bring this world to life, though the reader will judge with what success.

The study compares bureaucracies in six jurisdictions, and while the comparative design is discussed further in Chapter 1, the basic logic behind using the comparative method is that it is difficult to assess the character and significance of a set of arrangements, such as those governing bureaucratic participation in policy-making, without looking at how things work where the arrangements are different. Since we might expect at least some such routines and arrangements to be system-wide, assessing their importance and effects calls for cross-national comparative analysis.

Comparing more than two different bureaucratic systems generally requires extensive collaboration between scholars, whether in the context of an edited book (see e.g. Ridley 1979; Peters and Pierre 2004) or a book produced (if not written by) a cross-national team (Aberbach *et al.* 1981). The advantage of a single-author approach is that in such collaborations it is never entirely clear how much of the cross-national variation found results from the different perspectives of the collaborators. The disadvantage is that one person is unlikely to have as much familiarity with the politics, government, and administration of a country as a group. The methodology chosen here tries to get around the main disadvantage by concentrating on one relatively distinct and self-contained aspect of the administrative process (and, incidentally, one about which knowledge is limited in jurisdictions outside the US). It takes a few decrees in each country and tries to understand, mainly from talking to the people who wrote them, how they came about and how they were developed. The methodology is explained further in the next chapter. It builds on work I have done on the UK (Page 2001, 2003, 2009; Page and Jenkins 2005). Its true origin, however, lies in Richard Rose's (1977) *Managing Presidential Objectives* which showed how careful interview-based analysis of bureaucratic detail can be used to address much broader systemic political features.

The methodology to some degree ensured that the interviews were carried out over a protracted period, between 2006 and 2009. However, this is not, and cannot be, a study of change over time. With the exception, perhaps, of the United States, we do not know much about how regulations were made ten or twenty years ago in these jurisdictions, and certainly not enough to make fine-grained comparisons of how the process might have changed since. The book uses a series of snapshots taken at different times within a four-year period. In most of the systems there have been significant changes in political leadership since the time when the decrees I looked at were produced, and some of the decrees looked at have been altered, superseded, or revoked. Such changes are unlikely, however, to alter the fundamental character of the process of decree-making in each of the jurisdictions since the procedures tend to change slowly and have not generally experienced sudden transformation following changes in political leadership.

Another reason for doing all the spadework myself was that it was fun. Ninety-two officials in six jurisdictions were interviewed for this research. The simple fact is that, until I was sitting in the officials' offices, I had no real idea what they were going to talk about. While it was clear, for example, that one of the interviews was about decrees transporting lithium batteries (see Chapter 6), it was less predictable that the conversation would cover a big interdepartmental split, the role of quasi-regulatory bodies, and the power of video download sites like YouTube. Dull-sounding decrees often turned out to be far more exciting than any outsider could have imagined, and occasionally exciting-sounding decrees turned out to be more prosaic than their titles and contents would at first have suggested. I am extremely grateful to the officials interviewed in Brussels, Berlin, Bonn, London, Paris, Stockholm, Jonjöping, and Washington, DC. The interviews were conducted in French, German, and English—in most cases this meant the officials' native language except in Sweden and for some of the EU decrees.

What is often generally known as 'secondary legislation' comes under a variety of names. The main instruments are known variously as statutory instruments, rules, regulations, *décrets, arrêtés, förordninger, Verordnungen.* I generally use the term 'decree' and 'decree-making' in preference to 'regulations' and 'regulating' or even 'making regulations' because the term 'regulation' has come to refer to rules and rule-making more generally and I would like to make it clear that I am writing about particular documents with the force of law. Readers from some jurisdictions might find the term 'decree' a little odd. There is a risk that such a term is associated with authoritarian and/or arbitrary government, as suggested by Coleridge's 'In Xanadu did Kubla Khan/A stately pleasure-dome decree', the illiberal Carlsbad Decrees, or Michel Crozier's (1979) *On ne change pas la société par décret*. No such association is intended here: the term is used specifically to distinguish between the documents included in this research and the broader term 'regulation'. Occasionally this leads to some awkwardness, but this appeared to be the simplest and least confusing way of dealing with documents that go under different names in different jurisdictions.

Although the research itself was a solo effort, and all responsibility for the accuracy, quality, and value of the content rests with me alone, I was helped enormously by many other colleagues. Jack Hayward's advice, encouragement, comments, and constructive criticism shaped the project from start to finish. Elisabeth Åsberg arranged the Swedish interviews and helped me get to grips with the substance of the Swedish decrees and the French portion of the research simply would not have been possible without the assistance of Rémi Lataste. I am grateful to Christopher Pollitt and Hilka Summa for advice on developing the EU interview schedule. I am indebted to Steven Balla, Philippe Bezès, Michael Bruter, Alistair Cole, Philip Cowley, Mauricio Dussauge-Laguna, Neil Elder, Jean-Michel Eymeri-Douzans, Geoffrey Fry, Julie Gervais, Klaus Goetz, Charles Goodsell, Scott Greer, George Jones, Hussein Kassim, Martin Lodge, Anand Menon, Jan Meyer-Sahling, Cajsa Niemann, Jon Pierre, Rune Premfors, Maja Rasmussen, Jeffrey Weinberg, William West, Harold Wolman, and Rüdiger Wurzel for advice and comments on the work. The late and sorely missed Hans-Ulrich Derlien offered valuable insights that altered my approach to the German material and passed on the excellent research papers he wrote and helped to write in connection with Mayntz and Scharpf's (1975) study, of which only small portions found their way into the final publication. Four referees for Oxford University Press produced some useful guidance on developing the material. The research was supported by a small grant from the Economic and Social Research Council, Reference RES-000-22-1451.

Contents

1. Silence, Conflict, and Bureaucratic Power — 1
2. France: A Cross-Pressured Bureaucracy — 26
3. Britain: Bureaucrats and Imaginary Ministers — 47
4. Germany: Administration and Politics Revisited — 66
5. Sweden: Political Direction and Decree-Making — 86
6. Political Leadership in US Bureaucracy — 100
7. Regulated Bureaucratic Politics in the European Union — 123
8. Bureaucrats, Politicians, Choice, and Motivation — 146

References — 178
Index — 189

1

Silence, Conflict, and Bureaucratic Power

A CARD FROM THE PRESIDENT

Charles de Gaulle once sent me a Christmas card. The other leaders to whom I had sent cards—Mao Tse-tung and Ludwig Erhard—did not reply, but President de Gaulle did. Even at the age of 10 I wondered how much of the French president's effort went into sending his reply—whether he even saw the card I had sent and whether he himself signed the card he had sent, got someone else to do it, or had some sort of machine duplicate his signature. Yet such considerations were minor: it was there on an official card in an official envelope and with a signature that was not an obvious forgery. Whoever or whatever wrote it, the card bore the authority of the French president and to all intents and purposes it was a card from him.

In modern government the work of others is habitually passed off in similar ways as the work of its political leaders. This applies not only to symbolic gestures and speeches but also to significant policy issues. Ministers have decisions made in their name about matters as diverse as individual immigration cases, moving prisoners from one gaol to another, and who should sit on a technical scientific advisory board. If one takes a look at the official journals that publish rules and regulations such as the US Federal Register, the French *Journal Officiel,* or the German *Bundesgesetzblatt,* the diversity and volume of decisions taken in the name of ministers, political executives, or the organizations they head is striking. Of course, as we shall see, it is usually impossible for anyone not closely involved in putting these rules and regulations together to offer an accurate account of their importance or political significance just by reading them. Nevertheless, glancing at these journals in spring 2010 there were some issues likely to make minor headlines, such as a French *décret* addressing global warming by imposing a ban on recycling refrigeration fluids, a German *Verordnung* changing market entry for gas providers, and US rule changes on endangered species. There are also some less visible regulations changing herring catch quotas in the North Atlantic, arrangements for marketing cranberries, and rules governing the security of water supply to military installations, notification requirements for precursor drugs, the use of fog-horns on inland waterways, and the insurance of foreign cars and drivers.

Given the range of decisions made in their names, and the frequency with which they are made, it is to be expected that politicians spend only marginally more time on many of these decisions than Charles de Gaulle is likely to have spent on my Christmas card.

What difference does it make that politicians who are in charge of providing public services and regulating societies might spend little time on many of the decisions taken in their name? One view might be that democracy is being short-circuited: political executives lend their names to the decisions taken by others. These others are usually members of the bureaucracy who either make the decisions themselves, or are in turn heavily influenced by the preferences of others such as professional and lobby organizations. It was the absence of genuine political direction of bureaucracy rather than any inherent authoritarianism that led theorists such as Michels (1962) and Weber (1972) to offer their famously pessimistic visions of a bureaucracy crowding out genuine democratic political choice. For instance, Weber (1972: 835) offered a generally darker view when he wrote that with the growth of bureaucratic power the ever-expanding state is 'working to create the iron cage of bondage of the future into which people will feel forced to enter, much like the fellahin of the ancient Egyptian state, since they value a technically good, that is to say rational, bureaucratic administration that provides for their needs and that this providential bureaucracy should decide over the way their affairs are conducted. For it is exactly what bureaucracy provides.'

OUTNUMBERED BUT STILL ON TOP?

While fear of bureaucracy might once have been a 'raging pandemic' (Kaufman 1981*b*), Weber's pessimism appears to be somewhat out of tune with contemporary scholarly discussions of policy-making which tend to be rather more relaxed about the idea that bureaucrats exercise delegated power in this way. If we look at the more recent literature on bureaucracy, four rather different approaches to understanding policy-making might offer some reason for optimism that politicians remain in control, despite being heavily outnumbered by bureaucrats, and despite being responsible for a range of issues they can hardly be expected really to engage with in any depth.

Reasons to Be Cheerful

First, a large portion of the literature on *agendas and decision-making* offers, albeit with substantial empirical evidence, a variant of the older 'politics decides, administration implements' approach to the question of bureaucratic power in the policy process associated with Woodrow Wilson and many scholars since (Svara 1998). Kingdon (2003), whose work is central to the study of policy agendas, found in his analysis of US policy-making that bureaucrats were indeed key actors in the policy-making process, but rather as subordinates. In 247 interviews career civil servants were mentioned as 'important' actors in shaping policy one-third of the time but 'very important' only once. While civil servants may advise political appointees and others, the political level remains on top: 'It is quite common for the higher level appointees to define an agenda item and then to solicit the advice of careerists [i.e. career civil servants] in drafting the proposal. Bureaucrats are not the only source of such advice, but they are an important source.' While bureaucrats 'may have more impact on the specification of alternatives' than the definition of agendas, their impact is indirect since it is mediated through political actors such as appointees, legislators, and lobbyists (Kingdon 2003: 32). Baumgartner and Jones's (1993: 195) study of policy change points out that 'one of the most important instincts any bureaucrat or policymaker in the United States must develop is to pay attention to Congress' without whose support or acquiescence any significant policy proposals from agencies have little chance of success.

Second, a range of *institutional accounts of bureaucracy* in the past thirty years have suggested that any balance of power has swung away from bureaucrats and towards politicians. In 'Westminster' systems such as Britain, Canada, and Australia there has been the development of 'special advisers' who strengthen the policy role of ministers (Eichbaum and Shaw 2010). In Germany Goetz (2006) points to an increasing importance to bureaucratic careers of civil servants acquiring 'political craft'—showing their ability to serve politicians. Even though the interpenetration between political and administrative careers is long established in France,

> since the 1980s, politicization changed the rules of the game because the face-down between politicians and civil servants turned into a three-way game: ministers surrounded themselves with a large staff (sometimes up to 40 advisors in a large ministry such as Education) and networks of political advisors within the senior administrative management. A political administration in the true sense developed, monopolizing communication between politicians and managers. (Rouban 2007: 488)

Similar trends to politicization have been identified throughout Europe (Peters and Pierre 2004) as well as the institutions of the European Union (Wille 2010). In the United States the growth in the number of political appointments to the senior levels may have had perverse consequences, creating more layers between politicians and key parts of the organizations they lead which Light (1995) discusses as 'thickening'. Nevertheless it remains clear that 'political appointees began to displace career officers...[and]...brought increasing numbers of...special assistants along with them to do much of the work once reserved for civil servants' (Light 1995: 92). The literature on bureaucracy that emphasizes increasing politicization is mirrored by studies of political parties that see in the development of 'cartel parties' a closer interpenetration between state and party (Katz and Mair 1995).

Third, from a smaller and more diverse literature based on the *study of bureaucratic and political norms* can be taken a more benevolent understanding of how bureaucrats use their privileged positions close to the top of the executive policy-making hierarchy. Jim Sharpe (1976) pointed out that bureaucrats and politicians are not like strangers meeting for the first time at an international conference. They know each other and in their relationship with each other anticipate the other's reactions and adjust their own expectations and ambitions accordingly. Hood and Lodge (2006) use the metaphor of a 'bargain' to explore the different sets of understandings prevailing between top officials and politicians in a variety of jurisdictions. Politicians and bureaucrats each give up things in their possession to benefit from receiving something they desire from the other. One of the key 'gains' for a politician in such bargains is often the political loyalty of the bureaucrat; for the bureaucrat the benefit might be status or a generous pension. Of course, Hood and Lodge recognize that such bargains are not stable and that it is possible for both sides to 'cheat', but the basic position is a 'cooperative equilibrium' with 'high trust public service arrangements' (Hood and Lodge 2006: 158). Rhodes (2011: 129–30) found when studying 'anthropologically' the UK civil service that the most striking feature of the higher reaches of executive government was 'the permanent secretary's loyalty to his minister; perhaps the greatest crime in the civil service canon is to betray one's minister. Loyalty is a core belief and practice socialized into the newest recruit to the senior civil service. And that loyalty can spill over into, literally, devotion.' Colebatch *et al.* (2010: 233) conclude from surveying the diverse contributions to their edited collection that the 'authoritative instrumental view'—that those in authority in the bureaucracy can secure compliance from their subordinates—'has great normative power and this is how it should be'. One of the pieces of evidence they emphasize, for example, is the practice of 'officials looking for a "steer" from their political leaders; without which they are inclined to play it safe, and stick with the established positions'.

Fourth, a literature on *delegation* has transformed perceptions of the relationship between bureaucracy and politicians. In the first two-thirds of the twentieth century those who emphasized the growth of 'delegated powers' tended to be critics of a new bureaucratic 'despotism' (Hewart 1929; Allen 1956). Now delegation is associated with the opposite: a literature concerned with understanding how forms and instruments of delegation may be used to assert political control over a large bureaucracy (for an excellent review of the different generations of this literature see Krause 2010). Applying the analytical tools of the economist, the approach draws from the 'principal–agent' approach previously used above all for business analysis. It starts from the rather pessimistic insight, not all that different from that of Max Weber, that bureaucratic agents with their potentially superior knowledge (described as an 'information asymmetry') are able to avoid direct control by their political principals or that they even have power over principals. However, politician principals, through deriving appropriate 'contracts' or procedural arrangements, can constrain the discretion of their bureaucratic agents. In particular, more costly 'police patrol' forms of supervision, which require politicians to examine a wide range of activities by bureaucratic agents, can be replaced by less politically labour-intensive 'fire alarm' forms of control (McCubbins and Schwartz 1984). 'Fire alarms' refer to procedures that allow third parties—whether interest groups, other organizations, or even individuals who take an interest in a particular policy area—to raise the alarm with politicians when bureaucrats propose actions that they perceive to be at odds with what politicians would endorse or sanction. A prime example would be the 'notice and comment' provisions in the United States that require publication of draft administrative regulations, allowing interested parties to raise objections to them. Thus, despite being outnumbered by bureaucrats, politicians can remain on top of the decisions that matter because a range of policy watchers will draw significant issues to their attention. Politicians can even 'stack the decks' by creating alarms that are more likely to be triggered by some interests than others (McCubbins et al. 1987). Thus, for example, according to Shapiro and Guston (2006), 'peer review' procedures in US regulation privilege professional experts over other stakeholders.

Reasonable Doubts

These four literatures tend to offer us a more optimistic vision of the kind of political control that politicians heavily outnumbered by bureaucrats can exert, and so the question arises: for what reason do we raise the question of political control when a large volume of analysis tends to suggest it might not be particularly problematic? There are two broad answers to this question. First, for each of the four broad arguments to suggest that political control is not a substantial problem, there are four counter-arguments that call them into question. Second, the range of evidence on which the conclusions these four literatures draw is limited. Let us look at four counter-arguments to the somewhat more optimistic contentions.

First, the agenda-setting literature is based on a somewhat linear conception of the policy process: the big issues are decided in the early stages of agendas and alternatives and the decisions or choices made at this stage render subsequent choices subordinate to them. Bureaucrats generate alternatives in response 'to their superiors' agendas' and have a significant role in 'implementation' (Kingdon 2003: 31). Such a linear conception might tend to underestimate the role of bureaucrats in policy-making. It has long been argued that implementation can profoundly shape a policy (Pressman and Wildavsky 1973). However, in between the commitment to a policy and its implementation comes the elaboration of the instruments to be used—the precise design of the legal, financial, and organizational arrangements which go to make the policy. In the elaboration of instruments, the role of civil servants can be crucial because politicians are often unclear about what the policy should look like and delegate instrument development to officials and because in developing these instruments it is possible to revisit fundamental questions about the goals and structure of the policy.

While we do not exactly know how typical it is for instruments to be developed on the basis of broad if not vague intimations from politicians of what they should look like, we know that it is possible for many key features of policy design to become clear only at the stage when policy instruments are being considered by bureaucrats. In earlier studies of the UK I found, for example, that major reforms of, among other things, criminal law and employment rights were fundamentally shaped by the groups of civil servants charged with drawing up the legislation (Page 2003). In an examination of the specialist legal officials who draft primary legislation, Parliamentary Counsel, it was clear that fundamental issues of what a policy should look like—whom the law was to affect, what effect it should have, what kind of organization should implement or enforce it—were decided in the drafting process (Page 2009). Drafting was not the simple technical translation of the language of policy and politics into the language of the statute books. Rather it was, in terms of the kinds of issues at stake and its effect on what was actually enacted, as crucial a part of the policy-making process as the party, ministerial, or legislative deliberations that led to the political commitment to legislate. Moreover these studies also indicate that we should not assume that bureaucrats are largely uninvolved in agenda-setting activities: civil servants in the UK played an important role in placing on the political agenda measures that were later incorporated into party election manifestos (Page 2003). That this role of civil servants can be found in the United States is acknowledged by Kingdon (2003: 32) but discussed as the official working on policy ideas and waiting for the political appointees to 'elevate their ideas to the point on the policy agenda of receiving serious attention'. The UK evidence suggests that civil servants have a more independent ability to shape key aspects of new policy, not least where policy commitments are little more than broad expressions of intentions to be filled in by subsequent elaboration. Here officials play a key role in elaborating policy and politicians' appetite to become involved is often limited.

Second, the institutional literature pointing to increasing 'politicization' of bureaucracy largely reaches this conclusion on the basis of the increasing number of political appointees within the bureaucracy: more political appointees mean greater political control. Wood and Waterman (1991) certainly show that political appointees can shape the outputs of a US agency, as changes in agency leadership were followed by appreciable changes in the way the agency operated. However, more appointees does not necessarily mean more control. Political appointees can do a variety of things: they can manage relations between ministers and other ministers, legislators, parties, and interest groups, they can write speeches, and they can manage relations with the press. They can provide the minister with ideas for developing new policy. They do not, of necessity, bring about greater 'political' control because not all appointees have the job of supervising the bureaucracy. Moreover, Wood and Waterman's (1991) study focused on change in leadership at the top, and it was changes in the very top position to which the agencies appeared to be responding; the additional value of an expanded political leadership cadre is not altogether clear. In fact, Light (1995) argues that such 'thickening' of government, the expansion in numbers of higher leadership positions within the bureaucracy (in part generated by expanding numbers of political appointees), creates *barriers* to political control as it puts extra layers between the top leadership and the front line of the organization and 'fragments accountability'. More political appointees might mean more political control, but the case needs to be established rather than assumed.

Third, while investigations of the belief systems of bureaucrats might indeed find some strong evidence of a predisposition among bureaucrats to accept the legitimacy of the expressed wishes of politicians, whether through a public service bargain or some other mechanism, and act on them, this can only lead to extensive political control where the expressed wishes cover a large part of all the significant decisions to be taken in putting together a policy. As Geuijen and t'Hart (2010: 187) point out, Dutch national civil servants working in the European Union have to 'invent' their country's policy positions since there is often little by way of political steering. Their role is one of improvising (*bricolage*) where 'the civil servants in this process seemingly move seamlessly between acting as a unit or as a department civil servant involved in intra- or interdepartmental agency politics, as a domain expert involved in developing a professionally sound position, and as a "classic" civil servant serving his superiors and the hierarchy in general'. Similarly, in the UK, civil servants are often left to develop key details in legislation without direct instruction from their political leaders (Page 2003). While there may indeed be an acceptance among civil servants that political authority in principle trumps any bureaucratic wishes, political authority can remain silent over a vast array of public policy issues, leaving civil servants free to develop policy as they see fit.

Fourth, while we will look again at the principal–agent delegation literature further below, one of the main reasons not to accept the conclusion that it serves to sustain a high degree of political control is that the strength of its case is largely theoretical rather than empirical. Krause's (2010: 526) review of the field points to the 'chasm between theory and evidence in the realm of procedural rule-type controls' arising from the 'paucity of clear and consistent evidence supporting the efficacy of procedural constraints'. West (1997, 2004) for example, shows that 'notice and comment' in the US (one of the key 'fire alarm' procedures) does indeed serve to mobilize interests and offer them opportunities to shape regulations (and this is not a theoretical insight but rather lives up to the ostensible goal of the provisions of the 1946 Administrative Procedure Act). Yet the idea that the procedure allows for 'deck stacking' by protecting the constituencies served by 'original winning legislative coalitions is highly dubious' (West 2004: 73). Balla's (1998: 670) study of the Health Care Financing Administration 'demonstrated that physician participation in the notice and comment process did not influence Medicare physician payment reform in the manner posited by the deck-stacking thesis'.

UNDERSTANDING POLICY CONSTRUCTION

In part our pessimism or optimism as regards the Weberian perspective is likely to be shaped by what we are looking at when we consider 'policy'. If we regard policy as *political commitment*; the broad agreement to develop a particular policy programme—decentralization initiatives, tax reform, combating climate change, restructuring welfare or health systems—then we are likely to find that those who can mobilize political support, politicians and key policy activists and groups, are in the driving seat. Certainly bureaucrats can advise or even inspire politicians in developing political commitments, but it is hard to think of many examples of a broad policy commitment of this kind that predominantly reflects bureaucratic preferences, still less the dominance of bureaucratic over political values. In this sense the insights of the agenda-setting model that found only sparse evidence of bureaucrats in agenda-setting arenas, seem likely to hold. However, as discussed above, one key limitation of the agenda-setting model is that its vision of bureaucratic influence on agendas and alternatives as predominantly mediated through politicians and other 'political' actors omits a large amount of 'everyday policy making' (Page 2001)—developing the legal, financial, and organizational arrangements for policies—where bureaucratic influence might be expected to be larger and more direct.

A second reason for looking at this everyday form of policy-making is that political control is not necessarily a contact sport. Much of the empirical analysis of bureaucratic power centres on the question of who prevails in a policy process—whether the minister gets what he or she wants in some kind of direct opposition to what bureaucrats want.[1] Yet the argument that politicians can still influence without lifting a finger in any direct intervention is recognized by many approaches to political–bureaucratic relations, including principal–agent approaches (see e.g. Weingast 1984; see also Krause 2010). Bureaucrats might act in ways that politicians could be expected to want them to act without any direct instruction, possibly through some mixture of anticipating politician reactions, desiring to avoid conflict, or sharing identical views. As Kaufman's (1960) classic study of forest rangers showed, the ability to rely upon a body of officials who shared similar outlooks with each other and the federal leadership of the organization meant that direct supervision of the decisions of rangers was not necessary: rangers behaved no differently from the way they might be expected to behave if they had been under direction from federal headquarters. Highly effective central control need not rely on direct instruction or other forms of intervention.

In order to understand bureaucratic roles in policy-making we need to go beyond looking at instances where bureaucrats and politicians disagree or where politicians become noticeably involved in making decisions and take a wider look at the process of everyday policy-making, including examining cases where there appears to be little or no contact or conflict between bureaucrats and politicians. In particular this book focuses on three central questions. First, when do politicians get involved in making policy? We might expect them to be involved in the political initiatives that they themselves launch, but what involvement do they have in these more frequent everyday policy decisions? Second, what happens when politicians do get involved in such decisions? Do they get their own way or are they vulnerable to bureaucratic resistance and persuasion? And third, what happens when they *do not* become involved in such decisions? Does the silence of the politician leave the bureaucrat with the discretion to shape policies in ways that the bureaucrat wants?

What theoretical tools might we use to examine these questions? At first sight the questions seem to be natural principal–agent and delegation theory territory since the central concerns of this literature lie in understanding whether politicians can 'control policymaking and implementation when they apparently spend little effort at such tasks' (Krause 2010: 524) or in Weingast's (1984) words 'how do 535 people who are busy campaigning control 2–3 million bureaucrats?'. The reason for not using the methods of the principal–agent approach have in part to do with the fact that the approach

---

[1] The wishes of bureaucrats and politicians are usually assumed rather than established by investigation, as in the case of the assumptions that bureaucrats want increases in staffing levels and politicians oppose them (see Boyne 1986; for a challenge, see Hood *et al.* 1984), or that there is general recalcitrance of the bureaucracy to politicians' wishes, as in the case of Aberbach *et al.* (1981).

itself does not refer to a distinctive set of intellectual concerns or a defined empirical research strategy. The central intellectual concern is with the character, form, and uses of delegation—an intellectual concern that can also be found in mainstream public administration and public policy approaches. The empirical strategies used to develop, examine, or sustain its insights range from casual and passing reference to one or two cases, the systematic and detailed case study, and the comparison of a small number of cases to the multivariate analysis of quantitative indicators of 'discretion'. Rather the approach defines a mode of argumentation and set of widely shared findings, and it is the mode of argumentation and findings that one would be adopting by using the tools of this kind of delegation theory rather than anything else.

The mode of argumentation of this approach focuses on deriving hypotheses about expected behaviour from basic propositions about actors' interests that follow a logic similar to that found in economics. As such it has developed a set of insights, widely shared but not uncontested, such as the proposition that politicians tend to delegate where the costs of monitoring agents are high, and tend not to delegate where there are differences in preferences between legislators and bureaucrats. The insights have generally looked at political control as legislative control—in part because of the dominance of the US, one of the few countries in the world with a powerful policy-making legislature separated from the executive branch, and in part because of the preponderance of scholars of Congress in the field. One of the central weaknesses of the way the argumentation has been applied is that it has largely failed to offer a clear understanding of intra-executive political control—the control exercised by political appointees and their staffs. This failing poses strong limitations on its useability not only in countries, such as many in Europe, where executive and legislative powers are fused in party government, but also for its applicability in the US. As Krause (2010: 534) suggests:

> Because most of the advances in legislative delegation research emanate from students of legislative politics in political science, it is hardly surprising that considerably more effort has been expended in modeling the role of the legislature than of the executive branch. The extent of modeling of the executive branch in separation-of-powers models of delegation is often relegated to providing a unique ideal point for agency heads and presidents.... Such a focus, however, comes at a considerable expense to theory. Specifically, the modern delegation literature is primarily focused on understanding the supply of bureaucratic discretion, with little explicit concern for either the demand for or actual exercise of bureaucratic discretion.

Since our concern is with understanding the exercise of bureaucratic discretion, the attractions of the principal–agent approach seem more limited than might at first sight be expected.

Would it not be a worthy objective for research to fill the perceived gaps in understanding the patterns of delegation from a principal–agent perspective? From the perspective of an evangelist for the approach with some strong prior faith that the result from such an elaboration would achieve results unattainable by other perspectives it certainly would. However, since the approach concentrates attention on a narrow set of mechanisms—procedural rules and their application—to measure and understand delegation, it is somewhat more prudent to include at least the possibility that a wider range of institutions and processes might be at work here than procedural devices and develop an approach to the research that does not rule this wider range of possibilities out through excluding them right at the start.

WHAT WE MIGHT EXPECT

While the study of the development of decrees has not generated much empirical analysis,[2] there is still plenty in the scholarly literature covering the relationship between politics and bureaucracy to direct our attention towards a series of expected answers to our three central questions of when politicians become involved in everyday processes of policy-making, what happens when they do, and what happens when they do not?

When do Politicians Get Involved?

We might certainly expect the politicians who lead departments and agencies to be more involved in the policy-making process when they are developing key party or presidential priorities and key personal ones. However, aside from such circumstances, what shapes their involvement? One can think of three types of variables likely to affect the role they take in this respect: the *cues* for their involvement, their *disposition* to become involved, and the *institutional capacity* to become involved. These variables are likely to be related to each other, and distinctions are not always easy to make between them, but they are worth separating out.

Cues

Politicians might be prompted to become involved in making policy through cues generated by others. As the delegation literature suggests, some of these

---

[2] Even in the USA, where scholars have focused on later stages in rulemaking. Kerwin *et al.* (2010: 602) point out, that there is not 'a great deal of research' on the development of regulations.

cues for politician involvement can be legal and/or formal consequences of the decree-making process. 'Fire alarms' (McCubbins and Schwartz 1984)—procedures for consultation and approval that bring the issue to the attention of interest groups or legislators—can also act as a cue for political executive involvement. There are some circumstances in which politicians' participation is *mandatory*, as with the requirement under German law that a minister signs a decree before it can have the force of law. Indeed, it is a common feature of all the jurisdictions in this study that decrees are generally signed by a political executive. The requirement for the minister to sign a decree could prompt him or her to object to it or ask for a change in it.

Yet it is not only through bureaucrats following formal procedural requirements that an issue might be passed to a politician and thus a cue be offered to involvement. Accepted norms of bureaucratic behaviour not necessarily incorporated in formal rules might provide cues for political involvement. Politicians may also become involved because issues get pushed up to them. In particular the principle of hierarchy and its acceptance by bureaucrats might incline them to seek to involve politicians for two reasons. First, a basic principle of conflict resolution in a hierarchy is that any conflict between two units of a similar level, or two people of similar grade, can be resolved by the decision of the superior in charge of both units (see e.g. Downs 1967). Thus conflicts between two parts of a ministry or agency, where they cannot be resolved, may be passed up the hierarchy and eventually to the political leadership. We can extend this principle of hierarchy and argue that where a ministry is in conflict with another ministry and this cannot be resolved at lower administrative levels, the political leadership may also become involved to handle relations with the other ministry. Since politicians are superior to bureaucrats in hierarchical structures, they may push items to the top where there is uncertainty about which direction they should take in developing a policy. Thus they may offer cues for politicians to become involved by seeking guidance on how to develop a policy—it is not uncommon for UK civil servants to ask politicians for a 'steer' on how to develop policy (Page 2001). The cues might indeed be somewhat less predictable than the kinds discussed so far—through happenstance (say, a political colleague raising the issue with a senior political executive) or serendipity.

Disposition

How politicians respond to cues might be expected to reflect a disposition to become involved. For example, a party colleague mentioning a policy being developed in a minister's department could simply be ignored, or the intervention could lead to no more than a formal request by the minister for information on how the issue was progressing, or it could lead to the minister calling the policy in and seeking to deal with it entirely on her/his own.

Moreover, the disposition to become involved may mean that politicians do not need external or internal cues to seek to shape policies, but take an interest in them right from the start. What might affect politicians' disposition to become involved?

Most approaches to this question tend towards tautology: politicians are likely to want to get involved in issues that are 'political', with political issues being those that politicians take an interest in, usually because they could affect their re-election prospects (see e.g. Huber and Shipan 2002). Yet apart from this, one cannot easily stipulate what it is about an issue that makes it political. How many people are affected by the issue does not necessarily make it 'political' if what they are affected by seems to raise little interest. Many people are affected by changes in use of the multiplexes delivering digital signals to televisions in the UK, but that did not make them 'political' (see p. 51 below). Money is a poor guide too. While the decree covering the settlement of revenue sharing between German *Länder* meant the movement of billions of euros (see p. 75 below), it was applying a formula agreed years before (albeit contested in the courts at the same time the decree was being produced), and was widely regarded as a routine law that the minister merely signed without hesitation.

Contention and conflict is possibly the closest one can come to criteria that define whether an issue is 'political'. This corresponds not only to general conceptions of the nature of politics as conflict (Crick 1964), but also to perceptions of politicians and bureaucrats themselves (Suleiman 1975: 296–7; Aberbach *et al.* 1981) who, when asked in surveys, emphasize the struggle for power as a political role and the ordered 'management' of affairs as an administrative role. Almost any government policy or action might raise some form of controversy—changing the format of an expense claim form might irritate or upset some people—but that does not necessarily make it political. A working definition of political might be that a policy is related to controversies where significant support can be mobilized, whether this is in the form of support from the public or electorate, organized interests, or political and administrative elites themselves. While this definition offers no precise dividing line between what is and what is not political, it suffices to highlight a range of characteristics of a policy that might be expected to attract the attention of a politician.

By contrast the literature on technocracy strongly suggests that politicians are generally excluded, or exclude themselves, from technical discourse (Laird 1990). According to Schattschneider (1960) technical discourse is a classic strategy used to limit the number of people who can participate in decision-making (see Baumgartner 1989 for an application of this approach to French politics). Thus we would expect the disposition to intervene to be far weaker with technical issues than with those that allow politicians to make decisions on the basis of general political judgements.

Institutional Capacity

The institutional capacity for politicians to become involved in bureaucratic policy-making might also be expected to shape their involvement, as the institutional literature on 'politicization' discussed above suggests. One politician faced with a huge department covering hundreds of policy issues each year is hard pressed to get involved in many such issues. The more help a politician has, the more we would expect him or her to have the opportunity to shape the policy work that goes on within a ministry or agency. There is a variety of institutional arrangements for sharing out the political policy direction/supervision work of an agency or ministry. Such arrangements include multiple political executives, such as junior ministers in the UK and France or agency heads and assistant heads of different kinds in the USA, political civil servants in the USA, Sweden, and Germany (and to a lesser extent in France), political advisers in the UK and Sweden, and an organized *cabinet* with powers to offer direction to ministries and agencies in the name of the minister in France and the EU. Such assistance has the result that politician involvement is often indirect as it is given though others. This means that the question of how far the various types of auxiliary politicians reflect the goals, values, or wishes of the politicians on whose behalf they might be expected to act remains open (see Light 1995). The issue of senior political executive-adviser/junior political executive relationships is rarely if ever approached in the study of executive policy-making. However, even though such auxiliaries may not directly carry out the instructions of those they have been appointed to support, we would expect, *ceteris paribus*, that politicians are better able to be involved in policy-making where they have more assistance.

What Happens When Politicians Get Involved?

At first glance the answer to this question appears obvious. If a bureaucrat wants to do something and a politician does not want it, other things being equal, the bureaucrat will not be able to do it. If a politician wants something and it can be provided by the bureaucrat (the politician is not, in Heclo's (1977) terms, asking for the equivalent of making 'water run uphill'), then, again, other things being equal, the politician will get it. Examples of successful bureaucratic sabotage are extremely rare. Müller (2006) for instance undertook a systematic search for evidence of different forms of bureaucratic sabotage and found no significant examples of them in Austria over the whole postwar period. So, in a straight fight, where a politician in charge of a ministry or agency wants something (or does not want something) the bureaucrat is generally likely to accept this and act accordingly. However, another possible outcome of the involvement is that the bureaucrat changes the mind of the politician not to want something, or to want something else—one could call this in the jargon of social science 'preference shaping' (Dunleavy 1993) whether by direct engagement and argument or by more devious methods such as seeking to undermine the politician's preferred policy in the eyes of his or her colleagues.

The way the politicians initially become involved might also shape their subsequent involvement with any one policy. Politicians may also become involved on the terms suggested by the bureaucrats by, for example, being asked to choose between a range of options suggested by the bureaucrats, which biases politicians to accept the preferences of bureaucrats (see Bendor et al. 1987). Or the bureaucrats can reduce the chances that the politician will want to get involved more than he or she has to by making the issue appear dull and technical, thus decreasing the disposition to take any active involvement. The minister might be approached about the issue when work on it is nearly completed—after much time and resources have gone into developing the policy a politician might feel reluctant to undermine the work of his or her department (West 2004: 71–2). We might call any such attempt to shape the way politicians become involved a matter of *setting the terms of politician involvement*.

What Happens When Politicians Do Not Get Involved?

It is commonly assumed that when the politician is not directly involved the bureaucrat is likely to 'shirk'—to engage in behaviour that suits the bureaucrat's purposes but not those of the political leadership. It is possible to think of the types of motivations that might lead them to act in this way when not directly supervised or instructed. The public choice approach suggests that bureaucrats are motivated by *self-interest*: they follow the preferences that benefit most their own individual material well-being, whether this is pay, promotion, leisure, or a congenial working environment. It was, for example, the pursuit of better incomes and promotion prospects that led scholars such as Niskanen to assume that bureaucrats would favour the growth of government in the postwar era and could be regarded as a significant cause of the rise in public spending until the 1980s (see Niskanen 1971; Hood et al. 1984). *Socially acquired values*, those acquired through early or later socialization and/or membership of a social, political, or cultural group might shape decisions taken by officials. One of the main assumptions of the 'representative bureaucracy' literature is that social status and social experiences shape the way that bureaucrats think and behave (Sherif 1976).

Professional values might shape the way bureaucrats approach policy-making. One of the central assertions of the literature on professionalism is that acquisition of a body of knowledge and techniques as well as socialization into a group predisposes officials towards a distinctive way of seeing the world. Road engineers see the world differently from land-use planners (Laffin 1998). *Agency values* are another source of cues for bureaucrats in exercising policy discretion. The idea that different ministries, agencies, or sections have their own distinctive values is central to the 'bureaucratic politics' approach (Allison 1971). Moreover the notion behind political leaders 'going native' is that they adopt the priorities and objectives of the agency they are supposed to be supervising (see also Downs 1967). Or the discretion of bureaucrats may be *externally constrained*: in deciding what to do they seek to avoid opposition from (or to gain the approval of) a body outside the bureaucracy, whether, for example, a court, a state or local authority, an interest group, or public opinion.

All these assumptions tend to underline the expectation that bureaucrats, when left on their own and given discretion to shape policy, might be expected to act in ways that can (or do) work against the preferences of politicians. However, shirking/undermining is only one possible response by bureaucrats when politicians are not directly involved in their policy work. It is possible to envisage bureaucrats exercising discretion in ways that are supportive of their political leadership. Bureaucrats may try to base their exercise of discretion on the *anticipated reactions* of political and administrative leaders, or some other figure inside or outside the organization (see Page and Jenkins 2005).

The degree to which the values that orient bureaucratic discretion support or undermine the authority of the political leadership is crucial to our understanding of bureaucracy and its political control. Briefly summarized, one can say that where bureaucratic values are supportive, political intervention is less necessary to guarantee leadership. Under these circumstances it is possible for political as well as administrative superiors within an organization such as a ministry or agency to claim responsibility for things that their subordinates do, even if the superiors have had little or nothing directly to do with them. In fact, direct order giving might even be a rare activity among those at the top of bureaucracies, whether politicians or unelected officials. As Kaufman (1981a: 86–7) argued in his study of US bureau chiefs based on observing their daily activities over an extended period of time, what is

> seemingly missing from this portrait of chiefs at work [is] ... command ... Didn't the chiefs order subordinates to do things? ... Of course they did, but not in an obvious, authoritarian manner. Ordinarily ... chiefs did not find it necessary to impose their will by fiat. Not that they were unable to do so: the moral and legal authority of their office was a powerful enough implement. But they seldom had to express it in the form of outright orders.... Cracking the whip and

personally regulating the flow of work were not ways in which the chiefs spent their working days.

Postmodern scholarship includes this phenomenon of direct instructions not being central to the exercise of authority as a part of 'governmentality' (see Rose and Miller 1992), where shared ideas and conformity substitute for the exercise of command, but the phenomenon was in reality something recognized long before postmodernity. It can be found in the works of Herbert Simon (1945), Alexis de Tocqueville (1945), Niccolo Machiavelli (1961), and Max Weber (1972) among many others. Where the values are supportive the degree of direct intervention becomes less crucial for understanding the character of political leadership.

ANSWERING THE QUESTIONS

Comparative Research Design

The answers to each of these questions of politician and bureaucrat involvement in policy of this kind are certainly likely to vary. We might expect to find at least three sources of variation: the nature of the individuals concerned, the nature of the policy issue, and the characteristics of the political system. We might expect some individual ministers to be more prone to intervene and be more assertive when they do, while others are less so, as a preferred style of politics. Similarly, some bureaucrats may be more likely to try to keep issues away from ministers, to try and change ministers' minds when they cannot avoid it and indulge their own predispositions about how the policy should be shaped, while others are more deferential and more likely to listen, say, to interest groups.

While such individual characteristics might affect behaviour, bureaucrats and politicians generally act within an institutional, legal, and constitutional environment that varies from one jurisdiction to another. Thus, for example, the constitutional/legal arrangements for developing decrees in the United States offer different opportunities to politicians to get involved in policy-making from those offered to ministers in the United Kingdom. Indeed, the very nature of the executive political leadership differs as between the United States with its separation of legislative and executive powers and European countries where heads of ministries are generally members (or, where there is an incompatibility rule, ex-members) of the legislature. The impact of distinctive features of national systems might go beyond the institutional and affect the norms and patterns of expectations that bureaucrats and politicians have of themselves and each other. Crozier (1964) famously argued that bureaucracy was a national 'cultural phenomenon' and this broad thesis is sustained by recent work in the field such as that of Hood and Lodge (2006).

The policy issue itself might shape our answer to these three questions. It has already been suggested that some policies are likely to be more 'political' than others and thus attract the attention of politicians. Whether we can systematize this and argue that some policy areas, whether economic policy or animal welfare, attract the attention of politicians, while others such as plant diseases and building regulations do not, cannot be settled here. Ever since Lowi's (1964) classic it has been hypothesized that policies shape politics—the political processes vary from one policy area to another—mainly because of the different constellations of interest groups surrounding each area, as some policy areas are dominated by one powerful group, others by many competing groups, and yet others by different patterns of interest group activity (see Wilson 1989).

Since one might expect some of the answers to the central questions—when do politicians become involved in everyday policy-making, what happens when they do, and what happens when they do not?—to vary according to country and policy area, this study is a comparative analysis of six jurisdictions: the United Kingdom, France, Germany, Sweden, the United States, and the European Union. Because I had to read the laws, speak to the people who wrote them, and consult supporting material as well as secondary literature, the selection was in part shaped by the languages I was able to read and converse in. Interviews were conducted in English in the US, UK, and (to my regret) Sweden, but in French and German in France and Germany and in French, German, and (mainly) English in the European Union. These six jurisdictions are also systems about which we know much from secondary literature, and we know they have distinctive politico-administrative systems. Some stick out in cross-national comparisons because of their institutional structure (e.g. the US and Sweden each have peculiar forms of agency structures; France has a *cabinet* system imitated elsewhere such as in the EU, but not exactly replicated); some stick out because of the character of the top officials (e.g. the *grands corps* of France, the Oxbridge types of the UK, and the political officials of Germany) and some stick out because they have distinctive constitutional structures that give bureaucrats tasks and roles they do not generally have in other jurisdictions (e.g. the power of the legislature in the US; the Commission as initiator of legislation in the EU). If we are looking for cross-national variation, we have a good chance of finding it as the similarities between the main contours of these six bureaucratic systems are few.

Focus on Secondary Legislation

Although more likely to produce a less rosy picture of the relationship between bureaucracy and democracy than a focus on the broad political commitments to policy, in this research I look at the everyday policy-making that produces secondary legislation—the mass of rules, regulations, and decrees that fill up the bulk of the official registers of law in any jurisdiction. Secondary legislation was chosen because it is generally regarded as more likely to be the province of the bureaucrat than that of the politician alone. In fact, comparing two UK studies of legislation, one primary and one secondary (Page 2001, 2003), the differences between the two might not be quite as large as one might suppose, at least not in Britain. Primary legislation, procedural differences aside, often entails very similar processes to that of secondary as far as relationships between politicians and the bureaucracy are concerned. In both, middle-level officials are often left to develop detailed provisions with generally only infrequent involvement of political and administrative superiors. Nevertheless, if the main purpose is to understand the systemic features of bureaucratic power—i.e. what happens when politicians are silent as well as when they speak—then secondary legislation appeared likely to offer a reasonable way of exploring them.

There is the danger that secondary legislation, with its reputation for dull routine, is more likely to exaggerate the importance of politicians' silence than if one selected instruments such as primary legislation or white papers, more frequently associated with major policy initiatives, because dull and worthy secondary legislation matters less politically. The apparent dullness of secondary legislation is, however, somewhat exaggerated. As we will see among the small sample examined here, such decrees have been used to implement major party-political initiatives, have generated raucous opposition from powerful interests, and brought demonstrators out on the streets. Even if the tendency to dullness has to be conceded, this is no bad thing for a study that seeks to explore the rather neglected topic of what bureaucrats do when politicians are not looking over their shoulders. Since our understanding of how policy is put together, and of the role of politicians and bureaucrats in drawing it up, is generally based on a focus on the broad policy commitment rather than the detail of how policy measures are put together, looking at the everyday traffic in decrees is at a very minimum likely to offer a fuller understanding of how the interaction between politicians and bureaucrats works than a concentration on the broad policy commitments alone.

In fact, looking at policy-making within the executive from the perspective of everyday processes of decision-making offers an important corrective to the potentially misleading general accounts of how bureaucratic decision-making works in different countries. As will be discussed in later chapters, accounts of bureaucratic involvement in decision-making are often extrapolations based on limited understandings of how top civil servants behave or how policies that generated major controversies are put together. Yet top civil servants are not the main players in developing most policies within government, and much that government does raises, if at all, opposition or support from limited constituencies that are not usually enough to propel it to the attention of social scientists. We have many reasons to think that everyday policy-making might offer a different broader picture of the relationship between bureaucracy and politics in any one country. The constitutional rules, norms, and procedures governing its generation are different, as are the people involved, the pressures they face, and the reasoning they might be expected to use as they face them. Unless we understand everyday processes of government, we do not understand government at all.

The basic design of this research was to pick a small sample of decrees in each jurisdiction and talk to the people who wrote them. If we want to find out when politicians become involved with the bureaucracy, what happens when they are involved, and what happens when they are not, we have to ask the people concerned. There are no alternative direct measures that could be used to piece together answers to these questions—no statement of the history of the decree containing such details—and there are no proxy variables (e.g. length of the decree or its wording) that could be used to address them either. This strategy brought problems of its own.

One problem was that of the selection of the decrees to be included in the study. The notion of selecting 'equivalent' items of secondary legislation in the six jurisdictions is an attractive sounding idea but cannot be used as a guide here. Defining 'same', 'similar', or 'equivalent' is problematic. Two decrees from different countries in the same policy area, say agriculture, are not in any meaningful sense equivalent: for example, a US decree on beef slaughter differs in form, content, subject, and effect from an EU decree on import tariffs for agricultural goods. If one takes 'equivalence' to mean decrees trying to achieve something similar in policy terms, it is impossible to find particularly close equivalents across all six jurisdictions. In part this is because of differences in the politico-administrative agendas in them (it is rare for the same issues to be dealt with in decrees across all six at roughly the same time) and in part because of the way in which policy instruments work in each of them. In some jurisdictions what is done by a piece of secondary legislation can be done by primary in another and by codes of guidance in yet another. What is done by one decree in one jurisdiction can be done by several elsewhere. Decrees often deal with highly specific and limited issues in the development of a policy such that finding two, let alone six, that do precisely the same thing or even something close, would be difficult. If one took the four EU member states one could look for decrees implementing EU laws. This is not as easy as it sounds, as all the arguments raised above about equivalence apply here too. Moreover such a strategy would bias the study in those four countries towards EU implementation issues. It would also detach the four countries from the other two jurisdictions, the EU and the US, where for different reasons one would not necessarily expect to find 'equivalent' secondary legislation dealing with the same issues.

It was not possible to select decrees according to other measures of equivalence less directly related to their policy effect. We might be interested in looking at decrees with similar levels of politician involvement, yet that can only be discovered once one has spoken to the people writing them. Moreover, very few features of a decree one might have liked to have used to create a sampling frame—such as how contentious it is—can be accurately (or even for the most part approximately) assessed simply by reading it. Even characteristics that appear more susceptible to clear definition and classification, such as how 'technical' a decree is, cannot be deduced from the text alone. One might have thought that decrees that contain scientific jargon, formulae, and/ or tables of numbers could be classed as 'technical'. Yet this would be misleading as the key issue at stake in some decrees like these is a simple non-technical choice and the technical components a mere formality.

If one considers the methodology of the study—contacting and talking to people who write the legislation—then the choices become limited anyway as one has to select recent decrees in order to increase the chances that the people who wrote them are still in position (few civil servants in any of the jurisdictions were keen to talk about what they did in a former job) and that they can remember what happened. The strategy adopted was to select recent decrees that looked like they were related to policy decisions of some sort—a criterion mainly used to avoid investigating the formalistic uses of decrees such as the French *arrêtés* and *décrets* that confirm the appointment of named individuals to the governing council of a public body and the myriad of UK trunk road statutory instruments that designate new areas for no parking zones or changed speed limits. In selecting the decrees, I tried to get a broad spread across different ministries, insofar as it was possible to tell which ministry produced the decree (which minister signed the decree is not an infallible guide, as I found out). After the selection, it was a matter of securing the agreement of the ministries and agencies concerned. The variable numbers of decrees in each country (Sweden 7, Germany 6, EU 7, USA 10, France 10, UK 12) reflect, if anything, how quickly I managed to arrange interviews after initially contacting the ministry/agency concerned. When I did not hear from the people I approached connected with my initially targeted six decrees, I found substitutes. When the substitutes agreed and the original respondents later also agreed to participate, I found my sample expanding.

The respondents were bureaucrats—ninety-two were interviewed—mostly officials outside what are normally considered the senior ranks. Writing decrees is mainly a task for middle-ranking officials. Senior officials become involved usually, if at all, in the interdepartmental diplomacy or the higher politics of the policy process. However, gathering the information together, working out precise proposals that were to be contained in the decree, and drafting the decree itself were tasks normally carried out by people at this grade. The concern in this book is with how they went about their work, what considerations guided their approach to the policy problem, when they felt they needed to refer things to politicians, what happened once they referred things upward, how far they felt they could decide things on their own, and how they handled any potentially contentious issues. The politicians' perspective would certainly have been useful, but exceptionally hard to get and even harder to interpret. The prospect, for example, of interviewing President Sarkozy of France on a decree allowing Texas Hold 'Em Poker in French casinos (as Interior Minister he was responsible for this decree included in the sample) was appealing but unrealistic. Moreover, as I had found from earlier research (Page 2001), a particular decree with few exceptions forms a small part of ministerial activity (even though it could have taken weeks or months of a bureaucrat's time) and politicians have difficulty remembering details about it. Understandably politicians tend to talk about the key decrees that stick in their minds rather than the one systematically or serendipitously selected by an academic.

Small N Research

A second problem generated by the research strategy is the size of the sample. To extend the sample to any size that would allow statistical extrapolation to the population of decrees is likely to require the study of hundreds in each country. This might be possible with a large collaborative project, but collaborative projects in bureaucracy (and other subjects) bring their own problems. Guy Peters once remarked that the main independent variable in a collaborative cross-national study, above all one conducted through contributions to an edited book, was the author contracted to contribute to it. The small N design above all allowed me to control for that particular independent variable: a more or less equal familiarity with the material from all the countries means that the person drawing up the conclusions is the person who gathered the information. Moreover I wanted to write a book on comparative bureaucracy that did not depend on trying to piece together pictures of different national systems from secondary material of varying quality and vintage (see Page 1985) or on interpreting the individual perspectives on the question likely to be produced by an edited collection.

One reason why it does not matter that this is not a random sample is that the numbers of decrees included in each jurisdiction are too small for a random sample to be of any advantage. However, that points to a bigger problem: what can a non-randomly selected handful of decrees tell us about the big questions raised in this chapter? Because they are based on a tiny sample, the results cannot all be extended to whole jurisdictions, ministries, or policy areas. To some degree we might expect some of the insights yielded by even a handful of decrees to have wider validity in the country concerned. For example, the requirement that decrees be submitted to the Conseil d'État for approval is a general requirement for a large proportion of all French decrees and the procedures by which the Conseil considers decrees (the fact-finding and hearing stages and how they are conducted) are broadly common to all such decrees. Yet other results, especially those that relate to conventions and assumptions about appropriate ways of behaving, cannot with any confidence be extended to apply to the whole country (or to the whole ministry or to all decrees in a particular policy area).

The question about the appropriateness of the methodology thus becomes this: does it produce material that helps us address the central issues I have raised about bureaucratic and political roles in policy-making? The answer to this question must be that the proof of the pudding is in the eating: does the material and the way it is interpreted help us understand more about how bureaucracies shape, and how politicians can influence, policies largely developed within the bureaucracy? The question is certainly important enough to make the prospect of a decent glimpse at some answers, if not the answers themselves, worthwhile. This question of the validity of any conclusions based on a small non-random sample will be taken up again in the concluding chapter and cannot be settled here in advance.

PLAN OF THE BOOK

The logic pursued to answer these three questions will be what is often disparagingly described as 'inductive' in the sense of observing how things work and then seeing if the observations can be fitted to a particular pattern. The alternative, of course, is a deductive logic: setting up hypotheses derived from broader theoretical propositions and then testing them, knocking out the ones that don't seem to work, and offering a pat on the back to those that do.

The inductive method has been chosen over the deductive for two main reasons. The first is that few truly theoretical propositions offer us much help in understanding this world of everyday policy-making in such a way as to generate hypotheses. Some of the sub-questions outlined above can easily be framed in terms of the binary supported/not supported fashion characteristic of hypothesis testing, yet the insights on which such hypotheses may be based hardly go beyond what Lindblom and Cohen (1979) describe as 'ordinary knowledge'. For example, a hypothesis (set out earlier in this chapter) that greater institutional capacity is associated with a greater propensity for politicians to intervene in everyday policy-making is essentially derived from a commonsense 'ordinary knowledge' proposition (that in many cases the easier it is for you to do something, the more likely you are to do it) not true theoretical insight. To dress up such guesses as scientific hypotheses would be to attempt to mislead with the formal trappings of science. Second, and perhaps more important, it is impossible to understand how bureaucrats work if one focuses exclusively on a series of guesses about what one would expect to find plucked out of the air through such ordinary knowledge. Moreover, we know that the empirical record of public choice accounts of delegation is not strong. To be guided in empirical strategy by armchair theorizing about a world which is still largely unknown is harder to defend than the inelegance and unfashionability associated with non-deductive methods.

Related to this, a comparative study might aspire to dividing itself on a thematic rather than a country-by-country basis. This book could have been written this way. Indeed, early drafts of it were, but what it produced was difficult to read, if not unreadable. Comparing six jurisdictions based on fifty-two individual cases, would involve a rather breathless juxtaposition of the detail of each case and a reminder to the reader of the context of the case (even if the context had been set out before) which threatened to become tedious and bury the conclusions in detail. Detail is an important part of this research, and to keep it entirely as hidden wiring would miss its central point, but it should not take over the general comparative argument. The best way to present the material seemed to be on a country-by-country basis for the main exposition. The synthesis and comparison, although implicit and sometimes explicit in the country chapters, is primarily concentrated in the last chapter.

Each chapter will address the questions discussed above about how politicians become involved in bureaucratic policy-making processes, what happens when they do, and what happens when they do not. However, the empirical material is not presented in the form of six identically structured chapters for each country. This would have been cumbersome, not least because the features that are particularly relevant for understanding the role of bureaucracy in one country are less important in others. For example, some of the detailed provisions of the law by which decrees are produced are central to understanding the whole process of decree-making in the United States but only need to be outlined in the other countries. A uniform chapter structure would also have been more tedious to read, with six different countries presented in a repetitive structure into which they would have to be forced. The order in which countries are presented is not particularly important for the development of the argument: I have sought to juxtapose countries that differ significantly from each other in order to try and make the material more interesting for anyone reading this book from start to finish.

Each chapter develops the exposition of how things work in the country concerned by contrasting the picture presented by an understanding of everyday government with conventional accounts of politico-administrative processes. In doing so, each chapter develops the observation, discussed briefly above, that our conventional understandings of how bureaucracies work in any one country are based on the view from the top, on policies that generate major conflict or on how top officials behave or see their roles, rather than on everyday process of government. Occasionally the contrast between accounts gained by the study of everyday policy-making on the one hand and high-profile on the other is sharp, but for the most part the contrast shows how broad received understandings of policy-making have to be modified to produce an accurate account of how government works.

Each country chapter is structured using a basic pattern, even if the precise headings and subheadings are different. First, each describes the organizational and institutional context in which decrees are developed: who the bureaucrats are, and who the politicians are. Then the chapters broadly follow the process of policy-making, exploring how the decrees started life, how they were developed and drafted, and how they were approved and put on the statute book. However, it would be mistaken to consider the fifty-two cases without a clear idea of what one should look out for in them. To follow an inductive method is not to abandon theoretical argument but rather to make decisions about how theoretical insights should be used and applied. The final chapter will explore a range of arguments discussed already about the conditions under which politicians become involved and what happens when they are not involved—the impact of different cues, institutional capacities, what disposes politicians to intervene, the consequences of their intervention, and the way bureaucratic decisions are reached without intervention. The theoretical propositions are best discussed comparatively in the final chapter. This material will then be used in the conclusion to offer direct answers to the main questions posed in this chapter and to explore the implications of the answers I give for the wider understanding of bureaucracy.

2

France: A Cross-Pressured Bureaucracy

France's bureaucracy is the one that scholars and students of administration are most likely to know best after that of their own country. The seminal work of Crozier (1964) and Suleiman (1975) has done much to ensure that French bureaucracy is given substantial prominence in comparative studies and texts. Yet the view offered in both classics and texts is a view of the summit. It is the world of the *grandes écoles, énarques,* and ministerial *cabinets*; of *pantouflage, détachement,* and the notion of serving the *interêt général.* Of all the countries in this study, it is in France that one finds the clearest contrast between the generally accepted picture of how things work at the top and the revealed picture about how things work at a less elevated level. The view from the top is that the 'strong' French state is supposed to be resistant to the power of interests, except perhaps in a rather minor way—groups may play a role in 'implementation' rather than 'policy'—yet overall the French system is, certainly in European terms, distinctive because of its 'statism' (see Schmidt 2006). This 'strong' state is, however, far less apparent as one gets closer to the middle levels of the national bureaucracy at which policy is routinely made.

The picture that emerges from this examination of a sample, albeit small, of French secondary legislation casts strong doubt on the contention that the role of groups in policy-making is either exceptional or confined to 'implementation'. If the results apply even only to a limited extent outside the sample, this would certainly be sufficient to call the 'statism' of the French policy-making system into doubt and question whether the role of groups really is limited to 'implementation'. It is not claimed that the findings here are entirely unexpected. As we will see, some observers of the French state have cast strong doubt on this vision of a statist, interest-resistant, bureaucratic core and pointed instead to the importance of national interest groups and local 'notables' as powerful participants in French policy-making (see Hayward 1973, 1983; Cole 2008). Before discussing these findings, I have first to present them. In this chapter, as in the following five, I trace through the processes that gave rise to the decrees included in the sample. This is preceded by a brief account of the immediate environment in which bureaucrats help develop policy, without which it is difficult to keep track of the events described.

FRENCH MINISTRIES AND THEIR OFFICIALS

It is useful to think of the leadership of the ministry as a composed of two hierarchies closely intertwined at the top: one administrative, the other political. The administrative leadership of a ministry is the hierarchy composed of the top 'line' leadership even though these positions are in principle subject to ministerial appointment. The leadership structure in a ministry varies somewhat from ministry to ministry. In some, such as the Education and Budget ministries, the ministry is headed by the *secrétaire général*, the most senior civil servant in a line position with responsibility for the main units of the ministry. In others, such as Interior and Energy and Environment, the *secrétaire général* has more limited responsibilities. Ministries are divided into *directions générales, directions,* and *services* headed by *directeurs générales, directeurs, sous-directeurs,* and *chefs de service* in descending order of rank, each assisted by one or more deputies (*adjoints*). These top levels of the civil service, especially *sous-directeur* and above, are usually occupied by civil servants who have been educated for, and followed, an elite career path within the French civil service. They are usually members of a top corps (*grand corps*)—effectively an exclusive job placement organization that steers its members into leading administrative positions throughout French government and beyond—and are educated in one of the top schools providing access to the *grands corps*, above all the École Nationale d'Administration and the École Polytechnique (see e.g. Thoenig 1987).

The grade structure of the French civil service is complex—it is broadly divided into three categories, A (managerial positions for those with university degrees), B (intermediate positions for those with high-school leaving certificates), and C (junior positions for those without educational qualifications). The arrangements for the higher civil servants in the *grands corps*, who occupy the leading positions within the ministry, are regulated by special salary arrangements (the '*hors echelle*' scale) and by the norms and regulations of the corps to which they belong. As Eymeri-Douzans (2008) puts it

> Unfortunately for the analyst, this status of '*haut fonctionnaire*' is a social status and not a legal one: nowhere in the whole legislation on civil service could be found a precise definition of what is a '*haut fonctionnaire*'; however, the vast majority of public servants have a clear and shared common understanding of who is and who is not a '*haut fonctionnaire*'.

The *political* hierarchy is the group immediately surrounding the minister. A minister in France cannot be an MP at the same time, and ministers are not always MPs immediately before becoming ministers; seventeen of the thirty-nine members of the Fillon government in late 2009 did not have to give up a seat in parliament to take a government post. Ministers are assisted by a *cabinet*, one of the distinctive institutions of the French politico-administrative system. The members of the *cabinet* are not simply advisers. They are integrated in the command structure of the French ministry and have authority over the administrative hierarchy. Many of the members of the *cabinets* are *hauts fonctionnaires*. Cabinets are of variable size, and although the numbers are officially fixed, usually at around twenty, such limits rarely have any bearing on actual *cabinet* membership. Precise figures for numbers of *cabinet* members are hard to give because there are, as Eymeri-Douzans (2008: 68–9) shows, three types of members: official, unofficial, and hidden (*officials, officieux,* and *clandestins*). Official members are nominated by statutory instrument (*arrêté*), many of them are civil servants seconded (*détaché*) from their ministerial civil service jobs to serve in the *cabinet*. In career terms both administrative and political hierarchies are closely related through the *cabinet*: having served in a *cabinet* of a minister helps an administrative career. Moreover, ministers tend to recruit members of the high-status *grands corps*. Even the unofficial members of the *cabinets* are usually civil servants (although they could be outsiders given a temporary civil service contract) who are de facto *cabinet* members but not formally recognized as such in a statutory instrument or in the official count of members. The hidden members are scarcely traceable as they generally have no proper offices and do not appear in the telephone directories. These are usually people given sensitive political tasks. One of the main links between the political and the administrative hierarchies are the *conseillers techniques*, members of the *cabinet* given responsibility for specific parts of the ministry's work. These will provide the most usual contact between the services of the ministry and the ministerial *cabinet*.

INTERESTS AND THE ORIGINS OF DECREES

Most of the work on the decrees in the sample involved the administrative hierarchy. The French sample included five *décrets* and five *arrêtés*. Both types of secondary legislation look similar and can do similar things. The fact that there are so many of them (4,245 *décrets* and 17,854 *arrêtés* were passed in 2007) reflects the fact that many things that are effected by non-statutory documents elsewhere, such as arranging for the secondment of a named civil servant to a post outside the civil service, are done by *arrêté* or *décret* in France. The main difference between a *décret* and an *arrêté* is that the *arrêté* is issued in the name of a minister or ministers, a *décret* is issued in the name of the prime minister or, less usually, the president of the Republic (for a discussion see Bergeal 2004: 82–91). Several procedural differences governing the generation of *décrets* and *arrêtés* follow from this and these are outlined below.[1]

While a full exposition of all ten French regulations in the sample (listed in the Annex at the end of this chapter) would occupy much space, it is possible to highlight the main features of the ten decrees covering: Bird Flu, reforming arrangements covering restrictions on the movement of birds in captivity including poultry following bird flu threats; Casinos, liberalizing the operation of casinos and allowing Texas Hold 'Em Poker (Sklansky 2002) to be played in them; Champagne, altering the amount of sugar that could be added to the grapes in the production of wine in the Champagne region in 2007; Cosmetics, implementing a small change in EU law on permitted chemicals in cosmetics; Farmers, altering eligibility for payments under a pre-retirement scheme for farmers; Handicap, a major recasting of the *guide barème* reclassification of handicap conditions which affect, among other things, eligibility for social benefit payments (see Council of Europe 2002); Housing, which set the arrangements for the state buying back housing from those who had bought their homes under 'right to buy' legislation; Osteopaths, setting up transitional arrangements for student osteopaths who started their education under one regulatory regime and finished it in another; Rhine, an internationally agreed measure amending the hazardous materials regulations for transporting goods on the Rhine; and Soups, which changed the regulatory regime covering soup manufacture from a law-based regime to one based on a code of guidance.

Turning directly to how our ten decrees started life, whether *arrêté* or *décret*, the prevalence of interest groups as a significant impetus for legislation was, as has been mentioned, somewhat unexpected. This larger than expected role in originating decrees points to an even stronger role in their development. Such groups were usually described, euphemistically for normative reasons (see Suleiman 1975: 293–5), as some form of 'professional' body, usually as 'organismes professionelles' since terms such as 'pressure' or 'interest' group that would be used in the other five jurisdictions are more closely associated in French politico-administrative terminology with 'special interests' which are antithetical to the 'general interest' officials like to claim they serve. The English term 'lobby' is often used to impart guilt by foreign connotation.

In the Soups Decree the initiative to make the decree came from both European and domestic interests, above all the Syndicat national des fabricants de bouillons et potages (SNFBP, the French National Association of Soup Producers). In 2003 the European Federation of the Bouillon and Soup

---

[1] *Circulaires* (in different circumstances described as '*instructions*', '*notes de service*', '*recommandations*', '*directives*') are not examined here. While they may have a similar effect to *arrêtés* and *décrets*, especially where they explain and/or give notice of the government's use of its regulatory powers, they can also be advisory.

Industry produced a non-statutory *European Code of Practice for Bouillons and Consommés*. This differed from the French statutes governing the production of soups and stocks, above all, in allowing higher levels of salt to be added (12.5mg per litre compared with 10.0mg). The SNFBP approached the Ministry of Economics, Finance and Employment to ask that the law, originally passed in 1905 but largely unamended since 1954, be replaced by a national code of practice (SNFBP 2005) based on the European code of practice. The proposal was accepted by the officials within the bureau of the ministry as they believed that French practice should be in line with European practice, above all the *Codex Alimentarius* (Codex 2001).

A second decree in the sample, the Casinos Decree, among other things changed the rules governing slot machines and also allowed Texas Hold 'Em Poker to be played in French casinos. This decree arose, as one official put it, 'from the [unpublished] *Protocol d'Accord* negotiated with two associations representing the casinos: the Syndicat des Casinos Modernes and the Syndicat des Casinos de France'. A third, the Bird Flu Decree, changed the arrangements for the movement of poultry and captive birds during outbreaks or feared outbreaks of avian flu. The scheme it set up offered more flexible rules, less based on an assumption that wild bird flocks spread the disease. The *arrêté* also owed something to interest groups for its genesis, although an 'independent' (though ministry-financed) committee of scientific experts, the Agence française de sécurité sanitaire des aliments (AFSSA[2]), also played a part, as one civil servant put it:

> We [in the ministry] came to the view [after operating the existing rules for some time] that wild birds were not the prime source of avian flu infection but the trade in birds. So we said 'maybe we should revisit our preventive measures'. Maybe we are too strict in the way we handle this. The breeders asked us to revisit this and the AFSSA also gave us an opinion on this. We did not need to ask for it. We might have mentioned the idea to the AFSSA at informal meetings and said it would be a good idea to revisit the [old] decree's measures.

Later on, the ministry further relaxed the rules to facilitate pigeon racing after the French pigeon racing clubs, such as the Fédération colombophile française,[3] had called on the ministry to ask the AFSSA to evaluate the case for changing the rules.

---

[2] Since June 2010 the AFSSA no longer exists. It was merged in June 2010 with the health and safety agency AFSSET (Agence française de sécurité sanitaire de l'environnement et du travail), and is now part of the Agence nationale de sécurité sanitaire de l'alimentation, de l'environnement, known as ANSES.

[3] 'Grippe aviaire—Les colombophiles prêts à lâcher des pigeons illégalement[.] La Fédération colombophile française (FCF) a annoncé mercredi être prête à organiser des lâchers illégaux de pigeons voyageurs, en délivrant des "permis de lâchers", pour protester contre les "mesures injustes et abusives" prises par la France contre la grippe aviaire.' Agence France Presse, 18 July 2007.

The Osteopaths Decree came as a result of a wider package of reforms for osteopathy. Earlier decrees had stipulated the qualifications required to practise as an osteopath, and a process of designating particular educational courses as providing proper training had been started. However, the reforms left out, among others, those who had already started courses before designation had begun causing uncertainty about the value of their qualifications. The whole process of reform was started by interest group activity. While a 2002 law (*La Loi du 4 mars 2002 relative aux droits des malades et à la qualité du système de santé* known for short after the minister responsible as the *loi Kouchner*) had indicated that there would be regulation of osteopathy, none came. The process of regulation became bogged down in differences between the three major groups involved: the medical doctors, the physiotherapists (some of whom could additionally practise osteopathy), and those who were osteopaths only ('*les ni-ni*' or 'the neither/nors' as they were neither doctors nor physiotherapists). An official explained:

> In 2003 and 2004 there was a series of meetings of a *groupe de travail* seeking to advise the minister on what to do [about implementing the law]. There was the ubiquitous Ordre des médécins—the Conseil de l'ordre, the Agence nationale d'accreditation et de l'evaluation de la santé (ANAES), the associations of the physiotherapists and the doctors and osteopaths associations... The idea was to reach a consensual agreement on how to do the implementing regulations... They must have had about twelve meetings... The positions that different groups took in the group reflected their different perspectives... The whole thing was very contentious, each had their own perspective. They sought a political decision (*arbitrage politique*) that would allow us to start writing the implementing regulations. There was no ministerial decision and the thing stopped there—there was no consensus.

It was only, strangely, a Value Added Tax (VAT) appeal case that started the process moving again in 2006. The 2002 law envisaged classing osteopathy as a profession and not subject to VAT. Yet osteopaths were still paying VAT and the Conseil d'État decided, in a case (CE, 19 mai 2006, n° 280702) brought by the Syndicat national des ostéopathes de France, that the government was in default and had to introduce a decree. The decree in this case was not the one included in the sample—our Osteopaths Decree was at the tail end of this particular round of regulation as it aimed to clear up the anomalous position of those who were in training courses at the actual time of the reform. So while the direct impetus for this particular decree was not the interests involved (as we will see later, the osteopaths were actually against the legislation clearing up the anomaly), their involvement in initiating the general process of regulation was substantial.

The Farmers Decree continued an early retirement scheme for farmers 'in (financial) difficulty' that had been offered to French farmers during the

1960s to ease agricultural modernization. The government had been, since 1980, trying to phase out the scheme, although attempts to remove it had produced strong protests from farmers' organizations. Another decree, the Champagne Decree governing the amount of sugar that could be added to the crushed grapes in the production process, resulted from the work of the Syndicat général des vignerons de Champagne (officially relabelled in 2006 an 'organisme de défense et de gestion' but continuing to use its old name). This group of wine producers makes suggestions about levels of sugar to be added, depending on how much sugar is in the grapes for that particular year (*recolte*).

Interest groups had no direct role in initiating four of the ten decrees. The Rhine Decree changed existing laws on waterways transport on the river Rhine and was part of a regular review of these laws through international agreement, the *Accord européen relatif au transport international des marchandises dangereuses par voie de navigation du Rhin* (ADNR). As one of the officials involved said: 'Amendments are made every two years, whether for the French or the international rules. That is the way things go, every two years an amendment, and that is how things go with the ADNR.' The Cosmetics Decree was a straightforward implementation of an EU directive amending the list of substances that may be used in cosmetic manufacture. The Housing Decree set a price (expressed as percentages of purchase price) at which housing associations would buy back houses from tenants who had earlier bought them from the associations but who could no longer afford the payments or who had to move house. The impetus for this decree came from the ministry. It was required to give effect to a political initiative (developed under Nicolas Sarkozy when Minister of the Interior in 2006) aimed at improving access to housing.

The Handicap Decree amended the *guide barème,* the framework setting out how levels of disability are to be assessed. It defines how levels of disability based on the ability of the individual to live without help, expressed in percentage points from 0 (completely able-bodied) to 100 (comatose), are calculated on the basis of detailed descriptions of different conditions. This percentage is later used to assess eligibility for a wide range of support regimes and the level of support an individual may receive. The *guide barème* had last been overhauled in 1993, so the ministry's service wanted a new overhaul. As one official put it:

> the 1993 *guide*... became obsolete as there were new issues and new ways of dealing with them. Take AIDS for example. That chapter seemed rather hard to use. We heard about it from the services—they see the changes and asked the ministry to modify the guide.... The idea to update it started here in the ministry, in the service. That is our job here—to look at the issues that arise from the *guide barème.*

The initiative here was from within the ministry. While these four decrees might not have originated in group demands for some change in the law, as we will see, groups were substantially involved in developing them.

THE MINEFIELD OF APPROVAL

In any jurisdiction no bureaucrat, and certainly not one at the level at which such initiatives frequently develop, can get very far in producing a decree without some kind of support from a superior. Wherever the impetus for a decree comes from, in most cases some political support is required before any decree passes into law in any jurisdiction. At a very minimum a minister or equivalent normally has to sign a decree or fail to oppose it.[4] This generally means that an official working on a decree has to have some reason to believe that a minister will support it, whether this support takes the form of an explicit endorsement or of acquiescence. No official in any of our jurisdictions can commit the government to a decree without some reason for believing that it will be acceptable to the political leadership. Yet in France the process of getting political approval for the *arrêtés* or *décrets* in the sample occupied a larger amount of time and produced more changes to the final text than in the samples from the other countries except Sweden.

The basic principle of political approval is that matters are passed up the hierarchy: sending a proposal from a junior-level official direct to the minister (as is possible in the UK) is not generally possible in France. It should be sent to the *sous-directeur* and then it may possibly go further. How far up the administrative hierarchy it goes, and whether from the apex of the administrative hierarchy it is passed on to the political hierarchy, and how high it goes up the political hierarchy, depends on the nature of the proposed decree, above all its formal legal status and its political sensitivity.

While I have mentioned that our sample of French decrees includes two different types of instrument, *décrets and arrêtés,* there are some points that need elaboration to make the procedures comprehensible. There are different kinds of *décrets*. Some *décrets* are issued by the Conseil des Ministres (a small proportion estimated at below one in twenty and none in our sample); '*décrets simple*' (plain decrees) are issued in the name of the prime minister (or occasionally the president). On top of this, most decrees passed by the Conseil des Ministres and under half the plain decrees are *décrets en Conseil d'État*. This means they are subject to scrutiny by the Conseil d'État—the highest administrative court (Bergeal 2004). Thus the legal status of *décrets* means that

---

[4] Some regulations do not have to be signed by ministers or equivalents. Even where this was the case, ministerial approval was still sought.

they have to have approval from *Matignon* (the Prime Minister's Office), and this is not always a formality, as we will see, and some will also be sent to the Conseil d'État which is similarly no formality. *Arrêtés*, on the other hand, are ministerial orders. Ministries only have the power to issue such *arrêtés* where the power is explicitly delegated by law or where it concerns the internal organization of the ministry (hence nominations to boards and such like are effected by *arrêté*). Nevertheless, both the *arrêté* and the *décret* need ministerial and in some cases Conseil des Ministres and prime ministerial approval, and this is often sought *before* work is started on either type.

As regards political sensitivity, the *cabinet* of the minister is informed in general terms of any decree, although for non-contentious decrees the notification will be a formality with little subsequent discussion. If it is very contentious it will require ministerial approval, not just that of the *cabinet*. The main initial point of contact with the *cabinet* is usually the *conseiller technique* (specialist adviser) who has responsibility for the area concerned. An official described the process:

> You write to the *cabinet*—you have to let the secretariat of the *cabinet* know what is coming—we send them a note: here are the things we have to take forward, these are the issues, there are these options. This is all done by written note, email and by meetings. [ECP: *And what if there are disagreements?*] The people who sort out the permission are in the Secretariat of the *cabinet*. We sometimes get in touch with them beforehand to see what they might say.... There are *conseillers* in the *bureau de cabinet* with whom I get in touch, and in my area...one particular *conseiller technique*. They [the *conseillers* and the *cabinet*] are only interested in the overall issue, they are not that concerned with what actually appears in the text. We only have proper discussions with him if it has difficult political consequences.

As was discussed above, in the absence of a clear ministerial line, an earlier version of a decree governing the role of osteopaths could not be developed.

Political clearance can also be necessary to resolve disputes involving more than one ministry. Inter-ministerial consultations usually initially take place between two officials at or below the *chef de bureau* level who try to sort out any actual or potential conflicts at an early stage. In the Soups Decree, for instance, an official in the Ministry of Finance pointed out: 'This decree was simple. I sent it to the *direction* concerned with that aspect in [the Ministry of] Health—my equivalent in Health. We send them a letter saying what we want to do. They made a few minor remarks.' If interdepartmental conflicts are not resolved at this level, or through agreement between ministers, they are taken to *Matignon*. Inter-ministerial controversies require an agreement by the *services du premier ministre*—such an agreement is put in writing and referred to as a 'bleu de Matignon' or just simply a 'bleu', because of the colour of the paper it is written on. One official describes the process involved in getting the *bleu* for her decree:

The decision still had to be approved, and we had to put a proposal for a decree to *Matignon* and there was a meeting at *Matingon* with the representatives of the ministry concerned and other ministries represented by members of the *cabinets ministériels* among others. So here you had the Finance and Social Affairs ministries there. There was a meeting and it all went around the [central controversial] question... The ministry put the thing forward... the Budget Office was against it. They then accepted the idea because we had *Matignon* on our side. They were against... this decree because of the financial difficulties of the public sector.

While the *décret* procedure explicitly includes inter-ministerial consultation and conflict resolution by *Matignon*, no such formal provision is found with *arrêtés*. However, with sensitive issues other ministries, and the prime minister, can sustain objections. For example, with the casinos *arrêté* the Ministry of Finance 'imposed', according to one respondent, some significant changes in the decree at a late stage to combat problems that it saw in relation to money laundering. In the case of the Bird Flu Decree (an *arrêté*) the Ministry of Agriculture officials responsible for the decree were summoned to the Prime Minister's Office:

> ... we had a meeting in *Matignon*. It was a very sensitive issue especially for the breeders and it was about a big public health risk, so the issue was discussed in *Matignon*. The request came from *Matignon*... At the *Matignon* meeting were me, *conseiller technique* from the *cabinet* of the Minister of Agriculture, the Office de la chasse, the Ministry of Health and it was convened by the Sécretariat général du gouvernement (SGG). There were about 10 of us there in all. They called it because the measure was very urgent.

In addition to the general provisions for approval, there are also mechanisms specific to the issue area concerned. One decree, the Rhine Decree (a *décret*), was subject to a distinctive regime for its development that involved inter-ministerial consultation. Once international agreement (between countries through which the Rhine flows) has been reached on amending the transport regulations, it is submitted to a French inter-ministerial committee chaired by the Minister of Transport. In practice this committee is not a high-level committee and its members are usually at the level of *chef de bureau* or below, although senior officials may attend if the issue merits senior attention. The committee's decisions are usually made by a *chef de mission* rather than the minister. Another quirk of this particular regulatory regime is that the decree has to be issued by the Foreign Affairs Ministry. This is pure formality. While the law applies as soon as it is agreed by the inter-ministerial committee as an *arrêté* (in late 2006 coming into force January 2007), it took until February 2008 for the Foreign Affairs *décret* to appear.

One of the procedures for breaking inter-ministerial disagreements available in some sectors is the 'expert' advisory committee. The Agence française de sécurité sanitaire des aliments (AFSSA), mentioned earlier, had a particularly important role in resolving an inter-ministerial disagreement in the Soups Decree

> The Ministry of Health was unhappy about the salt issue [as the new code of practice to be introduced by the decree had higher levels of permitted salt than the old regulations]. We got in touch with the Agence française de sécurité sanitaire des aliments and they said that this was OK and so they [Health] agreed.... If the proposals had not got their support I'd have had to have gone to [*Matignon*]

The AFSSA had a wide remit and its views were sought in two of our eight decrees—Bird Flu as well as Soups. In a third decree, the Cosmetics Decree the Commission de cosmetologie, an 'expert group' of the similarly named, but distinct AFSSAPS (the Agence française de sécurité sanitaire des produits de santé responsible for approving medicines and medical products) offered its views on the decree. In a fourth decree, the Casinos Decree, an advisory body (the Commission supérieur des jeux) was consulted, but because of the political importance and urgency of the legislation (elaborated on below), it played little part. In a fifth, as has been mentioned, the Rhine Decree, it was an 'expert' international committee that drew up the decree and in both the Champagne and Housing Decrees 'expert' bodies were also involved. In only three decrees (the Farmers, Osteopaths, and Handicap Decrees) was there no recourse to an 'expert' body, though as will be shown below, an expert *ad hoc* working group was involved in both the Osteopaths and the Handicap Decrees. The advice of 'experts' is, in the French system, a common way of avoiding or deciding conflicts within and between ministries.

For some decrees, Conseil d'État approval is required. The basic principle is that once one has drafted the legislation and gained all the necessary approvals (including the approval of the prime minister through the *bleu de Matignon*, where needed) a copy of the decree is sent to the Conseil d'État for examination of its legality. The Conseil d'État will allocate a *rapporteur* from among its officials whose task it is to produce a report on the proposed decree and present it to the relevant section of the Conseil for a decision. In order that relatively junior officials from the relevant ministry can participate in this process of meeting with the *rapporteur* and attending the meeting of the Conseil, ministerial civil servants attend as *commissaires du gouvernement*, a formal designation that gives them some temporary standing in a highly status-conscious politico-administrative system (the device of nominating them as *commissaires* is also used to allow officials to be present at meetings with *Matignon* officials), although in formal Conseil d'État and *Matignon* hearings they attend simply to listen, not to speak.

The *minute* or note from the Conseil might accept the proposed decree without any changes, or it might also make specific proposals. The ministry then has to decide its response, which might be not to accept the recommendation. While the Conseil was not involved in the Casinos Decree in our sample (as it was an *arrêté*), for the parent *décret* it rewrote a complete section. In the sample, the Conseil made no comments on the Soups Decree and for the Osteopaths Decree it made a small suggestion (adding a category of people who should benefit from the decree) which the ministry accepted. On the Handicap Decree the Conseil d'État criticized the style of legal writing but nevertheless let the decree through.

> There were some problems with the Conseil d'État. It was written by doctors for doctors and not in a judicial style. More a pedagogical style rather than a judicial or regulatory one. [*ECP: Did the Conseil d'État demand changes?*] No, they asked us to make sure that next time we write it in a proper style and put our pedagogical explanations in other supporting documents.

The Conseil d'État itself is divided into sections, and the approval by one section, say responsible for the particular ministry issuing the decree, does not preclude criticism following litigation by another, the litigation section (*Section contentieux*). An official recounted how on one recent decree he had made, the Conseil d'État rapporteur believed that the decree was illegal (and was successfully challenged in the litigation section soon after it was passed) but passed it nevertheless because he accepted that the ministry had little choice but to approach the decree in the way it had chosen to approach it. He explained:

> We knew it was illegal, we all saw it was illegal, even the Conseil d'État. They validated it because it was a legal blind spot (*vide juridique*). You have to resolve it somehow. It was not a good solution, but it was probably our only solution. There was a risk it would be declared illegal. We had to do something [along these lines]—it was illegal, but it was legitimate.

ELABORATING DECREES

The role of interest groups in initiating decrees in France has already been noted. In a surprisingly large proportion of cases, seven of the ten, when preparing the decree the officials played a significant role in mediating between the interests and the state, or as mediators between different competing interests, or sometimes both. In the Casinos Decree, writing the *arrêté* was a matter of developing a written, but not published accord, reached between the casino owners and the Ministry of the Interior. The immediate implementation of the accord involved the development of a 2006 *décret*,[5] not among

---

[5] Décret n° 2006-1595 du 13 décembre 2006 modifiant le décret n° 59-1489 du 22 décembre 1959 et relatif aux casinos.

our sample, and the 2007 Casinos *arrêté* in our sample. For both decrees the role of the major casino owners' associations was important. Both decrees were developed by a working group composed of officials from the Interior and Finance ministries, among others, and the casino owners. The 'professionals', i.e. the owners, played a leading role in this process. As one official describes it:

> In the working group rather technical stuff was handled. The professionals know the subject. The texts were generally proposed by the professionals [i.e. casinos people]. We often tended to work on the basis of their drafts. The first draft (*rédaction de base*) came from the profession... Much of the text goes into great detail about individual games and they [the professionals] are the ones that know most about them.

The draft would be looked at within the ministry and its officials would, on occasions, make 'counterproposals' or object to parts of the industry's draft. The meetings of the working group would decide in the case of any conflict. The decision rules were described by an official as follows: 'If the official in the particular section responsible, the *chef de bureau* and the *directeur* are in agreement, then the proposal [in the draft] goes ahead.' Middle-ranking officials (*chefs de section* or *chefs de bureau*) participated in these working group meetings as *commissaires du gouvernement* (see above).

The importance of the interest group involvement was highlighted by the turn of events as the working party was finishing its work on the Casinos Decree. A cross-union initiative (FO, CFDT, CGT, CFE-CGC[6]) called a strike of casino workers for 31 December 2006 specifically to object to the changes in pay and working conditions brought in by the proposed Casinos Decree which, according to the unions, would involve 'twenty per cent reductions in staff'. As the CDFDT strike call put it:

> By offering the casino owners the possibility of increasing their profits and working with smaller workforces, Sarkozy is Father Christmas to the casino bosses and Scrooge to their employees.[7]

Sarkozy, who was about to start his presidential election campaign in 2007, was reported as offering the unions concessions at a meeting on 11 January[8] and instructed his officials to draw up a list of the points the 'employees did not accept. This list was gone through by the *cabinet directeur* and the minister

---

[6] Confédération générale du travail-Force ouvrière; Confédération française démocratique du travail; Confédération générale du travail; Confédération française de l'encadrement-Confédération générale des cadres.

[7] Notice CFDT Hôtellerie Tourisme Restauration, Dec. 2006, http://www.cfdt-htr.org/?p=754 'En offrant aux casinotiers la possibilité d'augmenter leurs profits en supprimant des emplois, Sarkozy s'avère être le Père Noël des Patrons des Casinos et le Père Fouettard des employés!'

[8] http://www.casinos-hits.com/news-page-68.html

himself. Most of what the unions wanted was given to them.' The casino owners, nervous that Sarkozy's departure from the ministry and possible replacement by someone less sympathetic to their views would jeopardize the deals they had already negotiated, were keen to see the *arrêté* published even with the union-induced changes, and even with some further changes 'imposed by the Ministry of Finance... we accepted them because of the time pressure, as did the profession'. The *arrêté* was signed 'in a hurry' in between the first and second rounds of the presidential election in May 2007—a process that involved rushed taxi trips around Paris to make sure signatures were gathered before deadlines were missed and days were lost (similar rushed final stages were found in two other decrees in the sample).

The Osteopaths Decree similarly involved major interests concerned and part of the conflict was also played out in public. The decree came as part of a prolonged process of developing a framework governing how osteopaths are trained and how they practise. At stake were two cross-cutting sets of interest conflicts. The first was the conflict between the medical professions and the osteopaths. As discussed above, the medical professions (doctors and physiotherapists) were allowed to practise osteopathy alongside their other activities. Those who were neither doctors nor physiotherapists, '*les ni-ni*', were trained solely as osteopaths. The osteopaths were concerned that their profession was being restricted and downvalued by the medical professions. The second conflict was between the interests of the established '*ni-ni*' against the large number of trainees who sought to practise osteopathy. The main decrees covering osteopaths (not in our sample) dealt with (a) setting up a system for deciding which osteopathy courses should be accepted as providing the qualification to practise; (b) specifying what osteopaths were allowed and not allowed to do on their own, and what they could only do under medical supervision; and (c) arranging for the transition from the old system to the new system of regulation.

For the main decrees governing osteopathy the officials in the relevant bureau of the Ministry of Health[9] got clear instructions from the Minister about how they were to approach reconciling the different interests.

> The *cabinet* decided. Rather the key people in the *cabinet* were the two *conseillers techniques*, one of whom was a doctor. We went to the *cabinet* in 2006—we were supposed to set out the departmental vision for osteopathy and how it fits [in the medical professions], the idea was to give them something to work on. The *conseillers techniques* had different visions and we argued the case. That allowed the minister to make a decision. We're a team—the arguments were put forward and the minister decided... Our vision in the bureau was that the profession was *partagé* (shared)—the practice [of osteopathy] was one that was shared by

---

[9] In fact there were two different bureaux involved, one for education and one for the general conditions of practice, later on the latter took on responsibility for education and qualifications.

different groups. The view that my division here in the ministry put forward was shared by the minister.

And when writing the main decree

> We had lots of meetings. We met the *directeur de cabinet* several times and held the meetings in his office. It was very political. The lines were pretty clear: doctors wanted a monopoly, the physios believed it should not be given to anyone else and the *ni-ni* wanted to make sure that the title of osteopath was exclusively for the *ni-ni*. We were the ones who discussed this with the groups.

The text had to be signed by the prime minister, and involved the officials in the *service* attending two or three meetings to finalize them. The '*ni-ni*' were extremely unhappy about the resulting decrees that also shortened the study period from between five and six years to a minimum of three years and in December 2006 students demonstrated in Paris and other French cities against the decrees.

The whole negotiation over osteopathy regulation was somewhat protracted, and the specific Osteopathy Decree in our sample was above all a by-product of this process. Those who already started their osteopathy courses had been the 'forgotten' ones, caught in a no-man's-land between the old and the new regimes, and the ministry wanted to make arrangements to allow them to practise. The need to make some provision for this group was made clear by the requests that arrived in the ministry from students, 'they wrote and asked what do we do, are the courses run by our school approved?' The officials concerned regarded this as a 'technical matter' and did not consult on it. It was sent to the *cabinet*, who agreed it and it was approved by the Conseil d'État (with some modification which the officials in the ministry accepted). After it was passed the *décret* was bitterly opposed by the osteopaths' associations who wanted to restrict the new entrants to the profession. They took the government to court as they claimed the ministry was only allowed by law to make provisions for those already in the profession, not those yet to enter. The ministry then had to introduce a piece of primary legislation allowing the measure before the issue came before the Conseil d'État.

In the elaboration of five other decrees the role of groups was significant if not quite so public. The Housing Decree, which set the level at which housing associations (HLMs) buy back the houses they sell to tenants, was not only based on a proposal from the HLMs. Once elaborated within the Ministry of Housing it was checked, as one official pointed out, with the HLM representatives:

> We decided what we thought would be best and then we tried a first attempt to write the decree, we clarified problems, and discussed them ... inside the administration. Once we had agreed on the draft decree we sent it to the representatives of the associations of the HLM. We met them, talked about

the decree. They provided the information. As it was based on what they were doing anyway, we wanted to make sure.

The Soups Decree also had a substantial input from the interest groups although the decree itself was straightforward (essentially repealing a 1959 law) and the code of practice that replaced it was written by the producers associations. The development of the decree itself consisted largely in getting the necessary permission from the Cabinet, explaining the decree to the Conseil d'État and dealing with the Ministry of Health's objections to the increase in salt content in principle permitted under the proposed new regime (discussed above), a point the Ministry of the Economy countered by underlining the industry's argument that salt content had actually gone down over the past ten years and that the maximum was largely irrelevant. The AFSSA's report in favour of the Ministry of Economy decided the issue. All of this was negotiated at a level below the *chef de bureau*.

For three of our ten decrees the task of writing involved translating the work of 'expert' committees into regulatory form, and such committees brought with them significant interest group involvement. The Handicap Decree, defining different degrees of handicap used to assess eligibility for financial support and services, was based on the work of several working groups, composed of medical professionals, officials involved in service delivery for the handicapped and social insurance, as well as representatives of disabled groups ('at least one for each type of handicap' as an official involved described it). Their work, which included developing new criteria for assessing handicap and testing them, started in 2003, finished in 2005 but took over two years to reach the statute book. The officials' work in producing the text was largely done in the working groups. 'We used the text that the working groups produced, did a proposal for a law'. The Bird Flu Decree followed the advice of the AFSSA (Saisine n° 2008-SA-0082 of 30 April 2008). The Champagne Decree resulted from the work of the regional wine producers as approved by regional officials at the Comité national des vins, eaux de vie et autres boissons alcoolisées on which the wine producers are represented. This particular decree, governing above all levels of sugar that may be added to the grape harvest in wine production, is an annual event and remains uncontentious. The industry's proposals tend to be accepted—in contrast to the more contentious issues of acreages that may be planted with vines in the *Appellation d'origine contrôlée* region.

This leaves just three decrees where the role of groups in their development was less prominent. Yet in all three cases groups played an important part in the process, even if they did not, for different reasons, have much directly to do with the *elaboration* of the decree once the relevant ministry had started work on it. For one of them, the Cosmetics Decree (dealing with adding chemicals to lists of substances permitted to be added to cosmetic products), the role of groups was limited not least because it was a simple enacting of an EU directive. The proposed decree, developed within the Agence française de sécurité sanitaire des produits de santé (AFSSAPS) itself, was not difficult to write as all the provisions were already in the directive. Nevertheless, the draft still had to be shown to an 'expert' committee, the Commission de cosmetologie within the AFSSAPS, for approval—a body with over twenty members (mainly scientists) and which includes three industry representatives and a representative of consumer groups. With the Rhine Decree, once the international committee (on which interests are represented) has reached an agreement 'the proposal is considered *bon*', as a ministry official on the committee put it, and the elaboration of the decree is straightforward, copying the agreement into a decree and going through the formality of getting it approved by the Foreign Ministry. The Farmers Decree, revolving around retirement payments to farmers, arose from a deal between the state and the farmers dating back to 1980. Farmers were consulted on, and opposed, the proposed decree, even though the proposal was something of a compromise, and the matter became political. The campaign against the proposed decree involved MPs writing to the minister but the ministry managed to resist it as, according to the officials involved, it managed to get the Prime Minister's Office on its side.

CONCLUSIONS

Looking first at what our ten cases tell us about the involvement of politicians and their auxiliaries in the world of decree-making, France has clearly a distinctive set of institutional arrangements that fall outside the conventional 'fire alarm' versus 'police patrol' distinction for monitoring administrative behaviour. Three of the ten decrees, the Casinos, Osteopaths, and Farmers Decrees, attracted very active participation from politicians and *cabinet* members in their elaboration (even if not, as in the case of the Farmers Decree, in their initiation). The *cabinet* system did not appear to operate as a fire alarm, alerting politicians to their dissatisfaction with what bureaucrats were proposing, since in all three cases the interests were already mobilized and highly visible. Neither was the *cabinet* acting as a police patrol, or at least if it was, it had a very novel feature: the people they were policing were continually 'grassing themselves up'—items were routinely referred to *cabinet* members as part of the development of a regulation by the bureaucrats writing them. Involvement came at the choosing of the politicians who, in principle, had the opportunity to become involved in any one of the ten decrees. A second distinctive feature of the French system was that 'involvement' in these three cases did not mean the offering of detailed instructions to bureaucrats, or the exercise of a veto over some of the things bureaucrats proposed, but rather the virtual takeover of the process of elaborating the decree by the political level—most clearly seen in the Casinos Decree with the close involvement of the Minister of the Interior in negotiating with groups involved.

What happened when the politicians were relatively silent in seven of the ten decrees certainly did not mean an absence of constraint on bureaucrats. There exists a range of limits which do not rely on the direct intervention of politicians or even the credible threat that they could get involved. The Conseil d'État, a judicial body, could and did intervene in the development of some decrees, albeit in a minor and rather technical way. More importantly for the content of the decrees, a range of bodies that rely effectively on hierarchical or legal authority for their effect constrained the actions of bureaucrats. It is not claimed that these bodies—'expert' bodies and consultative committees—were not 'political' in the broader sense of reflecting conflicting interests, but rather that they did not rely directly on ministers or their entourage to have an effect. In some cases (the Champagne, Cosmetics, and Handicap Decrees) officials were essentially acting as the secretariat for these bodies—translating their recommendations into law; in others bureaucrats took a more active role, albeit in different ways, in shaping the decisions of such bodies by affecting their agendas (Soups and Bird Flu Decrees) or actively participating in them (Rhine Decree). Such bodies were important in resolving interministerial disputes in two cases (Soups and Bird Flu) without invoking the authority of ministers or their *cabinets*.

Moving on to look beyond the specific concerns of bureaucratic–political relations, the findings of this chapter also cast a rather different light on the broader character of decision-making in France than one finds in significant (though not all) parts of the literature on the subject. For Schmidt (2006: 108), France is a 'statist' country, certainly in comparative terms. Unlike Italy, Germany, Sweden, and the Netherlands, it has 'traditionally provided interests with little access or influence in policy formulation'. This is not to say that there is not a large amount of lobbying and consultation in France (Schmidt 2006: 122). Yet like other apparently 'statist' countries, France has, she continues (Schmidt 2006: 108), 'accommodated [interests] in *implementation*' (my emphasis). This accommodation has taken the form, in France, of 'making exceptions' to the rules that are made without their direct involvement. However, unless one wishes to understand the whole of the decree-making process as a producing a series of exceptions to general rules, the evidence from this sample of secondary legislation directly challenges this statist view of policy-making in France. Such an understanding that rules are 'exceptions' would be somewhat perverse, not least because decree law is so closely related to the general 'rules' that govern French society. *Arrêtés* and *décrets* constitute, for the most part, the bulk of the legal codes and provisions that govern French society and public policy. Moreover, it is the nature of such administrative regulation that it is consistent with acts of primary legislation and generally applicable legal norms. The notion that such decrees are 'exceptions' would be extremely difficult to sustain.

The finding that there are close relationships between the administration and its interest group environment might appear to challenge a branch of scholarship that points to the persistence of a normative republican tradition of a 'strong state', which itself underpins common understandings of French bureaucracy outside France. Yet it is entirely consistent with another branch of scholarship that challenges such a view. Grémion's (1976) study of *le pouvoir périphérique*, while a study of centralization and decentralization, is above all a study of the role of the French administration—central ministries and field services—in relations with regional and local elites (for a discussion see Hayward 2010). Grémion offers a broad picture of an administration with close relations with its immediate environment, not of aloof separation.

> In fact, administrative segmentation coexists with the social segmentation of its environment and the one reinforces the other to create exclusive bureaucratic-representative islands ('îlots exclusivistes bureaucratico-representatifs'). The Ministry of Education and the teachers unions, the Ministry of Agriculture and the farmers, the Interior Ministry and the associations of local councillors are all examples of this. But such islands are not always to be found at the level of the ministry. They can also be formed at the level of a *direction* [within a ministry]: relations between the National Association of Chambers of Commerce and Industry and their sponsoring branch in the Ministry of Industrial and Scientific Development or between the Order of Architects and branches within the Ministry of Cultural Affairs are characteristic of these islands... (Grémion 1976: 328)

Moreover this vision, as close to interest group corporatism as it is to the traditional aloof 'strong state' (but fitting neatly with neither), has been elaborated by scholars since in a version of what Cole (2008: 140) describes as 'a state-flavoured version of neo-corporatism' (see also Jobert and Muller 1987; Mény and Thoenig 1989).

Cole (2008: 140ff.) describes the features of this variant of 'neo-corporatism': state 'accreditation' of certain interest associations, co-management of public authorities with professions (he uses the example of the role of champagne producers which, coincidentally, relates closely to one of the decrees in my sample), and professional self-government in social affairs and other areas that do not directly involve the 'technical state'—those parts of the state that remain dominated by the technical *grands corps*. The picture of this interaction as it operates lower down within a ministry appears less of an organized stable set of relationships sanctioned by the state. Certainly this chapter has examined decrees that have involved interests through the 'expert' and deliberative organizations characteristic of an ordered form of state neo-corporatism. However it has also outlined more haphazard and shifting relationships that are the inevitable result of the extreme diversity of the everyday types of public policies dealt with at the level below the *direction*: the pigeon fanciers, the Rhine transport companies, the '*ni-ni*', the casino owners, the soup manufacturers. Which particular sections of which ministry are likely to impinge on the activities of such groups is often difficult to predict, and thus policy cannot always result from the interactions of an enduring policy network.

This observation about the variability of state–interest group relations at this level takes us back to one of the very earliest studies of French interest groups. Ehrman's (1961) examination of bureaucrats' administrative regulative activity indicated a strong influence for organized interests. His work also points to a caveat to any conclusion that sees the bureaucracy as 'captured' by groups. There are many reasons why bureaucrats in France give great weight to interest groups in making policy decisions, including convenience, deference to specialized expertise, and even fear (Ehrman 1961: 549). Bureaucrats can also enlist the aid of groups to achieve purposes identified within the bureaucracy. Here the bureaucracy 'will seek to maneuver between the interests surrounding it' and he points to cases where 'the administration has tried to overcome resistance from powerful interests by gathering behind its program the support of competing groups'. Hayward (1984) developed this to argue that pressure groups selected as allies for state purposes could become 'pressured groups'. The relationship with groups is complex and variable, but perhaps the least variable aspect is that the group nexus is crucial to administrative regulation in France.

Bureaucrats at this level are significantly cross-pressured by a range of intra-bureaucratic, external, and political influences. While external interests play a large role in shaping the agenda and the form of many of the decrees in the sample, the bureaucrats writing them are severely constrained by a range of intra-bureaucratic processes. These include the direct steer from superiors from the administrative or political bureaucratic leadership (e.g. immediate superiors or *conseillers techniques* from the *cabinet*), the processes that of ensuring compliance with a range of dedicated expert and/or advisory bodies, conformity with legal principles and precedent through the Conseil d'État, as well as the requirements of inter-ministerial approval. On top of this the issue might be effectively taken out of the hands of the middle-ranking officials within the ministry entirely and handled by senior politico-administrative officials, as happened with the Casinos Decree and to a certain degree the Osteopaths Decree. Given that the form and content of the measure affects the degree to which some or all of these cross-pressures come into play, the overall result is highly unpredictable, making the notion that French policy-making at this level conforms to a form of corporatism, with the predictability and stability it implies, less plausible.

ANNEX: DECREES INCLUDED IN CHAPTER 2

Reference	Ministry	Short Name
Arrêté du 24 janvier 2008 relatif aux niveaux du risque épizootique en raison de l'infection de l'avifaune par un virus de l'influenza aviaire hautement pathogène et au dispositif de surveillance et de prévention chez les oiseaux détenus en captivité	Ministère de l'agriculture et de la pêche	Bird Flu
Arrêté du 14 mai 2007 relatif à la réglementation des jeux dans les casinos.	Ministère de l'intérieur	Casinos
Arrêté du 14 février 2008 relatif aux Appellations d'origine contrôlées 'Champagne', 'Coteaux champenois' et 'Rosé de Riceys' de la récolte 2007	Institut national de l'origine et de la qualité et Ministère de l'agriculture et de la pêche	Champagne
Arrêté du 22 février 2008 fixant la liste des substances qui ne peuvent entrer dans la composition des produits cosmétiques	Agence française de sécurité sanitaire des produits de santé	Cosmetics
Décret du 22 octobre 2007 relatif à la mise en œuvre d'une mesure de préretraite pour les agriculteurs en difficulté	Ministère de l'agriculture et de la pêche	Farmers
Décret du 6 novembre 2007 modifiant l'annexe 2-4 du code de l'action sociale et des familles établissant le guide-barème pour l'évaluation des déficiences et incapacité des personnes handicapées	Ministère de la santé	Handicap
Décret du 16 janvier 2008 relatif aux opérations d'accession à la propriété réalisées par les organismes d'habitations à loyer modéré et modifiant le code de la construction et de l'habitat	Ministère du logement (rattaché au MEDAD)	Housing
Décret du 2 novembre 2007 relatif aux actes et aux conditions d'exercice de l'ostéopathie	Ministère de la santé	Osteopaths
Décret du 27 février 2008 portant publication du protocole portant adoption des amendements au règlement pour le transport de matières dangereuses sur le Rhin (ADNR)	Ministère de l'écologie, du développement et de l'aménagement durable (MEDAD)	Rhine
Décret du 24 janvier 2008 relatif aux bouillons et potages	Ministère de l'economie et des finances	Soups

3

Britain: Bureaucrats and Imaginary Ministers

Policy-making in the UK civil service is generally associated with the genteel clublike world of the Oxbridge-trained mandarin, made famous worldwide by the television programme *Yes, Minister*. Whether this genteel world still exists in the same form, or whether it has been replaced by another more frenetic world, that of the political adviser, 'spin doctor', and policy wonk, made famous by another television programme, *The Thick of It*, is a matter for debate. Yet as earlier work (Page 2001, 2003; Page and Jenkins 2005) has suggested, much policy is made without having to intrude much in either of these rarified environments. In the UK rather less gets pushed up to the top, whether the administrative or political apex, than might be expected, and conversely these worlds tend to impinge on the daily routines of policy-making infrequently. How then, is it possible for policy to be under political control where hierarchy appears to be so unobtrusive?

The answer to this question is that it is certainly possible to be under a form of political control, and a very pervasive political control that does not tend to produce the kinds of cross-pressures on the bureaucrat that one finds in France. While ministers in the UK can and do issue direct commands to bureaucrats developing policy detail, such interventions are indeed rare and the key mechanism of political control lies in the anticipation or indirect divination of the wishes of the minister. The mechanism appears to be a long-enduring feature of British bureaucracy: it could be found in Herman Finer's (1935) account of British bureaucracy and Kingsley's (1944) classic study of 1930s Whitehall and remained a striking feature of British government decree-making seventy years later (Page 2001). In earlier days such divination was thought to result from the similarities in social background and thus social outlook between the political and administrative elites (Finer 1935; Kingsley 1944; Weber 1972). Whether or not this congruence in outlook really resulted from social similarities cannot be examined here. However, the social similarities have arguably declined and, more importantly, the officials developing policy in the cases examined in this research are at grades in the civil service substantially below those where social similarities with political

MINISTERS AND OFFICIALS

In the UK the political control of ministries is vested in the senior minister, usually of Cabinet rank and termed the 'secretary of state', and the junior ministers. The number of junior ministers depends in part on the size of the ministry. In the Home Office in May 2010, for example, there were, in addition to the Home Secretary, three ministers of state (the higher ranking of the junior ministers) and two parliamentary under-secretaries of state (the lower ranking of the junior ministers), the Department for International Development has one minister of state and one parliamentary under-secretary of state. Unlike the other jurisdictions covered in this research, there is no overt appointment of political officials or political recruitment of ministerial leadership teams. While the degree to which politicians can shape the appointment and promotion of career civil servants in the UK is a matter of debate, few would argue that the system of government offers UK ministers anything resembling the spoils system of the US or the ability to create a political staff of the kind created in the French *cabinet* system (see Greer and Jarman 2010). Since 1970 there has been an increase in the number of political advisers—political appointees given responsibility for advising ministers rather than acting in their name,[1] and in the period covered by the research in this book (the Brown Labour premiership 2007–10) there were around seventy special advisers, double the number Labour inherited from the Conservatives in 1997 (Gay 2010).

The nomenclature for civil servants ranks and grades has changed significantly in the past quarter-century and since different ministries have significant responsibilities for their own personnel policies there is some variability between departments, especially below the top levels (discussed in National School for Government 2010). The most senior career official in a ministry is still known by the traditional title of 'permanent secretary'. In some ministries (e.g. Treasury and the Department of Health) there is a second (deputy) permanent secretary. Below the permanent secretary the traditional positions (in descending order) of deputy secretary, under-secretary, and assistant secretary (formerly also known as grades 2, 3, and 5) are usually now described as directors general, directors, and assistant directors. Together these grades make up the Senior Civil Service (SCS). Appointment to the SCS can be made

---

[1] Jonathan Powell and Alastair Campbell were temporary and partial exceptions between 1997 and 2007.

from outside the civil service, but in the main ministerial policy roles the large majority of SCS appointments are internal promotions (Public Administration Select Committee 2010), and these promotions are made by civil servants overseen by the Civil Service commissioners rather than politicians.

Below the SCS there is significant variation between ministries (sometimes within ministries that are newly merged) as regards grading. The traditional senior principal and principal positions (old grade 6 and grade 7) generally have a wide variety of names including assistant directors and team leaders, and below them the old senior executive officers and higher executive officers in some ministries keep these traditional names and in others they are replaced by different names, often including 'head' or 'manager'. Most of the officials who took the lead in developing the decrees analysed in this chapter were in these grades immediately below the SCS.

INERTIAL BEGINNINGS

Policy is often conceived of much like a creative process with 'entrepreneurs' or policy wonks getting an idea and working it through. In fact the process of making the policy for many of the twelve UK decrees in this study seems to have no clear beginning or end. Many of our twelve UK decrees were moved along by the inertia of previous decisions. In part this is a consequence of what appears to be a UK approach to structuring legislation by first creating primary legislation and leaving key issues, including sometimes the question of whether the legislation should be implemented at all, to later secondary legislation or even non-statutory codes of guidance or codes of practice. The UK is not unique in this general approach of legislating and leaving details of its application to later, but the fact that so many in the admittedly small sample were of this kind suggests the possibility that UK legislators are more prone than policy-makers in other countries to leave issues 'to the regs' (i.e. to the 'regulations'), or decrees in the terminology applied in this book, when they devise primary legislation.

The pattern of developing primary legislation through decrees appears to be of two main kinds: either a straightforward putting the legislation into effect (four cases) or dealing with some problems that have arisen from trying to put the legislation into effect (three cases). In such cases the political impetus to develop such decrees, and thus political approval, is deemed by those developing them to have been given before the primary legislation was developed, often many years before. The work to put such laws into effect followed the momentum created at the time of the original legislation and the officials concerned needed no direct instructions to implement it. Of course, when it comes to the development of the decree the deemed ministerial approval becomes less straightforward, but for those writing decrees implementing primary legislation the response of one official when asked what led him to start work on the decree—it 'was a manifesto commitment and a ministerial priority'—was fairly typical.

Among the relatively straightforward cases, at least in their initiation if not development, was the Alcohol Disorder Zones Decree giving effect to the part of the Violent Crime Reduction Act 2006. This allowed local authorities to raise charges from local businesses selling alcohol in designated parts of inner cities to pay for alcohol-related problems in the locality (see DCMS *et al.* 2005; see Berman *et al.* 2005). No such zone was ever set up and the measure was discontinued after the end of the Labour administration in 2010. The Mesothelioma Decree implemented the legislation fulfilling the government's commitment to address the problem arising from the typically protracted process of securing compensation for those contracting mesothelioma—a form of cancer usually associated with exposure to asbestos. The Offender Management Decree simply tidied up the law to reflect changes introduced by the Offender Management Act 2007 and the Criminal Justice Decree rolled out still further across the country the application of section 29 of the Criminal Justice Act 2003 which allows for new ways of instigating criminal proceedings by a public prosecutor.

Among the less straightforward implementing decrees was the Casinos Decree as this had to implement the 2005 Gambling Act. The implementation was blown almost entirely off course by the fact that one central point of the legislation, to create regional 'super casinos', was dealt what turned out to be a fatal blow by a defeat in the House of Lords in March 2007 of the proposal to site such a casino in Manchester. The House of Lords voted against the Statutory Instrument that was supposed to allow it to be set up (see Ward 2007) and the Act had to be implemented around the wreckage of this defeat. The Home Information Pack (HIP) Decree arose from a commitment first announced by the Labour government in late 1999, and brought into law in the Housing Act 2004, to oblige sellers to produce a HIP covering essential details about the property, in principle to make buying a house less expensive. A series of technical problems meant that the housing market would probably be unable to produce HIPs in the precise timescale proposed (there had already been significant slippage in the timetable) and the HIP Decree in the sample introduced some further delays into the implementation of the scheme. The Animal Mutilations Decree had to revisit the implementation of the 2005 Animal Welfare Act in so as far as it concerned banning some surgical procedures on animals (e.g. docking tails from pigs) after an issue came to light (the laproscopic insemination of sheep) that made the ministry realize that they had made some significant omissions.

Inertia rather than direct ministerial instruction can be found in the placing of three other decrees on the regulatory agenda. One, the Energy Billing

Decree, implemented an EU directive and required energy suppliers to give more consumer information on their bills to consumers, including previous usage and charges. The timetable for implementation was delimited by the requirements of EU law, in the words of one official: 'we had two years in which to comply with the directive. The directive text was a half baked piece of drafting. It was done at the last part of the UK presidency and finalized at five to midnight by people who did not know what they were talking about.' Two further decrees, one changing the performance measures against which fire services will be judged (the Fire Services Decree) and another the performance measures for police forces (the Police Best Value Decree), were timetabled to be developed as the earlier performance measures were due to expire after 2008.

This leaves only two decrees that formed discrete policies in their own right rather than parts of a longer story of bringing legislation into effect or maintaining a pre-existing regulatory regime. One was the TV Multiplex Decree that rearranged the allocation of digital broadcasting by moving the British Broadcasting Corporation (BBC) off a multiplex channel that had been formerly exclusively reserved for it. The initiative for this proposal came from Ofcom, the regulator responsible for digital airwave allocation. Politicians had little to do with the initial impetus. A DCMS official involved described the genesis succinctly:

> It started as an Ofcom idea, they are the real owners of this. Digital switchover [the move from analogue to digital broadcasting] releases parts of the spectrum which Ofcom wants to sell. Terrestrial broadcasters say 'give us more spectrum and we'll provide digital' and Ofcom came back and said 'use your existing spectrum more efficiently'. The Ofcom position interested us as we were interested in using the spectrum efficiently. They said they would go away and come up with propositions on how to use the six multiplexes more efficiently. They produced the idea of Multiplex Four to be arranged so as to use MPeg4, which is more efficient. This allowed them to put on three high definition channels. [ECP: How did this get the go ahead as an idea?] At a meeting somewhere someone said 'OK, let's do it'. It was a defensive thing to begin with about what to do with the spectrum released by switchover. We signalled to them to do it [come up with plans] without talking to ministers. We talked to the minister when the proposal came in. James Purnell was the minister then and he knew the media. He was happy for the work to continue, so we would feel we got a bit of a ministerial mandate.

The second discrete policy decree, the Mental Capacity Decree, might have been included as an implementing decree since it came from a problem arising from the implementation of some earlier primary legislation. A European Court of Human Rights judgement concerning the rights of those detained under the Mental Capacity Act pointed to the need for the Mental Capacity Act of 2005 to contain provisions for those who lack capacity to make decisions to be represented by a friend, relative, or carer to help them.

This required primary legislation, though the secondary legislation was developed at the same time. This requirement to pass primary legislation (the Mental Health Act 2007) at the same time as the secondary legislation tended to make the involvement of ministers somewhat closer than in other cases, since a parliamentary slot had to be found for the legislation. But even here, as suggested by a health ministry official, it would be mistaken to believe ministers either initiated or drove the process:

> Ministers were alerted to this issue when the ECHR judgement came in. Ministers were informed as we went along and had to agree to reform the Mental Health Act. [*ECP: Was that because you had to get a legislative slot for the primary legislation?*] The contact with the minister was about the substance of the issue and the vehicle to be used was decided later. The timing was all a matter for the Cabinet committee and this sort of thing was out of our hands. We got a slot, although a little later than we thought we would.

The inertial character of the initiation of decrees in the UK sample explains why civil servants often seem distinctly self-starting when working on decrees, but can legitimately claim to be working to a ministerial agenda. They see their role as initiators of decrees as carrying out expectations of what they should do established by earlier decisions, whether these decisions are to set up and maintain a regime or set in motion a policy on which the government has already legislated. Even those two decrees that do not fit this pattern could hardly be characterized as ministerial initiatives since the TV Multiplex Decree arose from the plans of officials in the regulatory body and the Mental Capacity Decree arose from an ECHR judgement. Yet in none of the cases did the officials interpret their self-starting role as giving them any substantial discretion about whether to start work on a decree. If it is thus easy to understand how ministerial approval could in most cases be deemed to have been given without much direct instruction from ministers, how much discretion did officials have when developing the content of the decrees?

THE DEVELOPMENT OF DECREES

Ministerial Roles

The deemed political impetus to start work on the decree in the first place tended to carry over for most of the decrees into their development. It is true that the development of the decrees sometimes involved few significant choices for either officials or politicians. However, only two of the twelve decrees fell into this category. For the Offender Management Decree the changes to existing provisions were largely technical legal points, and the

Casinos Decree carried out decisions that had effectively been reached several years before when the primary legislation was being considered. However, in ten of the decrees there were significant choices to be made in how the policy was to be developed. In some of the decrees the minister made some direct interventions that shaped such choices, but these interventions were limited both in frequency as well as in the scope of the matters the politicians were interested in. One official even commented: 'I've never seen a minister over an SI [statutory instrument]. That is not to say that people don't see ministers over them. Some big things are done by SI and you might be expected to see a minister [for those].'

To begin with those cases where there was direct ministerial intervention aimed at shaping the policy development, we can find three positive initiatives where ministers defined what they wanted to see included in the decree that might not otherwise have been expected to have appeared in it. One was in the Fire Services Decree that created new performance indicators for local fire services. The idea was to move away from mandatory injunctions towards a more permissive regime. This particular idea was pushed by the SCS official supervising the team working on the framework

> The steer to reduce the burdens... came from the [SCS official in this ministry]—he has meetings with the FRAs [Fire and Rescue Authorities]. He wanted the number of 'musts' and 'shoulds' to be reduced—we cut them from 37 to 25. We had meetings with the director before we drafted the revised framework and he came along to the stakeholder workshops. It was a big deal and he took an interest in it. It was a high-profile document.

The draft involved the collaboration of different parts of the Department of Communities and Local Government concerned with fire services and the SCS official sustained his desire to keep the mandatory parts to a minimum.

> We asked policy leads to draft different chapters to update the previous sections. We said they should keep the 'musts' and 'shoulds' to a minimum, and we had the final say. You had a policy lead for each chapter and the policy leads felt it was their role to tell others what they should do. We did the introduction and the foreword. There was lots of pressure from our director to remove as much as possible from the compulsory bits, we went back and said we wanted to drop this or that bit.

The direct ministerial intervention came in one particular aspect of the new regime: the inclusion of gender and race equality in the performance targets: 'The minister was keen on the diversity agenda—that was big, and he wanted it included in there.' It was somewhat inconvenient as 'that meant additional musts and we were also under pressure to find and cut others in case we exceeded our targets of "musts" and "shoulds"... there was a strong steer from the [SCS official] and without that strong steer we would certainly have let more in'.

A second similar direct intervention came in the development of the Alcohol Disorder Zones Decree. As an official involved explained: 'The appeals issue—ministers took a view that we did not need an appeal mechanism. Hazel Blears [the minister concerned] said we should use the ombudsman scheme. We found out what the ministerial intention was and we drafted accordingly.' And something similar was found with the Mesothelioma Decree where the minister made it clear that he did not want administrative costs to be deducted from the lump sums paid to those suffering from the disease. In all three cases the direct ministerial involvement referred to significant but limited aspects of the development of the decree.

Given the substantial increase in the number of special advisers ('SpAds') appointed by ministers after 1997 and their apparent importance, they did not feature significantly in our twelve decrees. Significant though their role may be in a ministry, it did not extend to dealing with the everyday issues of the kind covered by the decrees in this study, even the controversial ones (for an alternative view see Rhodes 2009). Respondents were asked about the role of advisers. With two decrees, officials referred to the fact that advisers 'might have been involved' in discussing the primary legislation (since they were unsure if any discussion would have taken place without them) but generally for the kind of detailed elaboration of policy the role of advisers appeared limited. For the Alcohol Disorder Zones Decree, for example, when asked whether SpAds were involved at any time, an official replied they had not been. Even when the issue had to be taken through Parliament (some decrees have to be approved by vote of Parliament, see below) 'the discussions took place with government business managers and whips to get things through the house, but not advisers. We sent a written submission to the minister.'

Interpreting Unexpressed Ministerial Wishes

Officials used a variety of techniques to decide how they should structure the policy when faced with choices and where no direct politician steer was available. The most important of these techniques in terms of the frequency it was mentioned in our sample, was trying to divine what the minister would want the decree to look like were she or he faced with the choice. An official involved in writing the new police authority performance measures (in the Police Best Value Decree) pointed out: 'Ministers intervening or imposing a target or removing it? That would be an exception. There is lots of guidance and lots of places where ministers can say what their priorities are and what they are not so they do not need usually to intervene.' By this he meant that ministers make their views clear in a variety of forums—policy statements, green papers, House of Commons debates, through preparing the cross-government performance indicators in the Public Service Agreements

(PSAs). Moreover, ministers' private offices, staffed by civil servants, also offer guidance. As one official said: 'You get a feeling for where ministers are coming from through private office and things that are important to them.' (See also Page and Jenkins 2005; Rhodes 2009.) This highly indirect form of ministerial participation, by officials anticipating reactions based on a range of cues, could be found in most of the decrees where deemed ministerial preferences had a bearing on the choices to be made. In the Alcohol Disorder Zones Decree, for example, when dealing with a range of groups to develop the implementation of the scheme, the official concerned argued:

> I went to meetings with ACPO [the Association of Chief Police Officers], LACORS [the Local Authorities Coordinators of Regulatory Services] and the LGA [the Local Government Association]. They said their concerns had not been met. Representative organizations will have self-interested views. The challenge for us is to try and work out what is a legitimate and not a legitimate concern. [ECP: How do you do this?] The first thing is to ask yourself 'what do ministers want to achieve?' When...the minister at the time was taking it though the House, what did he want and what did Parliament agree to? It was 'polluter pays' [referring to an extension of the environmental legislation principle, that those who supply the alcohol should pay for the damage it causes, used by ministers to describe the policy].

In a similar way, the officials who had identified that the key HIP policy could not be implemented in time anticipated the reaction of the minister. Because they knew it was a high ministerial priority to bring the HIP scheme into force, to help sustain a case for delay they made sure they had independent specialist advice. One of the officials involved explained:

> we commissioned Ted Beardsell [the deputy chief executive of the Land Registry].... Ted reported, and his report confirmed there were big problems getting leasehold information researched—problems of timescale and cost. We went to ministers presenting the information and asked ministers what was the best way forward. We asked whether we should press ahead as planned or do we make some sort of amendment, although we recommended an amendment.

Of course, in saying that ministers tend to be more involved in policy-making by proxy, i.e. through their reactions and wishes as anticipated by officials, one must not lose sight of the fact that ministers are involved in the development of almost all decrees in a somewhat passive way in that decrees have to be signed by them. This means they will be kept informed of any decisions taken by officials through 'submissions' which generally set out the policy context, the problems, and the proposed solutions. There are key stages in the development of a proposal at which a minister is likely to be informed, even if this is a formality. Ministers are approached when questions of controversy arise, even if the minster's likely answer is already clear, not least so that the approval can be minuted. In the Mesothelioma Decree, for example, a policy official responsible for its development argued:

One issue is term renewal, that was why we sought a ministerial decision on it. And the question of whether ex-servicemen come into [the scheme] . . . These were the controversial bits. We took both to ministers. We knew these were issues that would be controversial, and you get the decision in writing. We definitely went to ministers on other things we thought may crop up and we then have a paper trail.

Apart from a paper trail for officials, a possibly more important consequence of seeking ministerial approval is to avoid ministerial embarrassment. If there is any issue on which the minister might be asked a question, by colleagues, the press, outside interests and organizations, she or he should know what is going on in the department. It is a key failing of the officials if the minister is not informed. Thus with anything remotely controversial or likely to alter substantially any policy measure, the minister will be informed before any significant amount of an official's time is devoted to it. Before an idea, or the fact that the department is thinking about an idea, becomes more widely known, such as through consultation with outside groups and organizations, the minister will be informed. If the officials have done a good job of anticipating the minister's reaction, the minister will simply indicate agreement to a submission. Usually such submissions set out the planned progress but they may also offer the minister choices. In the HIP case, for example, the submission appeared to offer the minister a choice (do nothing and let the HIP scheme go wrong or delay its implementation). However, even if it was a genuine choice, it was one of the very few offered to ministers in the twelve decrees in this sample.

Conceptual Divination

Other techniques, apart from trying to anticipate ministers' wishes, are used to decide how the legislation should be structured in the absence of a steer at the outset and direct intervention in development. For want of a better word we might call one of the more significant of these 'conceptual divination'—a form of divining the way ahead, using one or more simple and broad concepts, known to be among those that the minister or government approves of in this context, or even concepts believed to be a principle of 'good government'. Of course, such conceptual explanations officials offer might be *post-hoc* rationalizations of decisions adopted for other reasons. However, we have no way of distinguishing one from the other. One example of this conceptual divination has already been mentioned. With the Alcohol Disorder Zones Decree the minister was believed to be in favour of the 'polluter pays' principle applied to those who sell alcohol, by placing a responsibility on them to pay for any harm or extra costs alcohol consumption brings. This idea was used to judge proposed amendments suggested in the consultation, for example. Such central concepts often have to be balanced against others. In the case of the

Alcohol Disorder Zones Decree the central principle balancing 'polluter pays' was the potentially contradictory 'cost to business'. The official most closely involved in this regulation went on to say that the response to consultations with stakeholders was approached by taking the 'polluter pays' principle and 'working back—trying to find the best outcome with the least cost of regulation and cost of burdens. Sometimes you please all the people, sometimes not. Here we did not.'

A central concept in the Animal Mutilations Decree was 'necessary mutilations'—some mutilations were 'necessary' for animal husbandry. An official describes how one issue was taken up:

> The issue of tagging non-wild birds came up. Poultry breeders got in touch and we decided it was a good idea to talk to look into it. The welfare groups were a little worried about commercial wing tagging. They did not think it was necessary. They could be leg ringed, so it was a needless mutilation.... [ECP: How do you decide which side to take or how to go on this?] You rely on the expertise of your adviser. X [the veterinary officer] went and visited a duck farm and saw them do the tagging and made an assessment based on his expertise and assessed the welfare costs and welfare benefits. He suggested it should only be allowed for specific purposes and for 36 hours after hatching. The industry was only asking for that as they did not do it after 36 hours (actually they did not do it after 24 hours but we thought we needed some sort of margin as we did not want to be prosecuting people who did it 24 and a half hours after). It was also a process to be done 'for breeding improvement' as it did not need to be done in normal farms.

In the same decree officials decided not to include provision for permitting mutilations of camelids (above all including llamas) due to a principle of 'good legislation'. As one explained:

> The issue came up during consultation and we decided not to include them ... It was an agreed line. It was not something that was consistent with the principle of good legislation. You could not say it was needed now [because the procedures on camelids were not widely used at the time], it was to be there 'in case'. If it had been something needed now we might have spent more time on it.

With HIPs the central idea was the seller providing the buyer of a house with information the buyer would otherwise have to pay for, and this was balanced against 'reasonable' costs: 'This started off with good intentions—that the buyer should have good information. Providing it can cost a bit, so the question is whether there is an alternative way of providing the information with minimal cost.' With the Digital Decree the central issue was 'efficiency' in use of the digital multiplexes (see p. 51, above), and those developing the decree were confident that the principle gave them a clear view of what the minister was likely to support. When dealing with the BBC, unhappy with the proposed changes, the officials felt assured that they knew the minister's mind. 'The minister is always there over your shoulder [metaphorically speaking]. You try to avoid saying that you'll get the minister to ring up Michael Lyons

[BBC Chairman]. But if you ask him to... he'll do it. [*ECP: Did you ask him to ring him up?*] No... [but] we had a lot of brinkmanship the day before the consultation in May'.

Consultation

Conventional interpretations of British government have it that government officials are inveterate consulters (Jordan 1982; Jordan and Maloney 2001; but see also Cairney 2009). Indeed in every decree except one there was some consultation with 'stakeholders'—a term that refers to anyone deemed to have a significant interest in a particular policy area, whether individuals, groups, firms, or governmental bodies, even other parts of the same ministry. It is certainly a general principle of policy formulation that one needs to consult and the only exception in the twelve decrees studied here was the Offender Management Decree—those writing it did not feel it needed any form of consultation since it was a largely consequential decree tidying up existing law and not changing anything.

Consultation was one or more of three kinds. One form comes through consultation of a formally constituted advisory group (often called 'stakeholder' groups or panels). A second comes through informal or *ad hoc* consultations with interests as the decree is being developed, whether early or late in its development. A third is the a formal set-piece public consultation where the department produces a consultation document setting out the decree, inviting comments which are then collated and frequently published in a departmental response to the consultation.

In only one case did the consultation process play a significant role in shaping the content of the decree, and it did so less in changing officials' minds or shaping ideas about what should be done than pointing out issues for regulation that officials were largely unaware of. The original intention behind the Animal Mutilations Decree was to deal with one small matter: procedures surrounding the artificial insemination of sheep. The issue arose following a question from a firm of commercial sheep breeders about whether a particular procedure was permitted and it emerged that the issue was not covered in the existing mutilation regulations. Once it became known among the stakeholder group that a new decree was being proposed to cover sheep insemination, the veterinary officers raised the question of wing-tagging. There followed an informal consultation. An official takes up the story:

> Of course, we had to start the consultation before we actually wrote the consultation document.... Our thinking became clarified by the consultation and goats were added. Then we considered placing an embargo on any other points to be brought into the new SI as we were up against a time limit, we needed to get the SI in place by the start of the [sheep] breeding season.

Nevertheless, in the course of the consultation a range of other issues were added to the decree, including tagging of non-wild birds ('Poultry breeders got in touch and we decided it was a good idea to talk to look into it') and beak trimming. The camelids issue (referring primarily to the question of whether llamas should be exempt from some of the regulations) was raised, discussed at length, and dismissed.

In terms of changing minds over proposed courses of action, all three forms of consultation offered only limited guidance to officials developing decrees. The inclination was to accommodate interests, but this was generally only insofar as it was possible to make changes that did not significantly modify what the department had originally proposed or ran counter to what officials saw as the central concepts underpinning the legislation. Because formal set-piece consultations are initiated only after significant work has been done already on the policy and the minister has agreed to the thrust of the thinking behind the policy change, such consultations appeared less likely to have an impact than informal consultations and stakeholder groups. One official was quite blunt about what he expected from a formal consultation: 'We sent out the drafts to people before we went out to final consultation. We wanted to avoid the position where new feedback came in. The consultation did not come up with anything new.' An official commenting on the elaborate job the department had done in collating the feedback on a public consultation argued:

> We followed what was done previously, with something high profile like this you have to. We went through them all [all the comments received], went to the different policy leads [i.e. different parts of the Department responsible for different parts of the legislation] to draft the response to them and collated it all. The idea was to do the key themes and keep the whole thing succinct. The policy leads would say how to address the points. We made minimal changes and then got the final draft OKd by the minister.

Yet another came up with a similar argument that the department looked at the comments but felt considerable discretion as to whether they paid any attention to them:

> [*ECP: How did you decide which responses to the consultation to listen to and which not?*] We decided as a team. And we employed someone to categorize the responses. It was someone who had [previously] worked in the ministry... and then found he had some spare time (I think he set himself up as a [kind of self-employed professional consultant]), and we knew he was good at this sort of thing He brought the comments together clearly so you could look at them effectively. The team decided which ones we would take on board. The Grade 5 was not involved in the detail of this.

Part of the reason that consultations often make little difference is that the officials concerned believe they can usually accurately guess what the responses of different groups may be and tend to discount them in advance.

In much the same way that it is frequently argued by officials writing primary legislation that the objections or points raised by groups can be dealt with 'in the regulations' (Page 2003), it was not uncommon to find that officials offered groups the possibility of concessions 'in the guidance'—the official ministerial document accompanying some of the decrees offering advice on how the decree was to be interpreted or applied. As an official working on the guidance for the Alcohol Disorder Zones Decree argued,

> The guidance was where we had lots of discussions with the LGA and the industry [and others]. This was where the proposals fleshed themselves out. They asked lots of questions 'what about this, or what in this instance?'. You cannot address these things in the SI, but we said we'd include it in the guidance, and that is where they will be listened to. Will the supermarkets be captured in the legislation? We took legal advice from the lawyers and put it in the guidance.

Departmental Views

Given that 'departmentalism' is often assumed to be an important influence on decision-making, there was little clear evidence of its operation, although, of course, selective conceptual divination (e.g. deciding cost was either a big issue or not a significant issue when judging the merits of a proposal) could be a rationalization or justification of such departmental views. It came up in two decrees. In both, commercial interests were involved, but hardly in a way that entailed any significant cost issues. For the Energy Billing Decree the official closely involved pointed out:

> The August 2007 consultation asked if people wanted [the provisions to include information on past bills to be extended to business customers]. We were always clear we did not want to include business customers. We did not think it would have any influence in the business sector. We had some support—we include in the consultation a leading question [along the lines] 'should the provision be for private customers only and not business'. Certainly here [in BERR] we ruled it out early on.

Interdepartmental issues arose, albeit not directly in the decrees concerned (rather in the primary legislation made with the prime purpose of allowing the secondary legislation covered in the research), when officials were looking around for primary legislation already in the pipeline on to which they could add some clauses allowing their planned changes in the Mental Capacity Decree. Once they had managed to get permission, in one case reluctantly,[2]

---

[2] As one official said 'People defended their borders on bills. And our bill was not on [their issue], and [so they] were not keen at first until the minister [concerned accepted an approach from our minister]'.

they tended to work on their part of the bill entirely separately from the other department concerned.

Most of the officials writing decrees were generalists. The only significant specialist civil service involvement (as opposed to consultants and non-civil service agencies) was found in the Animal Mutilations Decree where the veterinary officer effectively made decisions about levels of pain and advised on the 'necessity' of different kinds of mutilation. In other cases officials simply mugged up on the detail necessary to do their jobs. As lawyers working on the TV Multiplex Decree put it:

> We had to learn more about DTV than we thought we ever needed to know. [My colleague here] could give you 20 minutes on Null Packets. We got a pretty firm grasp of the technicalities.

As we will see in Chapter 8, the argument that such generalism is unique to Whitehall is not entirely accurate.

LEGITIMATION

In a system where executive authority is based on party majorities in the legislature, the approval of ministers is generally enough to ensure that the decree is passed. However, there is a variety of checks on executive power in this respect and a high proportion of the decrees in the sample were to some degree affected by them. Most decrees have to be approved by Parliament, either by not being voted against ('negative resolution') or being subjected to a vote in favour ('positive resolution'), and the relevant parts of the primary legislation on which the decree is based specify whether a decree under its provisions is subject to a negative or affirmative resolution.

The Alcohol Disorder Zones Decree had to negotiate problems not only in the affirmative resolution procedure but also following criticism from the parliamentary committees that oversee all statutory instruments, whether negative or positive: the Joint Committee on Statutory Instruments (JCSI) and the Lords Committee on the Merits of Statutory Instruments. The decree was withdrawn once even before it was considered by the JCSI. The official who dealt with the issue explained:

> How our lawyers saw it and the JCSI saw it differed and we withdrew the regulations. It actually only got as far as JCSI's lawyer, not the JCSI, and we withdrew the regulation to tighten up the drafting. If we'd have said 'no, we'll carry on' we could have got a negative report on the SI.

A critical comment from the JCSI is not necessarily fatal for the decree. It can be ignored, for example, if the department is convinced that the criticisms would not indicate the decree failing in court or if it can be corrected by some kind of amendment later on. Nevertheless, it is more common (see Page 2001) to avoid difficulties with the JCSI. The concern about JCSI appeared to derive in part from the fact that officials do not like to see a 'defectively drafted' decree on the statute book, and in this case partly from the fact that an adverse JCSI report might make it harder to gain support for it when debated on affirmative resolution procedure in Parliament. The draft Alcohol Disorder Zones Decree was later relaid (in January 2008) and withdrawn again, this time following a critical report from the Merits Committee drawing 'the regulations to the special attention of the House on the ground that they may imperfectly achieve their policy objectives' (Merits Committee 2008: 3). There was also criticism from the JCSI (2008: 5) on the ground that the decree was 'defectively drafted' (at issue was the question of how those on whom charges were imposed could appeal against them). They were withdrawn again, relaid, and approved by positive resolution, albeit with a division in the House of Commons and a fifty-minute debate in the House of Lords.

The process of negotiating these problems was largely dealt with by officials in the same way that the original drafting process was handled—keeping the faith with the main principle of the legislation ('polluter pays'), changing the draft where necessary on the basis of the perceived likely wishes of ministers, and getting final approval through a submission. The contact with ministers on this issue was indirect, as an official put it: 'private office told us the minister was happy with how we proposed to deal with the JCSI's concerns and was keen to see us take this forward as soon as possible.'

The Animal Mutilations Decree was also subject to affirmative resolution but faced no difficulties from the JCSI. In this case, as in the Alcohol Disorder Zones Decree, the role of officials was to brief and support the ministers for the affirmative resolution debates, should it come to a debate. Civil servants will usually attend 'in the box' in Parliament. In the Animal Mutilations Decree there was an unusual breakdown of communication that nevertheless shows the kind of things civil servants attend debates to do since, as the official attending the debate said:

> it went to the House of Commons—it was not that bad. There was some briefing against it. The NFU [National Farmers Union] got an MP to ask about whether camelids [llamas and such like] might be brought into it—it was all about whether the artificial insemination provisions might be extended to other species—deer and camelids. The issue [had come up earlier] . . . and we decided not to include them and it was raised by an MP [in the debate]. Unfortunately the minister did not get my note in time [which was passed to him from the box] and said that he would write to the MP to tell him why it was not extended to camelids.

Overall, of the twelve decrees, five were affirmative resolution where the role of officials was anticipating criticisms and amendments and briefing on them. Three were drawn to the attention of the House by the Merits Committee and one was the subject of an adverse report in the JCSI. A further decree (Mesothelioma) was subject to the special procedure of the Social Security Advisory Committee (see Page 2001). In these cases the role of the officials rather than ministers or special advisers was the most important in handling criticisms (either by amending the legislation or some other response). Moreover, just examining JCSI or Merits Committee reports probably underestimates the role of officials in legitimizing decrees as important informal contacts may also be established between lawyers for the committees and officials drafting decrees. One official pointed to such informal discussions when he said:

> The Merits Committee—its remit is so wide, and it has widened into areas where our input [as lawyers] is required. Once they contacted us on something we did not think was part of their area. We told them that and they accepted what we said.

Thus officials can also get an idea of any likely objections by the committees before they actually draft the decree.

CONCLUSIONS

Unsurprisingly, the picture offered by this discussion of the everyday process of policy-making differs little from the picture offered by my earlier study of a different set of decrees in *Governing by Numbers* (Page 2001). Nevertheless, this view of everyday policy-making from the perspective of those most closely involved in it still contrasts with a 'top brass' perspective, the view from the office of the minister or permanent secretary. It is not unusual, of course, to see the top brass and the lower levels of the bureaucracy as largely separate worlds that do not seem to have any frequent direct interaction. In what he describes as an 'anthropological' study, Rhodes describes decision-making within the minister's 'court', largely the direct personal interactions with the minister's private office. Here he sees 'more discussions about the presentation of policy than of the substance' (2007: 30), the accounts of meetings appear to be more about the corporate affairs of the department and its relations with the wider political world than the substance of policy in issues facing the department. In fact his account of life at the top around the minister contains a series of clues that indicate that much of the everyday life of a minister and his or her top brass in Whitehall has rather little directly to do with the everyday practice of government as revealed in the bulk of the measures that government produces, such as decrees, guidance, direct instructions to public and private bodies, and regulatory decisions.

It is in the role of the top brass, the 'court', in this policy process that the view from the top gives a fundamentally different picture from the view from below. Traditional approaches to understanding the role of the British civil service tend to assume that the policy-making is done by the senior civil service (see Page and Jenkins 2005). Rhodes (2007: 26) makes it clear where he believes power lies in a Whitehall ministry in his musings on the last bit of his trip to see the minister *in situ*:

> On arriving at the department, it is immediately clear that I am entering the land of the official and the powerful. There are security guards on every door and everyone has to check in at the front desk to get a security pass... I was not allowed to walk through the building unescorted. My status as a professional stranger was all too clear. I was not one of them.

However, since it is normal for anyone entering a Whitehall building to pass through a security desk and to be escorted around the building, whether visiting a minister or a clerical assistant, the trappings of security should not be confused with the reality of decision-making.

Indeed, in this world anything approaching the humdrum of detail is repeatedly described as boring and tedious, 'done on autopilot' (see Rhodes 2011: 10). 'Autopilot' might well be how policy decisions are best made for those that lack interest in them, and it is quite understandable how the process of everyday policy-making should appear to take care of itself when viewed from the immediate environs of the minister's office. Every effort appears to be made by the officials for whom such policy cannot be taken for granted to make sure that their work intrudes only rarely into this elevated world. The policy-making world of officials outside the SCS works on the basis of a range of routines that allow decisions to be taken, sometimes contentious ones, without having to secure direct and explicit approval from the minister but allowing officials to claim with some justification, that they are doing what ministers want.

ANNEX: DECREES INCLUDED IN CHAPTER 3

Reference	Ministry	Short Name
2008 No. 1430 The Local Authorities (Alcohol Disorder Zones) Regulations 2008	Home Office	Alcohol Disorder Zones
2008 No. 659 The Police Authorities (Best Value) Performance Indicators Order 2008	Home Office	Police Best Value
2008 No. 1330 The Categories of Casino Regulations 2008	Department for Culture, Media and Sport	Casinos
2008 No. 1420 The Television Multiplex Services (Reservation of Digital Capacity) Order 2008	Department for Culture, Media and Sport	TV Multiplex
2008 No. 1370 The Fire and Rescue Services (National Framework) (England) Order 2008	Department for Communities and Local Government	Fire Services
2008 No. The Home Information Pack (Amendment)(No. 2) Regulations 2008	Department for Communities and Local Government	Home Information Pack (HIP)
2008 No. 1426 Animal Welfare The Mutilations (Permitted Procedures) (England) (Amendment) Regulations 2008	Department of Environment, Food and Rural Affairs	Animal Mutilations
2008 No. 1315 The Mental Capacity (Deprivation of Liberty: Appointment of Relevant Person's Representative) Regulations 2008	Department of Health	Mental Capacity
2008 No. 1263 The Offender Management Act 2007 (Approved Premises) Regulations 2008	Ministry of Justice	Offender Management
2008 No. 1424 (C. 63) The Criminal Justice Act 2003 (Commencement No. 21) Order 2008	Ministry of Justice	Criminal Justice
2008 No. 1163 The Electricity and Gas (Billing) Regulations 2008	Department for Business, Enterprise & Regulatory Reform	Energy Billing
2008 No. 1963 Mesothelioma Lump Sum Payments (Conditions and Amounts) Regulations 2008	Department for Work and Pensions	Mesothelioma

4

Germany: Administration and Politics Revisited

While Weber probably never said or meant it, the idea that bureaucracy and administration can and should be separated from politics and policy is associated with him (see Sager and Rosser 2009). The separation is widely regarded as the way in which political control should be exercised in a modern democratic system. Politicians make the choices and officials carry them out. This separation has something in common with another dichotomy, also often erroneously associated with Weber, that of facts and values. Applied to policy-making, this means that while bureaucrats can be involved in making policy, they bring facts and an understanding of technical issues to the policy process, while the politicians make the choices of priorities and values (see also Aberbach *et al.* 1981). This dichotomization of political creativity and administrative technical competence has been commonly applied to the policy-making process in Germany. The traditional notion of the German *Beamte* highlights the virtues that officials are expected to have of loyalty, obedience, and competence. Putnam (1973) highlights the traditional avoidance of involvement in politics found among German 'classical bureaucrats' and Dyson (1982) talks of the importance attached to *sachlich* (factual) discourse in the German policy style.

Recent literature has tended to point to change in the German bureaucracy to include a greater willingness to participate in politics in general and party politics in particular (see Goetz 1999, 2006; Knill 2001; Hood and Lodge 2006). Like Putnam (1973) before them, they tend to point less to a fundamental transformation than to a coexistence between a more politically oriented bureaucracy and a group with a more traditional *sachlich*-technical self-image, often on the basis of seniority, with predominantly very senior officials needing to employ 'political craft' (Goetz 2006) to advance their careers. Yet the distinction between the old and the new version of the role of bureaucrats in the policy process may be less of a contradiction than it at first appears.

As has been seen in the French and UK cases, the way the world immediately around the minister works appears to follow rather different rules to the everyday policy-making world which is the focus of this book. In France and the UK the relationship between these two worlds—the everyday world and the world at the apex of the politico-administrative system—is quite different. In France the role of intermediary institutions and procedures, above all the *cabinet*, appears make the traffic between the worlds frequent. French *cabinets* can identify key priorities and effectively take them over. The intermediary processes and institutions in the UK, including private offices and political advisers, appear to lead to less interaction between the two worlds and still make it possible to talk about the 'minister and his court' operating within a 'cocoon' (Rhodes 2009). As we will see, the traffic between the two worlds in Germany, on the evidence of the decrees in the sample, appears to be significantly more regulated than in France and the UK.

The six decrees included in this chapter cover a range of different issues. The Ship Safety Decree is an omnibus regulation containing various measures for different kinds of ships, including the provision that leisure boats have to carry radio equipment. Its most striking feature was its contribution to the ban on ships' captains drinking while in charge of a ship, an issue that had been prominent since the ship *ENA 2* crashed into the *Pudong Senator* in the Port of Hamburg in 2004. The Civil Emergencies Decree changed the legal liability of pharmaceutical companies supplying drugs under conditions of civil emergency when the strict regulations governing drug safety could not be observed. The Employee Insurance Decree involved a highly technical set of arrangements for the administration of accident insurance in the public sector. The Milk Quotas Decree governed the allocation of the additional milk quotas that became available in 2006, the Fiscal Equalization Decree set out the final calculations for distributing funds between the different *Länder* for fiscal year 2004 and the Noise Maps Decree implemented a European Union directive instructing the creation of noise maps in order to help deal with noise pollution.

POLITICS AND ADMINISTRATION

For the officials involved in the six decrees examined in this chapter, the separation between the world of politics and the world of administration was not a matter of avoiding issues that can be considered 'political', or even avoiding acting 'politically'. The civil servants interviewed were certainly not afraid of being involved in 'making policy'. Rather the separation helps delimit a sphere in which bureaucrats can do their work largely unhindered by direct political intervention, though safe in the knowledge that whatever they do will have to be agreed to by politicians at some stage. This space appears to be protected by a variety of measures, above all sets of norms about what politicians and bureaucrats should do and the formal procedural requirements of a gemeinsame Geschäftsordnung—a code of procedure for handling policy. This space appears to give bureaucrats significant latitude in developing policies, a latitude that is all the larger because a significant portion of federal rule-making requires securing agreement with the *Länder* or state governments. This means negotiating with the relevant functional bureaucracies in the *Länder* as well as the *Staatskanzeleien* or the core political executive organizations which may differ significantly in what they are prepared to agree to. Nevertheless, this space is bounded by a set of agreements and understandings, apparently shared by bureaucrats and politicians alike, possibly through a bargain arrangement (Hood and Lodge 2006), that significant political issues cannot be settled within the routine bureaucratic regulatory process, or even by seeking to get ministers onside. Rather such issues belong to non-routine political and political-administrative decision-making forums that surround the bureaucratic regulatory process. This set of arrangements does not separate politics from administration, but rather creates procedures and forums in which more contentious issues are decided, certainly with bureaucratic participation, separate from the routine procedures of bureaucratic decision-making.

FORM IS NOT EMPTY NONSENSE: LEADERSHIP, RESPONSIBILITY, AND THE GEMEINSAME GESCHÄFTSORDNUNG

A German ministry is headed by a minister, who is assisted by a junior minister (*Staatssekretär/in,* the slash indicating the masculine and feminine versions of this noun[1]) or in some cases two. These are by law members of the *Bundestag* (although junior ministers in the Federal Chancellor's Office do not have to be). Parliamentary state secretaries are not part of the hierarchy of German ministries in the sense that they cannot, like their UK counterparts, sign decrees. The administrative hierarchy of German ministries is headed by *politische Beamte* ('political officials'), normally described as 'political appointees' as they are appointed and dismissed by the minister. The level at which this form of political appointment takes place is predominantly the most

---

[1] I will use the masculine forms of nouns relating to position and rank. Under a quarter of civil servants working for the federal government in the formal category of the higher civil service (*höherer Dienst*) are women. To use the feminine forms might imply greater gender equality than actually exists.

senior ranks of *Ministerialdirektor*[2] and above who fill the top positions in a ministry: *Abteilungsleiter* and *Staatssekretär*. Although the term 'state secretary' is applied to two separate positions, one filled by a politician and the other by a bureaucrat, the top civil servant is a *beamteter* ('administrative') *Staatssekretär* and the junior minister a *parlamentarischer* ('parliamentary') *Staatssekretär*. Between two-thirds and three-quarters of the approximately 130 in this group of *Abteilungsleiter* and *Staatssekretäre* will change following the election of a new party to government as there are limits to the numbers of officials who can be replaced[3] (see Goetz 1999). The positions that the *Ministerialdiretkoren* fill are usually those of *Abteilungsleiter*, with the *Abteilung* being the highest level unit below the ministry, these are divided into subunits headed by *Unterabteilungsleiter*, usually at the rank of *Ministerialdirigent*. The *Referat*, arguably the most important unit for the development of everyday policy, is headed by a *Referatsleiter*, usually someone of the grade of *Ministerialrat*. All these top bureaucratic positions belong to the higher civil service, the *Höherer Dienst*.

In the pioneering empirical work (Mayntz et al. 1973) that led to Mayntz and Scharpf's (1975) classic study of German bureaucracy, the importance of the *Referat* was already clear and there is little reason to believe its position has declined. Mayntz et al. (1973: 82ff.) distinguished between top-led ('central') initiatives, initiatives from the level of the *Abteilung* ('semi-central'), 'decentralized' initiatives from the level of the *Referat*, and initiatives emanating from outside the bureaucracy:

> The initiative to develop policies comes predominantly from the *Referate*. A minority of the officials in the *Referate* even said when asked that if it were not for the *Referate* taking the initiative the 'process of developing policies would come to a complete standstill', while the majority also recognised that leadership at the central and semi-central levels also play a role. (Mayntz et al. 1973: 82–3)

The importance of the *Referat* is further underpinned by the formal legal provisions surrounding policy development.

It is not possible to understand how ministries work, and how officials make decrees, without understanding the rules and formal provisions governing German administration. As the members of the student duelling club in Heinrich Mann's *Der Untertan* (1952: 50) put it, 'Form ist keine leere Wahn' ('form is not empty nonsense'). The strong link between law and policy that has been commented on by many outside observers (cf. Johnson 1978; Dyson 2010) is especially apparent in administrative procedures. While

---

[2] In principle the *rank* of the civil servant (e.g. *Ministrialdirektor*) is different from the precise *position* in the ministerial hierarchy (e.g. *Abteilungsleiter*). In practice they are closely related.

[3] The mechanism for replacement involves putting the official to be replaced into temporary retirement (*einstweiligen Ruhestand*). There are usually financial limits that constrain the numbers of appointments at this level.

respondents in every country in which I conducted interviews, with the partial exception the UK, made frequent reference to the legal framework within which they operated, in Germany the reference to law was especially noticeable. All respondents had copies of the legal texts relevant to the decree in question open on their desks and referred to them frequently when discussing their work.

Officials also referred to the gemeinsame Geschäftsordnung (GGO) of the federal ministries that regulated how they do their work (for the version current at the time of the interviews see Bundesministerium des Innern 2000). They did not have this open on their desks, rather they knew it as if by heart and presumed that anyone interested in how things work in German ministries knew it too. The main responsibility set out in the GGO is that a decree is prepared on the basis of a *Vorlage*, or submission, that gets passed up the hierarchy until there is agreement on what the final text should contain. The *Referat* has to prepare the *Vorlage* and get it approved by the Cabinet through the Federal Chancellor's Office (*Bundeskanzleramt*). The GGO (at *Anlage* 2) sets rules for procedures in handling policy. It even contains guidelines covering the colour of pen that officials in different positions should use to write on documents that will be passed up and down the hierarchy: *Referatsleiter* in black biro, *Unterabteilungsleiter* in brown, *Abteilungsleiter* in blue, *Staatssekretär* in red, and the minister in green.

The GGO sets out in some detail the form that the submission has to take and the questions it should address. Before the *Vorlage* can be submitted for eventual approval by the Cabinet, it has to go through the procedures of approval within the ministry and then the process of approval with other ministries. The GGO specifies that the ministry should involve other relevant ministries and, where appropriate, the *Länder* in the early development of the decree (paras 45(1) and 47(1)). The decree also has to be submitted to the Ministry of Justice for approval of the legal content. Once it has been approved by the government, if it concerns a matter for which the *Länder* have responsibilities and their approval is needed, it is submitted to the *Bundesrat*.

A central concept in German administrative procedure is the notion of administrative responsibility for a policy. The term is *federführend* and literally means 'having control of the pen', with a *feder* being an old-fashioned quill or fountain pen.[4] The term comes close to the idea that a particular ministry or part of a ministry is the 'policy lead' in UK terminology. In formal terms (art. 18, GGO) 'an organizational unit holds the pen for an issue if the issue is predominantly within its responsibility as defined in the formal division of

---

[4] A sign that the term might be spreading outside Germany is that the term has started to appear in this context in English-language publications and was also suggested when a respondent in the European Commission, a UK national, described himself as 'holding the pen' for a particular policy area.

responsibilities or if it is determined to have this responsibility in a particular case'. The term applies to a ministry as a whole—thus one ministry generally holds the pen for any particular piece of legislation even if it cuts across the work of several ministries—and applies to units within the ministry, defined as the general term, *Ressort*. A *Ressort* is an important idea in the German administrative system as the *Ressort* is not only used to describe administrative units in formal documents, it has long been considered by scholars to constitute the basic unit of identification for German officials as contained in the term *Ressortpartikularismus* (an enthusiastic identification with, and loyalty to, the *Ressort*). A *Ressort* is a slightly elastic term that simply means the units within an organization, here the ministry, who work on a particular functional area. In most cases this means a particular *Referat* or group of *Referate* within a ministry. Joint responsibility can be assigned too, although it is more common to find *Ressorts* than ministries sharing responsibility. In practical terms, the provisions about holding the pen mean that responsibility for taking the lead rests with a ministry and a particular *Referat*, or possibly with two *Referate*, within that ministry.

One of the sample of six decrees involved some conflict about where responsibility for policy development should lie. The issues at stake and how these were resolved highlight the importance both of the *Referat* and of the rules surrounding bureaucratic policy development. *Referat* within the Environment Ministry identified the need for the Noise Maps Decree following the introduction of Directive 2002/49/EC relating to the assessment and management of environmental noise. The official from the Environment Ministry explained:

> [ECP: *How does it work with a law like this?*] You have a directive that is passed in Brussels, the question becomes: what is it that needs transposing here? You do an analysis of this and look at what needs to be done, if anything, in German law to get rid of any barriers that there are. [ECP: *Was this a tough decision?*] Yes it was quite tough, there were one or two things . . .

Part of the difficulty was that the directive involved several ministries, above all Transport and Environment, and jurisdiction had to be resolved. The episode illustrates that which particular *Referat* takes the lead, i.e. is *federführend*, can be both contentious and important for the subsequent development of the decree.

As one official describes it, there was a wrangle over whether the federal level itself should be *federführend*, and which particular ministry should be responsible. This wrangle was not just a petty struggle over administrative turf but had far-reaching implications for the type of law that would result:

> We were made *federführend* for this. Responsibility was contested—maybe that is not the right word but it was not straightforward. . . . This [European] directive concerned airports, roads and such like. There was some talk that airports should be done through airport law, and roads through highways law and so on. But then

we faced the problem, we have federal responsibility for federal roads, but not for state roads. That meant we faced the question: did we want to have a federal transposition and then leave it to the *Länder* to do their own transposition via transport legislation? The Transport Minister did not really want all that either, and we certainly did not.... [W]e have an overall law for noise pollution at the federal level... But the decision to go via the general law on pollution was partly about legal competencies: we could have legislation at the federal level and we could develop it at the federal level as environmental law. We could not do this under transport law. Once it was clear that they wanted federal transposition and that we had the legal powers to do it, the *Federführung* almost automatically came to us in the ministry.

The wrangling over *Federführung* 'lasted quite a while', and the federal and state ministers involved in the debate were concerned 'not just about who did it, they wanted to know *how* we were planning to do it before they decided to accept that it be done through environment law and thus by us'. A mismatch between the formal structuring of legal responsibilities and the organizational divisions of the Agriculture Ministry meant that the Milk Quotas Decree in our sample was in principle shared between two *Referate* within it, but effectively only one took the lead. In the other four decrees the question of who took the lead was largely unambiguous.

The importance of the notion of *Federführung* is that it highlights, if not defines, the notion that the responsibility for developing a proposal lies with the *Referat*. This means that, once it has been defined as the part of the ministry (the *Ressort*) that holds the pen, it is up to the *Referat* concerned to come up with a proposal in the form of a submission or *Vorlage* which will need to be passed through the procedures of intra- and intergovernmental consultation set out in the GGO which specifies the form and content of the *Vorlage*.

THE ORIGINS OF THE DECREES

The importance of the *Referat* as the origin of the decree can be seen in each of our six German decrees. None of the decrees came from direct instructions from a minister. The Ship Safety Decree was something of an omnibus decree covering a range of issues, including some that involved controversy: the requirement that leisure boats carry radio equipment, the consumption of alcohol by ships captains, and the powers of the Federal Maritime and Hydrographic Agency (Bundesamt für Seeschiffahrt und Hydrographie). As one of the officials involved explained:

> You catch me just as I'm doing a ninth regulation [*Holds up a typewritten page with the heading 'things that so far need to go in the ninth regulation'*]. This *Referat*... is one that coordinates the legal work that is done in the different

sections. This regulation is an omnibus regulation and it includes all the bits that the specialist *Referate* [*Fachreferate*] think they'd like to see put into a law. That's the way much of our legislation is here in this area—omnibus. There are two regulations in particular that tend to get amended almost each year [and this is one of them].

This particular decree was, however, certainly not consequential. The change in the powers for the agency involved transferring its direct responsibility for ship safety to the trade associations (*Seeberufsgenossenschaften*) and leaving the agency with a supervisory role. This was something the Ministry of Transport had been advocating for a few years, and the agency itself had opposed it. When asked why this part of the decree was raised now, an official replied:

> Well it was an accident. It started some time after 1994 that we wanted this, but it was too strongly opposed. But as more people left [the agency] that changed things. We all have to make savings and nobody was going to support them getting more [money].

The alcohol provisions of this decree addressed a problem raised in an earlier (2005) decree that reduced the permitted level of alcohol of anyone in charge of a ship carrying a dangerous cargo to zero. The same official handled the 2005 decree and the modification a year later:

> [*ECP: Did you get a request from the* Fachreferat *to change the alcohol provisions?*] Yes, sort of. I have a list of things that need to go in the regulation in a general way '*Alkoholproblematik* [The alcohol issue]—reduction of permitted blood alcohol levels'. [*ECP: So what do you do then?*] Well I also get other background material—looking at what position the federal government has taken on it or who has said what about it in the Bundestag and so on. And there is material you get from other sources. For instance, there is the annual meeting of the people running the transport courts. They have an annual meeting, to which I go, they've got it in Goslar. They discussed alcohol misuse last year and had a proposal and I had that to work with too. You get background material from diverse sources.

While the issue of the reduction of permitted blood alcohol levels was prompted by the well-publicized *ENA 2* incident where a tanker collided with a container ship in the port of Hamburg in 2004, and while there was considerable discussion of the issue by MPs, there was no direct instruction to regulate, still less to modify the decree the next year. It was identified as an issue that needed to be addressed at the level of the *Referat*.

With the two decrees reflecting changes in EU legislation the *Referat* was the source of identifying and moving to change the law. The Civil Emergencies Decree exempted pharmaceutical companies from liability during periods of civil emergency. This decree was prompted by earlier changes to the German law on medicines made to reflect a range of European laws, above all Directive 98/34/EC on the provision of information in the field of technical standards and regulations. A Health Ministry official describes how it happened:

> We were not specifically told we'd have to change the law. Each *Referat* is responsible for its own bit of the law. We are informed about the results of the EU deliberations. This is done through a variety of means. Internally mainly through email. We are informed as the thing is progressing so it was not really a surprise. We get reports from the Permanent Representations [in Brussels], our colleagues who are there in Brussels tell us by email what is happening, and there are EU papers (Presidency papers) and such like. This was going on for about three years, so you would not be surprised by it if you were paying any sort of attention. You know in the *Referat* that there is a provision that you will have to set into German law.... We noticed this change in the law, and the associations (pharmaceutical companies, insurance interests) also got in touch to tell us.... We had to produce this regulation otherwise we would have to have changed all our contracts with pharmaceutical companies to try to allow for the EU legislation.

The Milk Quotas Decree also arose from EU legislation, but this time it was a Council Regulation (No. 1788/2003 of 29 September 2003 establishing a levy in the milk and milk products sector) that gave member states additional quotas and these had to be distributed among farmers. Again the initiative came essentially from within the *Referat* in the Agriculture Ministry, but this time, because the administration of the scheme involved the *Länder* as well as the federal government, the whole issue had to be approved by the *Länder*, who gave the direction that the decree should take. The role of the *Länder* in other decrees was also significant, but in this particular case the role in *initiation* was greater than in the others that involved federal–state agreement. The nature of the decree meant that *Länder* agreement was needed to develop it and the *Referat*'s proposals which were to form the basis of the discussions with the *Länder* had to be approved by the minister. An unofficial minute of the deliberations made by one respondent describes the process:

> Resolution of the [*Land*] ministers of agriculture meeting of 7 October in Bielefeld which decides to distribute the additional quotas to active milk producers in the years 2006/7 to 2008/9 in three equal steps of 0.5 per cent; the basis of the decision was a paper from *Referat* number 423 [of the federal ministry] which discussed the different options for distribution and the difficulties accompanying each of them. The paper had been extensively discussed with the *Länder* and interest organizations (*Verbänden*) and had been approved by the federal minister... on 7 September 2005.

Of all of the six decrees, a ministerial, albeit rather indirect, role in initiation was found only in this one, and this role itself was limited to the approval of the *Referat*'s paper initiating discussions with the *Länder*.

Two of our six pieces of legislation were essentially consequential decrees which themselves involved no policy discussion or deliberation. The Fiscal Equalization Decree affected a highly sensitive and politically important issue, yet the decree itself was uncontroversial. It was just one of a series of decrees passed each year regulating the nationwide tax sharing and equalization scheme designed to compensate for the strong differences in the tax bases of the different *Länder* and their consequent ability to afford to pay for public services—it involved around 28 billion euros in 2004. This decree, although issued in 2006, made final adjustments to the equalization scheme for 2004. It set final figures for receipts of turnover tax for each *Land*, the amounts that each old West German *Land* had to pay to the 'unity fund' to support new *Länder* of the East, and the final sums for the fiscal equalization part of the arrangement, according to which wealthier states such as Hessen, Baden-Württemberg, Bavaria, Nordrhein-Westfalen, and Hamburg pay money to the poorer states (Berlin, the area covered by the former DDR, Bremen, Niedersachsen, Rheinland-Pfalz, Schleswig-Holstein, and the Saarland). Although the decree covered large amounts of money, and the issue was at the time highly contentious, with Berlin taking a case (and losing) to the Bundesverfassungsgericht in 2006 (BVerfG, 2 BvF 3/03 vom 19.10.2006, Absatz-Nr. (1–256)[5]), the decree itself was simply applying the formula to audited outturn data for 2004. As one of the officials producing the decree pointed out, this is an annual routine:

> We get the final figures from the (state) Audit Offices around late summer or autumn. We do the calculations and then it is a formal procedure.... the calculations are made according to strict formula. This is done in this *Referat* [section]—there are six of us in it. It gets fed into a computer programme, but it is not that complicated and could be done with a calculator.

The Employee Insurance Decree was even more straightforwardly consequential. It concerned the transfer of responsibility in 2003 for accident prevention for federal employees to the Ministry of the Interior: 'the federal Ministry of the Interior was made responsible for accident prevention and we had to change the regulations'. Both decrees fell to the particular *Referat*, or division within the ministry, and in so far as it was anybody's initiative, it came from the particular *Referent* or desk officer responsible for ensuring that the decrees were in order.

One has to be careful in interpreting the results of a small number of cases in any country, and it is especially hazardous in the German case as, with six decrees, it covers the smallest number of our six countries. One respondent suggested:

---

[5] Available at http://www.bundesverfassungsgericht.de/entscheidungen/fs20061019_2bvf000 303.html (accessed Jan. 2012).

We have a variety of reasons for coming up with a regulation: because it was wanted by politicians (*es kommt von der Politik*), because there is a need to change the law because something else has changed or something new has come up ... [or because] an EU [has] to be transposed into German law.

We do not have a decree that *kommt von der Politik* in the sense of being ordered directly by ministers or even political officials in this sample, and this is not to suggest that direct orders from politician cannot initiate decrees. We do, however, have four decrees that involved degrees of political controversy that nevertheless involved the *Referat* anticipating what might eventually have become an instruction that regulation was needed or wanted or initiating the decree itself. The German system of administration has formal and written sets of arrangements, generally observed in practice, that enable bureaucrats to play a major role in initiating and also developing decrees through regulating their relationships with politicians and political appointees as well as with each other. These formal arrangements and protocols, many of which are found in the Geschäftsordnung of the federal government, covering issues such as *Federführung*, specifying the content of a *Vorlage* and procedures for shepherding decisions through the hierarchy, help create a significant space within which bureaucrats themselves can take the initiative. As suggested in the discussion of the controversy over *Federführung* in the Noise Maps Decree, issues that cannot be decided by such protocols belong to political arenas of decision-making which involve senior officials and politicians. The importance of this demarcation between bureaucratic and political procedures and its property of allowing bureaucrats significant space to develop policy becomes even more apparent in the development of decrees.

THE DEVELOPMENT OF DECREES

Once responsibility had been established, the *federführende Ressort* was effectively left alone to get on with the whole job of developing our six decrees, not only the technical issues of determining details and form, but developing the policy and negotiating with relevant interests and securing the ministerial support needed to give it a chance of reaching the statute book (*Bundesgesetzblatt*). In two of the decrees there was very little that remained to be decided. As already mentioned, the Fiscal Equalization Decree simply involved 'running some figures through a computer' and feeding these into an existing template for a decree, and in the Employee Insurance Decree the decree simply had to bring together earlier decrees and guidance into a new one. However, where the content of the decree is contentious this can mean a significant amount of negotiation and deliberation with groups and other institutions and it is the responsibility of the *Referat* to carry this out without much direct control from administrative or political superiors. This can be clearly seen in the Noise Maps Decree.

Immediately the EU directive requiring noise maps was passed, the *Referatsleiter* in the Environment Ministry drew up a paper setting out the broad approach to be taken (an *Eckpunktpapier*, a 'cornerstone' paper, which is a common first step in developing a submission that has any potential for controversy). The paper was circulated to the *Länder* and other ministries. An official involved set out the issues that needed to be settled at this stage. Foremost was whether the ministry should take a creative approach and do more than merely implement the directive, using it to help shape wider aspects of environmental policy:

> [ECP: *How long did this process of discussing the* Eckpunktpapier *take?*] It took a long time. Here in the ministry we were not clear on what the broad approach (*Konzept*) to the implementation of the directive should be [there was also a primary Act of Parliament that implemented the EU legislation too]. Were we going to do a [straightforward] one-to-one transposition—you know, like they do in Italy. One-to-one implementation is hardly a work of art (*Kunststück*).... There is another way—we tried to approach it by integrating it into a mature system of environmental law and wanted to do more than a one-to-one transposition. We used to have the 'one plus' rule in Germany—to do a bit more for the environment than was set out in EU law. Earlier it was easier to do 'one plus' implementation. We thought of ourselves as a densely populated industrial country with serious problems in the environment and this demanded more of us. But that has declined and economic pressures have tended to push us towards a one-to-one implementation to remain competitive. It is a matter of transposition or effective implementation. In the *Eckpunktpapier* that is what was hard fought over, even here in the ministry. In the end the *Eckpunktpapier* saw something more ambitious than a simple transposition. But the size of the 'plus' was more contentious.

The consultations on the draft law that followed the *Eckpunktpapier* involved a series of hearings (also in part regulated by the GGO) at which economic and environmental groups as well as the municipal associations and the *Länder* were represented. The involvement of the political level—political officials and ministers themselves—was at the instigation of the officials in the *Referat* conducting the negotiations. As an official explained:

> [ECP: *Did you involve the political level in this?*] At points in the hearings you get issues coming up and we have to present them and say what the problems are and what options we see for dealing with them. [ECP: *Do they approve what you recommend?*] Well normally they do, but that is because you are not coming up with ideas out of the blue. You know what is going on at the top and how they react to things so you take that into account when you are working out the way to go. You know it because there is a weekly meeting of all *Abteilungsleiter*

(the *Abteilungsleiterbesprechung*) institutionalized each week. You have the minister, the state secretary, the Parliamentary state secretary there and this has minutes (*Protokoll*) and I get a copy of the minutes and I can have some influence on what is minuted by discussing things with the *Abteilungsleiter* beforehand.

He added 'man muss immer den Blick nach oben haben, und den Blick ins Land' (you always have to keep an eye on what is going on at the top, and in the *Länder*). The negotiations with the *Länder*, and securing their approval, are particularly problematic.

With primary legislation there are procedures for reconciling differences between the federal and state government in the final law. With secondary legislation, failure to get *Bundesrat* approval where it is required means that the decree fails—it cannot reach the statute book. This places the *Länder* in a strong position in the development of such legislation. Even where it is not constitutionally required, as an official responsible for part of the Ship Safety Decree suggested, it is still prudent to involve the *Länder* if there is the remotest chance that they might find something to object to in it (in fact this Ship Safety Decree did not even need to be placed before the Cabinet, just signed by the minister), because 'if the minister sees there is opposition to anything, he won't sign'. In the case of the Noise Maps Decree, *Land* consent posed a particular problem because the federal officials in the *Referat* were discussing not only with different *Länder* but different ministries and agencies in the *Länder*, including environment, transport, and finance. Moreover, in general the political leadership of the *Länder* were unenthusiastic about anything that meant more than the minimum required to comply with the EU directive. Although it is possible to negotiate with the specialist services (*Ressorts*) in the *Länder*, this does not necessarily guarantee *Bundesrat* support:

> [ECP: *Did your discussions with colleagues in the* Land *environment ministries give you a good idea of what comments you would get from the* Bundesrat?] Well they would be the first to tell you that they don't really know. They give their views as specialists (*Fachleute*), but it is not the *Ressorts* (specialist services) that count in the *Bundesrat*, so what is decided can also come as a surprise to them. In the *Bundesrat* what is decided is not the product of the environment ministries, but of the *Staatskanzleien* (the central political executives running the *Länder*). It can be that the transport ministries have other ideas than the environment ministry and they get their way with the *Staatskanzleiein*.

The negotiations with the *Länder* focused in particular on costs and on what areas were to be included in the noise maps. The ministry's original proposal, as this was not specified in the directive, was for agglomerations with populations greater than 250,000, but some *Länder* objected. Eventually, an official explained, 'we ended up with a qualitative formulation around the notion of "significant sources of noise". This meant the *Länder* had the capacity to regulate for themselves how much mapping went on.' Even the negotiation over *Bundesrat* acceptance carries on at the level of the *Referat* without being referred upwards, as an official involved in the negotiations made clear: once the *Bundesrat* had made its recommendation, 'we looked at this and we talked to colleagues in the transport ministry, always at the level of the *Referat* and we made a formal proposal to accept it'. In part the federal ministry had to accept the *Bundesrat's* recommendation because time was running out if Germany was to meet EU deadlines on transposition. Again, the proposal incorporating the *Bundesrat* recommendations, once worked out, was then put to the political leadership 'the proposal would say "this is where we are with this, transport says such-and-such and we suggest such-and-such". The proposal will be done in writing. The political leadership might call you in to talk to you about a proposal like this, but they did not call me in personally on this one. I did bring it up at the ALB [meeting of the *Abteilungsleiter*].'

This basic pattern of the officials in the *Referat* working largely on their own initiative to develop the decree is found in the other two decrees that involved some degree of controversy, the Ship Safety Decree and the Milk Quotas Decree. Part of the Ship Safety Decree took away the direct regulatory powers of a federal agency against its wishes (the Federal Maritime and Hydrographic Agency, Bundesamt für Seeschiffahrt und Hydrographie). The official responsible described how this provision was worked through:

> I present to the political leadership what I want, the pros and cons, who is in favour and so on, in a *Vorlage*. And the *Vorlage* goes through the hierarchy. You put things through the hierarchy early because if an MP asks the minister why we are doing this, the minister has the answer there. We did this three months before the regulation was passed.

The other parts of the decree were developed with little reference upwards until the regulation needed to be signed. On the alcohol issue:

> The [seamen's] unions also got involved in this one. The issue was that people can be at sea for weeks, and the unions did not want a form of regulation that meant that people, especially captains, were completely unable to drink at all. You cannot say that they should not drink when they are 'on duty', because captains are always 'on duty' as long as they are on the ship. So you have to open up the possibility for people to have a drink. That was a bit difficult to formulate in words. So together with the Ministry of Justice we sought a formulation that reconciled them—that you could have a drink when you were sure that nothing bad would happen—calm sea, nothing to do, and such like.
>
> [*ECP: Was the minister brought into this discussion as the unions became involved?*] No, the minister did not know anything about all this till he had to sign. We did the *Vorlage* and that is what he saw. We had sorted out the problem at the *Referat* level. We did not get the *Abteilungsleiter* involved either. Not the

Staatssekretär either. The negotiations with Justice and the unions were independent activities done here in the *Referat*.

She continued: 'We get all the work done here and then it goes up the hierarchy. *Everything is done at the level of the* Referat.' The same applied for the other potentially contentious part of the decree—the obligation for sports boats to carry radio equipment. '*Referat* XX had to deal with the sports boat people, and that was quite contentious, so I gather. But they did all that, I just got the result and had to put in the regulation.'

For the Milk Quotas Decree the *Abteilungsleiter* involved explained that much of the work is done in the *Referat*:

> The ... principle was discussed in the *Abteilung* and we made a *Vorlage* for the minister. *Vorlagen* start off ususally in the *Referat*, it becomes a *Vorlage* of the *Abteilung* once I have had a look at it and anyone reading it can see who was involved in it: my name goes on it, as does that of the *Referatsleiter* and the *Referenten*. The next level in the hierarchy looks at it and can amend it. We colour code signatures and comments: *Referatsleiter* is black biro, *Unterabteilungsleiter* in brown, the *Abteilungsleiter* in blue, *Staatssekretär* in red and the minister in green [*as specified in the GGO Anlage 2*]. The higher level always has the possibility to ask for a conference (*Rücksprache*). This was not a difficult case. There was no conference, but conferences take place quite often. When I go in to *Rücksprachen* I take my specialist people with me if I can. The minister can appreciate better what the technical issues are, the technical people can bring additional technical issues in, and it is psychologically necessary for the technical people to see that they are being listened to and understand what happens to their advice.

The process of developing the decree shows further how the *Referat* takes the initiative in developing and securing agreement for the decree within a structured process of reference upwards to administrative and political superiors and outwards to other *Ressorts* and the *Länder*. There was preparation of the ground for the changes in milk subsidies through the regular meetings of officials at different levels. Federal and state secretaries in agriculture ministries meet twice a year, as do the senior officials responsible for market policy (*Amtsleiter für Marktpolitik*) as well as the federal and *Land* ministers.

The basic political decision structuring the Milk Quotas Decree in particular was proposed in a paper written in the *Referat* which was agreed (in a formal minuted decision) at the October 2005 meeting of the ministers of agriculture conference. The paper itself was formally approved by the federal Minister of Agriculture and contained a report on the consultations with the *Länder* and interest groups as well as the discussions with other *Ressorts* in the ministry. In the subsequent process of developing the decree the *Länder* were consulted again, although the consultations took place between the *Referenten* in the relevant *Land* ministries and the federal ministry and rarely had to be taken higher: as one official put it, 'if the *Referenten* on their own can solve the problem it does not usually need to go higher. This is a sort of filter process—subsidiarity even.' During the process of developing the decree the Bavarian government put forward a proposal placing a cap on the amount of additional allocation for any milk producer—this was worked into the draft within the *Referat* after the *Referat* had gained political clearance with the *Länder* as well as the minister.

GAINING FORMAL APPROVAL

Since the procedures for approval are well understood—for the most part they are set out in the GGO but also through other conventions and understandings—the process of gaining approval for a draft and processing the draft itself are less distinct than in other jurisdictions. It is normal to secure the agreement of those who have to approve a decree long before it is finished by involving them. Issues are 'vorbesprochen', discussed before they formally get passed up or along for approval, during the drafting of the decree. This idea that one does not spring surprises on those one wants to approve one's draft is, of course, common practice in all jurisdictions in this study. However, in Germany, to a greater extent than in the other jurisdictions, the existence of such procedures appeared to offer other ministries and *Ressorts* a bigger stake in policy development than elsewhere.

The constitutional provision for approval of decrees requires the approval of the federal Cabinet under some circumstances—decrees issued by the federal government as a whole, decrees of 'general political significance', and where there are disagreements between ministries (article 62, para. 3, of the GGO). As discussed above, some decrees require *Bundesrat* approval. The main constitutional approval mechanisms, where applied (three of the six decrees required *Bundesrat* approval, and five required formal approval by the Cabinet through the *Bundeskanzleramt*), only produced changes in one of the six cases—the Noise Maps Decree (discussed above). However the significance of these two main formal requirements is far wider than this suggests as they underpin a range of requirements that other *Ressorts*, ministries, and external organizations be consulted.

Even where there is no formal requirement to refer a decree to the *Bundesrat*, *Länder* have to be consulted. In the Ship Safety Decree, for example, the constitutional provision for approval was that the minister needed to sign it. The procedure did not require federal Cabinet approval. Neither did it need *Bundesrat* (i.e. *Länder*) approval, although those writing the decrees took great pains to secure the agreement of *Land* transport ministries. When I suggested this was a matter of courtesy, an official set me straight: 'article 47, paragraph

1, in connection with article 62, paragraph 2, sentence 1, of the GGO says that the *federführende Ressort* is obliged to involve the *Länder* in developing any regulation that affects them irrespective of whether the regulation requires *Bundesrat* approval'. It did not prove contentious in this case, though as we have seen in the Milk Quotas and Noise Maps Decrees *Land* participation had greater influence.

Appendix 8 of the GGO sets out a range of ministries that must be consulted when a decree is being drafted and the circumstances under which they should be consulted (e.g. the Interior Ministry 'or ensuring that legal provisions are consistent with the Constitution (*Grundgesetz*)'. The most prominent of these in the sample looked at here, as well as in the sense that its role is emphasized in the GGO, was the requirement that the Ministry of Justice be consulted on, and involved in, the development of decrees from the point of view of their constitutionality (as with the Interior Ministry) and, even more likely to broaden its areas of intervention, of their compatibility with general principles of German law.

The Ministry of Justice played a significant role in all but one of our decrees. In the Ship Safety Decree an official describes a disagreement:

> Yes, we did have something of a dispute with the Ministry of Justice about the method we used to formulate the provision over alcohol. You see, Justice is concerned that anything that involves some form of punishment—fines and such like—fits a general conception of *Strafrecht*. The problem was that in Justice they did not really appreciate what the issues were when it comes to dealing with people who are at sea. It was a bit difficult.

The Ministry of Justice also had a direct influence on the Milk Decree (albeit indirectly through the earlier decree it supplemented) as well as the Noise Maps Decree where the issues at stake related to questions of how to frame the constitutionally sensitive issue of federal–*Land* collaboration. It participated directly in the development of the Employee Insurance Decree, insisting that the decree, which itself changed little in policy terms, corresponded to what it saw as correct principles of formulation (which proved somewhat onerous for those writing it). In the Civil Emergencies Decree the Justice Ministry became involved in reconciling EU law with German law principles of liability and negligence among others.

A Ministry of Justice official's complaint rather underlines the degree to which the principles of the GGO are observed:

> Unfortunately not everyone holds to the things set out in the GGO. [The *Referatsleiter* in this case] was very good at holding to the four weeks needed to check the legality of the decree [and stipulated in the GGO], but he was rather the exception. It is normal for us only to have three weeks, and in politically urgent and important cases we might only get four days to check the constitutionality [of the proposed regulation].

The reason why officials observe the GGO in this case, albeit possibly leaving less time than recommended for the Justice Ministry to go through the draft, was suggested by another Justice Ministry official: 'If we don't get enough time to do it we have to state that the "examination of the legal principles in the proposal has not been completed"... and the thing cannot be brought into effect... I have had to do that once.'

CONCLUSION

It is quite possible that in some circumstances the notion that politics is perceived as separate from administration denotes a particular kind of subordination to politics in which bureaucrats either avoid, or are prevented from, becoming involved in policy development. In Germany a host of rules sets out a range of formal procedures that require bureaucrats writing decrees to seek approval from political bodies—federal and state politicians and their officials. The rules further stipulate how other ministries and public sector bodies need to be approached. Moreover, with politically sensitive issues the broad principles of the decree can be discussed in explicitly political decision-making forums which serve to limit the discretion that those writing decrees later on can exercise. Nevertheless, the same rules can place the relevant section of the ministry, the *federführender Referat*, in the driving seat in the development of decrees. Where there were broader political issues, as in the Noise Maps Decree, the Milk Quotas Decree, and to a lesser degree the Ship Safety Decree, these had been settled through formal agreement *before* the bureaucrats started work on the decrees. These broader political agreements made clear a range of key issues that structured the subsequent development of the decree and the officials tended to take the initiative in shaping the decrees, dealing with interests, other *Ressorts,* and ministries, as well as the *Länder.*

The requirement that such decisions are taken in political forums does not exclude the bureaucrats from the process, rather it legitimizes their participation in it. They prepare the ground for such discussions and put forward papers which aim to structure the decisions taken in them. Moreover, the further conventions and rules governing who has to be consulted, how, and when, make it possible for bureaucrats to exercise substantial initiative and discretion, safe in the knowledge that the formal rules offer opportunities for political control even if such direct intervention is not obviously more obtrusive than in the UK or France.

The separation of politics from administration associated with the 'classical' bureaucrat of Putnam's study in the 1960s has often been argued to have been superseded by the more political bureaucrat of the decades following (a trend that Putnam (1973) himself thought he could see beginning, see Page 1985).

This trend appeared to be reinforced by the apparent decline of the *Juristenmonopol*—the tendency for nearly all top civil servants to be trained in law—at around the same time (Derlien 2003). Yet as Derlien (2005) later shows, the German bureaucracy changed less than one might have expected, even when one adds the 'New Public Management' changes of recent years into the evaluation—it is 'Weberian despite modernization'.

If we consider the relationship between rules that appear to delimit the political discretion of bureaucrats discussed in this chapter and bear in mind Derlien's (2005) suggestion that it is the distinctive legalist culture of German bureaucracy that makes it persistently 'Weberian', this can help us understand a point about German bureaucracy that has remained an unsung paradox: while Germany had the reputation of being the country of the unpolitical 'classical' bureaucrat, its bureaucracy was distinctly political. Appointments to the top of the bureaucracy were political even in the early years of the Bonn Republic (carrying on a tradition dating back at least to the nineteenth century). Indeed, the group dominance of political appointments was one of the famous criticisms of the 'sickness' of the postwar German democracy (see Eschenburg's (1955) 'domination by interest groups' (*Herrschaft der Verbände*) thesis). Moreover, the evidence we have suggests bureaucrats played central roles in developing policy, not least shaping the postwar German welfare state (Hockerts 1980). The evidence of this chapter suggests the possibility that, even below the very top ranks, the German 'classical' bureaucrat might not have been as shy of politics as often thought. Rather the adherence to rules, even those that give primacy to political institutions, offers and for a long time might have offered, a significant array of legitimate opportunities to play a substantial role in policy-making.

ANNEX: DECREES INCLUDED IN CHAPTER 4

Reference	Ministry	Short Name
Achte Schiffssicherheitsanpassungsverordnung vom 28. Juni 2006	Bundesministerium für Verkehr, Bau und Stadtentwicklung	Ship Safety
Verordnung über die Zulassung von Ausnahmen von Vorschriften des Arzneimittelgesetzes für die Bereiche des Zivil- und Katastrophenschutzes, der Bundeswehr, der Bundespolizei sowie der Bereitschaftspolizeien der Länder (AMG-Zivilschutzausnahmeverordnung—AMGZSAusnV) vom 16. Oktober 2006.	Bundesministerium für Gesundheit	Civil Emergencies
Verordnung zur Regelung der Unfallverhütung in Unternehmen und bei Personen, fur die die Unfallkasse des Bundes nach § 125 Abs. 1 Nr. 2 bis 7 und Abs. 3 des Siebten Buches Sozialgesetzbuch Unfallversicherungsträger ist (Bundesunternehmen-Unfallverhütungsverordnung—BUV) vom 6. April 2006	Bundesministerium des Innern	Employee Insurance
Vierte Verordnung zur Änderung der Milchabgabenverordnung vom 2. März 2006	Bundesministerium für Ernährung, Landwirtschaft und Verbraucherschutz	Milk Quotas
Vierunddreißigste Verordnung zur Durchführung des Bundes-Immissionsschutzgesetzes (Verordnung über die Lärmkartierung) vom 6. März 2006	Bundesministerium für Umwelt, Naturschutz und Reaktorsicherheit	Noise Maps
Zweite Verordnung zur Durchführung des Finanzausgleichsgesetzes im Ausgleichsjahr 2004 vom 15. Februar 2006	Bundesministerium der Finanzen	Fiscal Equalization

5

Sweden: Political Direction and Decree-Making

The Swedish politico-administrative system is commonly regarded as distinctive in two main respects. First, its administrative design is based on agencies. While 'agencification', the organizational separation of policy formulation (a ministerial function) from service provision (an agency function), has been regarded as a core component of the admittedly amorphous term 'new public management' (see Pollitt and Talbot 2003), the constitutional and administrative structure of Sweden has been based on a separation between ministries and boards since the seventeenth century (see Elder 1970). Second, the 'Swedish Model' of policy-making traditionally has been characterized as 'consensual' and 'consultative' (Anton 1969). Arter (1999, 2006) points to the three Cs of the policy-making model in the Nordic countries—'compromise, cooperation, and consensus'—and argues that these are features particularly noticeable in Sweden. Since at least the 1980s the traditional 'Swedish Model' has been argued to be in decline. However, while under challenge its basic features appear to have persisted into the twenty-first century. As Bergh and Erlingsson (2009: 72) argue, the 'well-known characteristics of policy-making in Sweden, traditionally used to explain the development of the extensive welfare state', can also be used to explain the subsequent liberalization. The 'old explanations and characterizations of Anton and others ("Policy making Swedish style") are still valid' (Bergh and Erlingsson 2009: 87).

It is certainly not in contradiction of such characterizations of the Swedish political system to point out that the role of bureaucrats in the seven decrees covered in the sample is limited. Bureaucrats, and in particular the bureaucrats at the level of those where the detailed everyday policy is made, have not been especially pivotal actors in accounts of the deliberative processes that characterize the 'Swedish Model'. Marier (2005), for example, discusses the role of Carl Gunter Scherman, the Director General of the (then) Pensions Agency as a major player in securing pension reforms in Sweden in the 1990s. However, his power as an official stemmed from his connections with the Centre Party and it was substantially through this linkage that his ideas for reform reached the political agenda; 'once it became clear that the political parties were seriously seeking a solution, Scherman, who was not formally involved, disappeared from public debates' (Marier 2005: 530). The evidence from this chapter rather supports the view, highlighted among others by Heclo and Madsen (1987: 32), that the 'principled pragmatism' of the Swedish policy-making system is essentially a *political* bargain rather than a technocratic or bureaucratic one, a 'mutual integration between political partisanship and policy development' creating a form of 'structured democratic participation and collective political control over society' that have 'fed on each other and expanded simultaneously'.

From the perspective of the officials involved in writing our seven decrees, it becomes apparent that the level of political direction of bureaucratic activity is strong—and in this sense the Swedish case is remarkably unlike the other five jurisdictions in the study. A range of features of the Swedish politico-administrative system facilitate such close political involvement. Consequently, before getting to our seven decrees, this chapter first discusses the size of Swedish ministries and the political and administrative hierarchy at their apex. It then goes on to discuss the origins and development of the decrees which tend to have a strong common theme largely absent from the remainder of the jurisdictions covered in this book: the direct and continuous involvement of political officials and advisers in the detail of everyday policy development.

SMALL IS BEAUTIFUL

The basic organization of the executive in Sweden is distinctive. As Premfors and Sundström (2007: 38ff.) suggest, one of its central characteristics is the unusual position of the minister. The central organizing principle of the Swedish executive is the *government*, the collection of around twenty ministers. Authority for government policy, even policy as developed in and administered by an individual ministry, generally comes from the collective decision of the government (Larsson and Bäck 2008: 176). The collective executive organization of Swedish government is the Government Offices (*Regeringskansliet*) and ministries are departments within it. Indeed the term 'ministry' in not used in Sweden, but the Swedish 'departement' is generally rendered as 'ministry', even in official translations, and the term will be used in this chapter. As the publicity material for the Government Offices puts it: 'The Government Offices form a single, integrated public authority comprising the Prime Minister's Office, the government ministries and the Office for Administrative Affairs.' In principle, it is the government and not the individual minister that makes decisions.

At the head of each ministry is one or more ministers (*minister* or *statsråd*). In 2011 Employment, Justice, Education, and Finance had two ministers, Health, Enterprise, and Foreign Affairs three and Health four. While all ministers in pluri-minister ministries are members of the government, areas of responsibility for different ministers are usually defined, and one is designated as the 'head' of the ministry (*departementschef*). The senior administrative official in the ministry is the state secretary (*statssekreterare*). Generally each minister in pluri-minister ministries has at least one state secretary. There were five state secretaries in the Finance Ministry in early 2009. State secretaries are political appointees (the position has been political since the late 1970s: see Premfors and Sundström 2007: 49), although they tend to have backgrounds in senior positions in the wider public sector not just ministries. In addition to the state secretaries there are other political appointments. Each minister also has a staff of political advisers (*politiskt sakkunniga*) and press secretaries, around half a dozen people. Of the 4,600 employees of the Government Offices including the Prime Minister's Office (*stadsrådberedning*), around 200 (4.3 per cent) are 'political appointees' (this includes state secretaries). Not all 200 will have direct contact with civil servants. Many advisers have roles writing speeches and liaising with the party (for a discussion of different kinds of political adviser roles see Premfors and Sundström 2007: 49). Nevertheless, the organization of the ministries is such that they have higher concentrations of political appointees than the other countries in this study. As an official in the Ministry of Agriculture put it:

> This is a very small ministry, 150 people, and every Monday there is a briefing with the minister.... [M]ost issues are discussed with the minister directly. I'd say that one in three civil servants in this ministry has contact with the minister each week. There is some contact with the state secretary and maybe some with advisers.

(For a discussion of the 'politicization' of the Swedish civil service, see Pierre 2004.)

Swedish ministries are small in comparison with their counterparts in most of Europe. For instance, the Swedish Ministry of Agriculture had 150 employees in 2009 compared with 700 in the German equivalent (Bundesministerium für Ernährung, Landwirtschaft und Verbraucherschutz), 1,000 in the Commission's DG Agriculture, 8,300 in the UK's Department for the Environment, Food and Rural Affairs, 36,000 in the French Ministry of Agriculture. Certainly this variation reflects the size of the country, the range of functions that each ministry serves in addition to agriculture as well as the precise nature of the services the ministry offers by way of supporting and implementing agricultural policy. Yet above all such differences in number reflect the organizations deemed formally to employ civil servants: French civil servants in regional offices of agriculture are ministry employees, many UK civil servants in field offices are employed by agencies and not the ministry. In Germany the federal structure means that not all public officials in the agricultural sector are employed by the federal government. Moreover in Germany the division of staff into separate institutes and organizations (the *Behördenaufbau*—usually under variable forms of tutelage of the ministry) means that over half the federal employees in the agricultural sector are only indirectly ministerial employees.

In Sweden the tiny size of ministerial staff is almost entirely explained by the basic centuries-old structural principle of the Swedish state: what is termed its 'dualism' (see Premfors and Sundström 2007: 18–36). This means that central government departments are small ministerial bureaucracies with the main task of developing policy and supervising the general principles of its delivery, while the delivery of the policy itself, as well as monitoring and adjusting the process of delivery, is a function of agencies. The principle is not, like the UK counterpart of 'agencification', a set of organizational practices that can be advanced or retracted according to the views of the government or even minister at the time (Talbot and Johnson 2007). In Sweden the agency principle has strong constitutional underpinnings: individual ministers do not have direct constitutional authority over agencies, only the collective government can offer direct instructions to them (Elder 1970; Elder and Page 2000). Even here the government is prohibited from instructing on how an agency 'shall decide in a particular case relating to the exercise of public authority vis-à-vis a private subject or a local authority or relating to the application of law' (paragraph 7 of the Instrument of Government). While the separation has many consequences for the way Swedish government works (Larsson and Bäck 2008: 187ff.), for our purposes the importance of the structure is that it creates a small ministry in which the political leadership and their auxiliaries form a large enough portion of the people working in it to enable a level of political supervision of the policy work of the ministry that is not found in the other five jurisdictions.

The most senior career civil service positions are the heads of corporate services (*Expeditionschef*), legal services (*Rättschef*), and in some ministries heads of budget (*Budgetchef*). Some ministries have other senior positions specific to them. Below the top come the heads of units (*Departementsråd*) and then varieties of executive officers (*Kansliråd* and the most numerous *Departementssekreterare*).

Depending on how one counts them (whether one counts regionalized agency structures as separate agencies or part of a single national arrangement), there are approximately 390 agencies. Their employees outnumber ministerial officials by approximately forty to one (see Office for Administrative Affairs 2010). The agencies play an important part in the administration of national public services. They played, however, only a small role in the development of our seven decrees and the notion that the allocation of executive functions gives agency career bureaucrats (as opposed to their largely politically appointed directors general) political power was certainly not apparent from the seven decrees in the sample.

POLITICAL LEADERSHIP AND THE ORIGINS OF DECREES

The most striking feature of the seven decrees examined in Sweden was the importance of what might be termed the 'political' level in initiating and developing them. The Women's Organizations Decree, which set up a scheme to offer large increases in financial support to organizations supporting women's interests and promoting equality, came from a committee report (*Kvinnors organisering*: SOU 2004: 59) commissioned by the Justice Minister Mona Sahlin and written by Lena Josefsson, a former Cabinet Office press secretary, consultant, and municipal official. The decision on what to do with the report was clearly a matter for the minister, as an official involved in writing the decree made clear:

> The commissioner's report is sent to the minister and she decides whether to make something of it. The state secretary is involved in whether to go on with the report—to take things further. They can also decide to leave it to gather dust.

Similarly the decree that sought to make the Free Year programme more attractive had clear party-political origins. The (now discontinued) programme, initiated in 2002, allowed an employee to take a sabbatical year away from work and to be replaced by an unemployed person. The 2005 Free Year Decree arose from a degree of mistrust within the governing parties. At the time, the Social Democratic government was dependent on the support of the Greens and the Left Party. All three parties had political advisers in the Ministry of Industry, even though the Greens and the Left Party were not formally part of the government. The presence of advisers from several parties in a ministry is not unusual for Sweden (Pierre 1995). The Social Democrats placed less value on the whole Free Year policy than the Greens, as an official explained:

> This regulation was a simple one.... The Greens want the Free Year legislation and this regulation is what the Greens wanted. The Left Party thinks it is OK, but the Social Democratic Party in its heart does not like it. It does not like it much because it does not create new jobs—that is its problem. [*ECP: Is it a secret that the government does not like it?*] Well not that much of a secret—everyone in the area knows that.

The idea was to give priority to the long-term unemployed, unemployed people with a disability, and immigrants. The direction given to the officials was quite specific:

> This regulation, like others, started with a political will—the politician [Hans Karlsson] and his advisers let us know 'this is what we want you to do'. It was all quite informal. Sometimes they give a general hint, sort of 'try something in this direction' or 'we ought to think about doing something for the disabled', but this one was quite specific. In this case they were quite clear that these three groups could be the ones to get the benefits of these regulations. They are the ones who are the most disadvantaged in the labour market.

The two other employment-related decrees had a clear political impetus. The Public Employment Decree aimed to give young graduates a chance to gain positions in state agencies. It was announced in the budget—a common way of the government announcing and committing to policy initiatives great and small. An official argued, 'this was a political impetus, from the Social Democrats. The word came from the Budget Ministry. They told us that this is a political issue and we have to make it work.' The Unemployed Graduates Decree, which sought to increase the number of school-teaching positions for new graduates was similarly initiated by political advisers who, as one official recalled, 'floated the idea' to the officials. He continued:

> we called up the [educational] institutions—did they think there was a need for this? Could they get the students? Can we recruit? They said 'yes'—of course they were optimistic about this as they could see some extra money for them in it. [*ECP: So it seems to have come from the political side—the politicians or the advisers?*] The politicians have lots of people working for them. They are working away all the time at political initiatives and they came to us and asked what we thought of it. They are the real motor in the whole process. They have some knowledge in the area—most of them as much as we have.

The Electrical Goods Decree implemented an EU directive (and thus had to be introduced into Swedish law to comply with Sweden's legal obligations) requiring manufacturers to take responsibility for the safe and environmentally friendly disposal of their goods. Even though one might imagine the origins of this decree to be less dependent on political support, the decree was the subject of direct political instruction. As the official involved explained:

> I don't think we would have produced Swedish legislation going this far without the political push from Brussels and the political will this created here. We would have thought of the consequences in terms of bureaucracy and would not have carried on. Without the Commission proposal the political will to compromise in Sweden would not have been as strong and there would have been no legislation if it had been a matter of doing this domestically.

Another EU-related decree, the Farm Payments Decree, amending the arrangements for the Single Farm Payments (SFP) to farmers, was produced in a similar way to the original and more controversial main SFP legislation: close consultation with the political level. An official involved describes the process:

> In the four to five days of negotiation (pre-parliament) [surrounding the original SFP legislation] we reached a compromise. A decision was reached between the parties about how to implement.... One point was about the level of support in each region. This was based on the calculations we had then.... But when farmers started applying for SFP in 2005 there were new farmers who had not applied for arable premium before and those who had who had applied for new pasture land: the calculated levels of support were not in line with what was actually coming up, so the regulation had to be amended. How did we find out? We heard about it in the videoconferencing meetings with the SJV [Statens jordbruksverk, Swedish Board of Agriculture] ... It opened up the discussions between the Social Democrats and the Left and the Greens. Then we had to have discussions all round about how to deal with it. This meant a discussion for around three or four months. This was done at the political level but we put forward calculations and factual material.

The only exception to this strong role of the political level in initiation was the Swedish Rescue Services Agency decree which changed the governance arrangements for this agency with 800 employees (no longer in existence as it was merged with two other agencies in 2009 to form the Civil Contingencies Agency). The decree came at the initiative of the agency:

> The idea that new arrangements were needed had been mentioned for a while as we see the agency quite often, but the agency itself came along and asked us if we could write a new one. [ECP: How exactly was this put forward?] We used to meet the Director of the Legal Secretariat in the agency and he hints what the agency would like us to do. When we have talked about it he sends us the written paper. We talk about the request, the director and I, and the director talks to the DG for Legal Affairs—the top administrator here, and I presume that he has contact with the state secretary. The director and I often meet with the DG so she will tell us to do the job. It was not a written paper instructing us to do it, but [an oral request].

DEVELOPMENT AS LEGITIMATION

The importance of the political level in decree-making is not confined to initiation. It continues with their development. Indeed it gains additional importance because of the elaborate arrangements for interdepartmental consultation required by the process of developing and legitimizing them as they have to be approved by the government as a whole. In particular, there are two procedures: *delning*, sending out draft decrees[1] to all other ministers and ministries prior to government discussion of it, and the separate process of *gemensam beredning* (formally termed 'joint preparation' or 'joint drafting procedure') that can precede it in cases where more than one ministry is involved, and this often involves the Ministry of Finance.

The constitutional position of ministries, the routines for inter-ministerial discussion, the fact that ministries remain small, as well as the close proximity of everyday working relations between ministers—they lunch together on a daily basis (Ruin 2000)—means that inter-ministerial deliberation forms an important part of developing decrees. The near-ubiquity of inter-ministerial consultation on decrees creates further pressures for political involvement since in all six jurisdictions in this study, not just in Sweden, cross-ministerial issues, or more specifically those issues that cannot be resolved at lower levels in the hierarchy, tend to be pushed upwards. In Sweden this can mean to the state secretary or ministerial level. Moreover, since officials engaging in inter-ministerial negotiations seek to make sure that they are on firm ground when speaking for their ministry, it is not unusual to run even quite routine matters past the political level, often the political advisers.

Several features of working life in a Swedish ministry further serve to increase the possibility of political involvement in the development of decrees. The smallness of ministries as well as the tendency of ministerial offices to have communal areas in which officials working in different divisions can sit and take coffee or eat packed lunches together, as well as the weekly meetings most state secretaries have with staff in their offices, afford many opportunities for formal and informal contact between officials writing decrees and the political level (see also Heclo and Madsen 1987: 15; Larsson and Bäck 2008: 183). In the Free Year Decree, for instance an official involved said:

> Once I did a draft I passed it on to my boss... You have to let everyone in other ministries know about this. I did not pass it specifically on to the state secretary before doing this. I might have told him informally that I had done it at the weekly meeting. The state secretary meets senior people every week and people like me would go along when there is a particular reason for doing so, if we were involved in something that needed political approval. The state secretary probably did not actually see the paper. In this case he was so personally involved in the thing he knew it by heart and did not want to hear about it. Anyway,... approval by the state secretary would only take 30 seconds in a case like this if he had seen the paper.

This followed a period of development of the decree that closely involved the Greens and the Social Democrats:

---

[1] The process applies to the drafts of all decisions taken by the government, not only decrees.

> For the past four years the Greens and the Left have had people here in the ministry. Not part of the government but they have people in all ministries. Here we have them as advisers. When a regulation like this is proposed, and when it is worked out (we have to talk to other ministries, finance ministry etc.) and we talk to the Green and Left people.

In this case the conflict between the Greens and the Social Democrats about the aims of the Free Year Decree produced some slightly bizarre results. Once the aim of the decree, to specify particular groups (the long-term unemployed, those with disabilities, and immigrants) had been set out, the Greens became concerned that this might prove too restrictive for the free year programme to work at all, so the solution was to include a provision in the decrees that 'striving to assign certain individuals' to the scheme 'shall not affect the chances of others to be assigned'. An official commented:

> It looks funny this regulation—the 'striving' part. This is where the Green Party comes in. The regulation sets the three priority groups. Well, the Greens said that this will reduce the number of people who can take advantage of the free year. They put these fears to us. 'Yes', we said, 'other people can get the benefit of the free year.' 'Are you sure?' the Greens came back. 'Yes', we said, 'you can expect to have advantage from the free year even if you are not in one of the groups.' But the Greens were not convinced. To calm them down, as they were really wanting the free year to be a successful policy, we put in this provision. It is a rather strange provision and I don't really know what it means.

The close involvement of the political level in the day-to-day development of decrees can be seen in the Single Farm Payment Decree. Respondents pointed to the intense political bargaining that surrounded the main decree governing Single Farm Payments (not in the sample): the working groups, the intense inter-party bargaining, the involvement of the prime minister. However, the same kind of intense party involvement also accompanied the somewhat less controversial decree adjusting one element of the original decree—the one in our sample. As one of the officials described it, as soon as the problem surrounding the old decree was discovered, the old tensions between the Greens, Left, and the Social Democrats reappeared.

> Yes, there is a Green person here in the ministry—she was very much involved in the process, though I would not say that their opinion was the one that counted. We gave broad technical background material. But the decision was a political one. The amendment means that more money is taken from region 1 and 2 and given to other regions. The politics was similar to the discussion in the main reform.

It is worth noting here that, although the Jordbruksverket (Swedish Board of Agriculture), employing 1,200 compared with the 150 employees in the Ministry of Agriculture, is responsible for administering the Single Farm

Payment, its officials had little direct involvement in the deliberations about either the main decree or the amendment. The Jordbruksverket official most closely involved said:

> I was not part of the working group so I was not party to the discussions about the different types of interests and conflicts over the choice of the model—that is something for the [ministry] to sort out. [*ECP: So you had nothing really to do with the conflicts at state secretary level and the like?*] We only worked on this to provide information.

The Unemployed Graduates Decree not only began life with political impetus, the political level remained closely involved in its development. One feature of this decree, that it needed to be included in the annual budget statement and cleared with the Ministry of Finance, meant, according to an official involved, that

> The discussions with the ministers and advisers then focused on the Budget Bill. Before we could get the regulation it had to be put in the Budget. Once parliament made the decision on the budget it was clear what we had to do.... Although we could start writing the regulation before the formal decision to include it in the budget. We have a lot of contact with parliament and we knew in November that the budget decision would be approved. The political level here in the ministry wrote in November and told us—since we knew it was coming we could write the regulations. If we were unsure we would not have written them.... [*ECP: Did advisers handle the contacts with the Finance Ministry?*] No we have contact with Finance Ministry all the time. You work things out with them. If there is disagreement you move it to the political level but that was not necessary in this case as we had the decision from the politicians that this is what they wanted to do.

When issues came up that needed political approval, such as, for example, the decision to introduce this scheme by means of a legislative instrument, this was discussed closely with the political level, though not invariably the minister:

> You mention it at the weekly meeting with the state secretary and the meeting with the minister. [*ECP: Do you always raise things first with the state secretary then pass it on to the minister?*] Sometimes the state secretary will say 'you don't need to contact the minister on this one' or they could say 'well you'd better pass this one on to the minister'.... [In this case] [t]he meeting with the state secretary made it clear that we'd have to have an ordinance. I think the minister was asked, but that would largely have been as a formality.

In the Public Employment Decree, creating posts in government agencies for the unemployed, the political level became closely involved when the *delning* (interdepartmental consultation) revealed interdepartmental disagreements. An official takes up the story:

> When we went to the formal *delning* a question that came up a couple of times was that of the agencies that were moving outside Stockholm. There were attempts by one or two to get us to put something in that would give extra advantages to those moving out of Stockholm as they had something of a need, as those that were relocating did not take all their Stockholm officials with them—older people, perhaps, who would rather stay here and take early retirement. They wanted us to write in [something covering this], not in the law but in instructions to the [Agency] implementing the law.... That is the only issue we had to refer to the state secretary and she said to keep the regulation as it is. The suggestion did not come from the political level—it was officials that were suggesting this. But when you get an issue like that it has to be dealt with at a political level.

Even the Rescue Services Agency Decree, which originated from the agency bureaucracy rather than from the political level, and which effectively did little more than tidy up existing law, had to be referred to the political level on several occasions. As a lawyer involved put it:

> At some stage in drafting you take the draft to the political advisers, and later I talked to the political advisers, ... before I sent it round to other ministries. They get it—they are on the email list so they know what is going on. If there is something controversial we check with them orally anyway. If there is no big problem that's OK, if there is, they take the issues up.

The political level did not, in fact, make any decisive intervention in shaping the content of the decree. The main interdepartmental disagreement in the decree, over how child safety was to be treated, was resolved between the three main protagonists, the Health, Defence, and Social Affairs Ministries, without reference to the political level, not least because, as the official continued:

> I think the state secretary knew what we were doing. We meet every week and tell him what is going on ... After we sent out the *delning* but before the government decision we came to an agreement [on the child safety issue]. It was done at the administrative level all the same. We told the state secretary it was a problem, but did not have to get him in to solve it.

Even in the most non-contentious of the decrees, and even where the political level has little effective contribution to make, the decree is developed under its close gaze.

For the Women's Organizations Decree, the close political involvement in initiating the decree also continued throughout its development. In part this might have been expected in any of our six jurisdictions. The decree was part of a wider process of policy-making: first came the production and passage of primary legislation and the decree only implemented it. Moreover, the matter at stake involved sensitive party-political issues: the question of whether women's sections of parties should be eligible for financial support. On top of this, the original proposal from the commission of inquiry was put through the *remiss* procedure of consultation involving sending round a draft of a policy proposals to all organizations and individuals likely to be affected by them (see Anton 1980; Eriksson *et al.* 1999). The *remiss* process itself involved politicians and their appointees and advisers to a far greater extent than the UK and the US—countries with a similar convention of open public consultation. As the leading official involved described it:

> When compiling the reports on the *remiss* you sometimes have to talk to the political executive and you give them shorter documents as you have to summarize. The reporting on the *remiss* takes place through a series of internal working documents. The minister will end up with a short briefing on his/her desk. There are several meetings with the state secretary and political advisers. [One of the issues that came up was a] critical one and you have to make sure you have it right.... We get the minister's view on things fairly early on when we are coming up with the terms of reference, and also you get the minister's view through the state secretary. If the consultation is interpreted as saying 'let us do it this way', the state secretary says 'no, I don't think so'.

The Electrical Goods Decree, which imposed significant costs on the electrical goods industry, caused significant disagreement between the Environment Ministry and the Industry Ministry, yet the disagreement was resolved largely before officials started work on the decree. The decree went through the *remiss* procedure despite the fact that it dealt with a decree that implemented an EU directive and the close involvement of the political level at this stage is typical of the other Swedish decrees and entirely atypical of the other decrees from other countries in the study. As an official describes it:

> We needed to consult the people in the relevant division. We also consulted companies. The producers were involved all the time we were developing the decree.... We invited them to meetings and drafted texts and sent them to them and asked what they thought. When we got it as close as we thought we could get it to the final text we sent it out for general and formal consultation. No political points came up in the *remiss*. We had meetings with the state secretary once a week and with the minister too once a week. They asked if everything was going smoothly and we said we saw no problems. If we see no problems and have a clear idea what the minister wants, we don't bother ministers with things.

The *remiss* or consultation procedure itself involved politicians and their auxiliaries far more closely than consultations in the UK and the US.

CONCLUSIONS

Sweden is unusual among the six jurisdictions in the study from the perspective of the close involvement of political officials in the everyday policy-making within the bureaucracy. In Sweden issues that in the other five jurisdictions might have been expected to have remained the province of bureaucrats alone, and not to have attracted the attention of politicians and their auxiliaries, brought about close interest in the work of ministerial officials by ministers, the state secretaries, or special advisers.

At first this might be a surprising finding because of the presumed 'consensual style' of policy-making in Sweden. Where bureaucrats and politicians share values about the direction of policy, one might assume that politicians are prepared to delegate more to their civil servants, much as Kingsley (1944) argued in his discussion of the British civil service, and Huber and Shipan (2002) in their cross-national discussion of 'deliberate discretion'. It is less surprising when one considers that consensus is not necessarily a consequence of value convergence among the principal policy-makers, but appears in this case to be a product of the procedures for resolving conflicts and of the adherence to these procedures in the development of policy. The administrative structure of Swedish government, the small size of ministries, the large numbers of political appointees relative to other ministerial staff, the informal working arrangements within ministries, and importance of a range of interdepartmental procedures to the production of policies all tend to bring ministers and their auxiliaries into the decision-making process on a routine and everyday basis. The frequency with which political leadership was involved in the initiation, development, and legitimation of decrees was striking, even on the basis of the small sample of decrees included in the study. This finding is, of course, entirely consistent with the scholarly views of the 'consensual' style of Swedish government being a political accommodation discussed in the introduction. What is surprising is how far this political accommodation permeates the process of everyday policy-making through the working routines and procedures of the administrative system.

One might suppose that where less experienced politicians seek to do jobs traditionally elsewhere carried out by bureaucrats—developing the logistics and detail of running government programmes and putting policy priorities into effect—that the quality of government might suffer as politicians put forward proposals of detail in areas in which they are unqualified. There is nothing, however, obvious about the cases suggesting that enhanced politician intervention produced 'bad government'. In one of the cases, the Free Year Decree, the weight of political initiative managed to produce a decree that appeared to do little other than offer cosmetic satisfaction to the parties whose advisers were pushing for it. Yet legislation has symbolic uses in all the jurisdictions included in this study and this particular decree hardly constitutes a strong argument against close political involvement precisely because it did almost nothing of substance. On the other hand the politician-led implementation of the Single Farm Payment Decree and the wider process of restructuring the whole scheme in Sweden in response to changes in the Common Agricultural Policy did not produce the major policy disasters that the same issue produced in the UK (NAO 2006; see also Tiessen and van Stolk 2007 for a comparison between German and UK implementation of the same directive).

ANNEX: DECREES INCLUDED IN CHAPTER 5

Reference	Ministry	Short Name
Förordning om producentansvar för elektriska och elektroniska produkter, SFS 2005:209	Miljödepartementet	Electrical Goods
Förordning om ändring i förordningen (2001:1300) om friåret. SFS 2005:173	Näringsdepartementet	Free Year
Förordning om ändring i förordningen om EG: s direktstöd för jordbrukare, SFS 2005: 1227	Jordbruksdepartementet	Farm Payments
Förordning om statsbidrag för kvinnors organisering, SFS 2005:1089	Justitiedepartementet	Women's Organizations
Förordning om tillfälligt stöd för nyanställningar vid statliga myndigheter, SFS 2005:899	Finansdepartementet	Public Employment
Förordning om särskild lärarutbildning för arbetslösa akademiker, SFS 2005:1235	Utbildningsdepartementet	Unemployed Graduates
Förordning med instruktion för Statens räddningsverk SFS 2005:890	Försvarsdepartementet	Rescue Services Agency

6

Political Leadership in US Bureaucracy

While the degree of political intervention in Sweden may have been surprising, we would probably expect political control of the bureaucracy in the US to be elaborate—more so, perhaps, than in any of the other jurisdictions. Not only is the United States one of the few systems that affords its legislature true legislative power—power to initiate and amend legislation even against the wishes of the executive. It also has an extensive system of political appointments that sees a massive turnover at the top of the executive branch when a new president comes into office. The policy process itself is generally characterized as pluralistic, with legislative and executive politicians and interest groups shaping policy in a process far more open than the more constrained executive-dominated policy process in European nations. The role of the bureaucracy in this process appears to be limited. Kingdon (2003: 44), in his seminal study of agenda setting, argues that while nobody 'dominates' the pluralistic process of policy-making,

> To the extent that anybody is important it is elected officials and their appointees. The president and the top appointees who make up his administration, for instance, do come as close as anyone can to dominating the agenda-setting process. Key members of Congress and their staffers are also figures very much to be reckoned with. On the other hand, career civil servants seem much less important.

Rather 'the power of bureaucrats is often manifested in ... implementation activity. Because careerists are so involved in administration, they have little time left for pushing new ideas' (Kingdon 2003: 31).

While the evidence on the ten decrees examined in this chapter does not directly challenge the overall conclusion that political executives and congressional actors are extremely important in the US political system, it does offer at least a qualification to it. The role of political leadership in developing rules is central, and more important perhaps than any of the other countries. This is in large part because the system of rule-making includes a series of checks and balances, enshrined in the 1946 Administrative Procedure Act (APA) and other related laws, that make it very difficult to put anything even mildly controversial into a decree without offering interests inside and outside government extensive opportunities to comment on and oppose it (for a discussion of the constraints on discretion see Kerwin 1999; West 1984). However, this central importance of political executives does not mean that the process is politician- or political executive-led. The role of the bureaucracy in rule-making is extensive. The US terms 'rules' and 'rule-making' will occasionally be used in this chapter but they are interchangeable with 'decrees' and 'decree-making'. The US decrees included in this study suggest that the *agency*, above all the career bureaucracy, is an important source for generating a decree in the first place and its content as it is being developed. In order to get its decree issued the agency thus has to negotiate the checks and balances set up by the APA (among other laws and procedures), and this in turn highlights the importance of securing political support for agency proposals which can serve to trump the opposition to them.

This chapter begins by outlining the, for a European audience, rather unusual and, at the edges, fuzzy definition of who the 'politicians' are in the context of the US executive and goes on to examine how few of the selected decrees were actually initiated by them. The development of decrees has to follow procedures specified in, among other places, the APA, and what these procedures mean for the development of decrees is outlined in the fourth section, and the fifth and sixth sections examine how rules are produced and the role of political support in producing them. The conclusion highlights the distinctive features of the bureaucratic role in the US system of rule-making.

POLITICAL LEADERSHIP AND CAREER OFFICIALDOM IN AMERICAN FEDERAL BUREAUCRACY

The general model of European executive political leadership, as embodied in the idea of a minister heading a ministry, is based on the fusion of the legislative and executive branch. In the US, with their separation, the nature of political leadership is quite different. Even in a semi-presidential system such as France, ministers tend to be politicians who have been elected to a national or at least local office: fourteen of the sixteen ministers in the 2011 Fillon government were members of the Assemblée Nationale immediately before their appointment. In the US, the political leaders are the political appointees, usually appointed in the name of the President, who head executive organizations. Their formal status varies—for instance, some are presidential appointees subject to the approval of the Senate, others are formally 'non-career appointments', and others are 'Senior Executive Service positions filled by non career appointment'. As Heclo (1977) observed over thirty years ago, identifying which position is filled by a political appointee, and what kind of political appointee, is not very easy. The pattern of leadership—how different organizational units of government are structured and how administrative and political leadership is organized—is extremely difficult to encapsulate in a brief description.

However, taking the main administrative political leadership positions, the cabinet secretary responsible for a department and the offices, agencies, and bureaux within that department, is an appointment made by the president subject to the advice and consent of the Senate. The personal staff of the secretary contains a large portion of political appointees, including senior appointments such as a chief of staff, special assistants, and senior advisers. Many of the cross-departmental services, such as the finance office, the office of general counsel, and the office for legislative liaison, are headed by political appointees, and their assistants and staffs contain large numbers of political appointees. The under-secretaries and assistant secretaries within departments, usually responsible for particular sets of functions (e.g. rural development in the Department for Agriculture or aviation and international affairs within the Department of Transportation), are generally political appointees, as are the heads of the bureaux, offices, and agencies that make up departments. In addition, the heads and other very senior positions within 'independent' agencies, agencies with special administrative law status such as the Securities and Exchange Commission, the National Transportation Safety Board, and the Federal Communications Commission (FCC), are also presidential appointees serving fixed terms and only removable by the president 'for cause'[1] (i.e. after significant shortcomings such as neglect or incompetence can be legally established and not at the president's discretion). The designation of independence is also important for the rule-making process because one of the key checks on departments and their agencies, review by the Office of Management and Budget (OMB) and in particular its Office of Information and Regulatory Affairs (OIRA), does not apply to the independent agencies, including the one in our sample, the FCC.[2]

The subunits of cabinet departments which, as we will see below, are the key units with which US federal bureaucrats identify themselves, go by different names: these include bureaux, services, administrations, agencies, and offices. The heads of these subunits are generally (but not always) political appointees whose positions are designated by a variety of different names. Some are

---

[1] The term 'independent agency' is often used rather loosely. There is a specific meaning in US administrative practice that generally refers to an agency with three main characteristics: 'the President's ability to remove an agency head only for cause ... freedom from oversight by the President's Office of Information and Regulatory Affairs; and a multimember design' (Barkow 2010: 26).

[2] Though some specific OMB checks, including those resulting from the Paperwork Reduction Act, apply to them. See Lubbers (2006).

headed by an assistant secretary or deputy assistant secretary, a high-rank political appointee; others are headed by officials given the (to European ears) misleadingly junior-sounding title of 'administrator' or 'associate administrator'. Even greater diversity of names can be found in the 'independent' agencies.

Political appointees are often people who have some knowledge of, or association with, the area to which they are expected to give political leadership or some prior experience in government. The fact that this is not always so, however, is highlighted by the case of Michael Brown, who resigned in 2005 as under-secretary in charge of the Federal Emergency Management Agency (FEMA) after his inexperience, according to critics, was thrown into spectacular relief in his inept handling of the aftermath of Hurricane Katrina. The officials heading the agencies and departmental subunits in the sample of decrees included in the study generally fitted the pattern that has tended to dominate political appointees since the 1970s—people with some contacts, possibly indirect, to the policy area in which they deal and/or experience in government (see O'Connell 2011). For example, the inspector general of USAID at the time of the interviews, Donald A. Gambatesa, was an ex-secret service agent appointed to a law enforcement role in USAID, then to a position as deputy director of the United States Marshals Service, where he served for four years before returning to USAID as its inspector general in 2005; the administrator of the Pipeline and Hazardous Materials Safety Administration (Department of Transportation), Carl T. Johnson, was president of the Compressed Gas Association; and the under-secretary in charge of the Food Safety and Inspection Service in the Department of Agriculture, Richard Raymond, was a former chief medical officer in Nebraska.

Most very senior appointees are paid on the basis of the 'Executive Schedule' pay framework. This marks them off from 'career' officials—those who make a career within the civil service, having at one time been appointed through a competitive civil service recruitment process—as well as less elevated non-career officials. Career officials can be employed under two main frameworks: Senior Executive Service (SES) and the General Schedule (GS). The SES framework also covers a range of non-career positions. Some senior positions are 'career reserved' and can be filled by appointees from among career officials. Non-career appointments are those that can be filled by appointees from outside government, though there are rules on how this may be done. Appointments can be made only to certain designated positions ('general' positions), have to be approved by the federal Office of Personnel Management, and no more than a quarter of an agency's SES allocation can be appointed in this way. Below the SES is the General Schedule which covers some of the lowest paid jobs in the federal civil service, starting in principle at $19,247 per annum in 2008 on GS1 (though under 0.5 per cent of the federal workforce falls in this low grade and the one immediately above it, GS2) and runs up to GS15 (with a top 2008 salary of $140,348). Some GS positions (these are found mainly at the top ranks of GS14 and 15) may be appointees, but this is almost exclusively a career grade.

The ranks of career officials are not easy to determine from the formal title of a job. The job description 'analyst' can apply to someone doing little more than clerical work and to someone helping make decisions on contracts worth millions of dollars. While 'administrator' is now usually reserved for a major leadership position, variants such as 'assistant administrator' or 'deputy assistant administrator' can describe someone who sits at the right hand of an administrator or someone who is a few rungs below that. The use of adjectives denoting a sharing of a position (such as assistant, associate, or deputy) have little specific meaning. Moreover there are other job titles that often give no real clue, or often a false clue, as to their seniority: 'chief', 'coordinator', 'special agent'. Most of the officials directly responsible for taking the work forward in the ten US decrees covered in this chapter were between five and seven rungs from the very top of the department in which they served.

THE LIMITED ROLE OF POLITICAL EXECUTIVES IN RULE INITIATION

Our ten decrees cover a wide range of different issues. Three were particularly controversial. Two because they entailed potential costs for businesses—the Alien Substitution Decree affected immigration arrangements for key incoming workers and the Lithium Decree involved the question of possible additional transport costs for carrying lithium batteries as air cargo. The third, the Salmon Decree, was not only significant in its own right, as it concerned the obligations on federal agencies to protect salmon habitats in the Pacific Northwest, but it was also related to wider questions about the non-implementation of the 1973 Endangered Species Act. Three other decrees concerned publicly visible issues, but appeared to generate less intense controversy. The Bovine Spongiform Encephalopathy (BSE) Decree changed arrangements for the slaughter of cattle in the wake of the international spread of the disease and its potential spread to humans, the Criminal Checks Decree sought to introduce more rigorous checks on the suitability of individuals volunteering for government service (e.g. as carers, helpers, or youth organizers), and the Katrina Decree sought to implement the lessons learned from study of the performance and role of communications services during the hurricane catastrophe of 2005. Two made significant changes to existing programmes: the Mentor Decree extended to the US Agency for International Development a scheme enhancing the capacity for small firms to gain business from federal contracts; the Exchange Visitor Decree reformed the legal requirements for those coming to the US on a range of cultural and training programmes. The ninth decree, Community Connect, made a minor change to a scheme aimed at providing broadband to rural communities, and the Privacy Act Decree essentially tidied up the law without changing anything following the transfer of some records in the Department of Justice from a paper-based system to digital storage.

None of the ten decrees in this part of the study were simply implementing a new piece of primary legislation. All sought to make some changes in existing decrees, ranging from the marginal and consequential to the substantial and major. One of the striking features of the US decrees was the extent to which the impetus to make these changes came from within the agency or department rather than from a political initiative or direct pressure from outside government. Initiation did result from stimuli external to the agency, in the form of the relevant part of the agency reacting to an outside event, or identifying a problem outside. However, the important point is that it was civil servants inside the agency who did much of the identifying and reacting.

The Department of Labor's Employment and Training Administration (ETA) had long been concerned about the fraudulent use of permanent work and residence permits ('green cards') granted to foreign workers, with the certification by the Department of Labor an important part of the green card application process. Firms could apply to hire a named worker for a particular job. If the named worker decided that s/he did not want the job or was unable to take it, the company could use the green card for someone else. This practice, known as 'alien substitution', was used by companies, especially some of the large multinational IT companies, to help recruit foreign workers who could be attracted to work for them by the prospect of being offered a green card (Branigin 1998). The Department of Labor was not concerned about such 'legitimate' use of alien substitution. Rather it had been for some time concerned about the development of an illicit market in green cards. Money could be made from applying for green cards in the name of one person (sometimes fraudulently) and selling them on to someone who simply substituted their name for the original applicant (see *Washington Post* 2002). As an ETA official explained:

> How did this begin? We knew for a long time there was a problem—it's there in the title 'reducing incentives' [the subtitle of the decree was 'Reducing the Incentives and Opportunities for Fraud and Abuse and Enhancing Program Integrity']. This [alien substitution] procedure is important—it gets you a lawful permit to stay. We had information here that was telling us that there was fraud. The department knew, the administration knew. Everyone knew. These things were being sold as a commodity. We had a wealth of information on that. Then it boiled down to two things: (a) legally, how to deal with it—the procedural thing and (b) [dealing with the companies that would be affected by the change.]

> We got comments from . . . counsel [for X Corp—a large multinational IT company] down. This touched the largest companies in the world. It especially affects IT companies. And they pay their lawyers a lot of money. They are good. They also have lobbyists and they know how to work the system. And they did.

In the Salmon Decree, the designation of 'critical habitats' for migrating salmon derives from the 1973 Endangered Species Act (ESA as amended in 1978). This required that all species listed as endangered should have their 'critical habitats' mapped and officially designated as such. In such designated areas federal agencies may be limited in what they can do by way of 'authorizing, funding or carrying out actions that destroy or adversely modify' critical habitats, and they have to consult with the Fish and Wildlife Service (or National Marine Fisheries Service) on any planned activity. While this is confined to federal agencies, it means, for example, that anyone who needs a federal licence to exploit the land by logging is indirectly subject to the provisions of the Act. For many years, especially under the second Bush administration, designation proceeded slowly and the administration sought to justify this, in the court cases brought by environmental and other groups, by claiming that the other provisions of the ESA rendered critical habitat designation redundant—above all that listing a species as endangered had the same effect as designating a habitat. In particular they argued that it was therefore unnecessary to analyse the economic impact of critical habitat designation, as required by the statute, because there was none. A series of court decisions challenged the administration's stance. Officials within a regional office of the Department of Commerce's National Marine Fisheries Service took it upon themselves to seek to remedy this defect in the way the ESA was being implemented. The breakthrough was to determine the different standards between listing a species and designating its critical habitat. As an official described the genesis of the rule

> I read the 5th and 10th Circuit Court decisions and started the thing from scratch. I got a bunch of us together here in Seattle. It was a two-day meeting with forty or fifty people there. We invited people from [the Department of the Interior and] a couple came along. It was facilitated by a contractor who also did some of the economic analysis. [The economists made it clear] that . . . from an economist's point of view there has to be a difference between the two standards and that you can use a cost-effectiveness approach to determine whether to apply critical habitat.

We will examine later the struggle that followed to get a decree out of this initiative despite the indifference and even opposition of other parts of the Department of Commerce and its political leadership as well as other parts of the administration.

Other more straightforward replies that 'the agency had been wanting to change the law for some time in this way' could be found in the changes brought about in the Mentor Decree from USAID which introduced a scheme (a 'mentor protégé scheme') aimed at letting smaller businesses have greater chances to secure overseas aid contracts. Moreover, some of the slightly more mundane decrees were, as might be expected, the product of internal agency reviews of existing laws. The Privacy Act Decree from the Department of Justice (DoJ) was effectively a consequence of a merger between different parts of the DoJ which required the legislation governing the data they held to be amended to reflect this. As its author put it:

> We took three systems that had been on paper and consolidated them into a database. So there were two things to do in this rule: merge the three systems into one and move it over to NSD [the National Security Division]. This was required by the Privacy Act. It was something I knew we'd have to do as part of the move. Privacy Act Administration is my jurisdiction.

The US Department of Agriculture's (USDA) Broadband Decree amended the existing rules governing grants to consortia set up to facilitate broadband connection in rural areas to allow more communities to take part and widen eligibility criteria. This resulted after the USDA's Rural Utilities Service had been, as an official said, 'operating the program over a couple of cycles' and 'we saw patterns emerge that are painted by our own experience and by applicants who had not got the points they needed—the grant works on a system of points. While they might be quite poor in that particular state, nationally they might not be as bad off.'

Two of our decrees started life as recommendations of bodies outside the agency. In formal terms the Exchange Visitor Decree started life as a report from the Congressional audit body, the Government Accountability Office (GAO). Even though the GAO appeared to have a major role in setting the process of rulemaking in motion, the agency itself could claim a significant role in agenda setting. As an official involved put it:

> This regulation is part of a series—which was the one you were interested in? Ah yes, this one. [ECP: The GAO report started this off, right?] The GAO, that we could say is part of the story.... It is useful if you have a policy you want and they come along and give their 'guidance' on the policy.... [ECP: So you had been thinking about this one before the GAO Report?] Oh yeah! If there is a GAO Report then you know the issue is well known to the agency 99 per cent of the time. They don't find anything new. What the report looks like is swayed by the attitude of staff giving them the brief.

In the other case where an external body was involved, the agency could claim less credit for having started the rule-making process. The Department of Transportation's Lithium Decree sought to address the problem of the instability of lithium batteries, used to power portable electronic devices such as laptop computers. These batteries, especially when damaged, can short circuit and catch fire. One incident at Los Angeles International Airport (LAX) in April 1999, when a shipment of two pallets of batteries caught fire, led to a National Transportation Safety Board (NTSB) recommendation that 'the Pipeline and Hazardous Materials Safety Administration [PHMSA]... within the FAA [Federal Aviation Administration] evaluate the fire hazards posed by lithium batteries in an air transportation environment and require that appropriate safety measures be taken to protect aircraft and occupants' (see NTSB 2008). The NTSB is headed by a five-person board—a chairman and four members, all presidential appointees—overseeing the work of 380 employees given the statutory mission of 'conducting objective, precise accident investigations and safety studies... [and] advocating and promoting NTSB safety recommendations'. As a PHMSA official pointed out, the NTSB's recommendations are not mandates: 'It comes down to our office level to respond to the recommendation. We don't have to agree—we can disagree with it, but we'd have to have a good reason for this'. As an FAA official baldly described it: 'LAX in 1999 drew attention to the lithium issue. The NTSB made recommendations. They report to Congress so you cannot ignore them.' Although this appeared to have been an issue known to the agencies involved, it required the NTSB to put the issue of further regulation on the agenda. While an official from PHMSA pointed out, 'we had done a lot of work on lithium batteries over the years and this was on the horizon', he added, 'I don't know if we had much we were trying to get through before we started [on this one]'.

Of the ten decrees, only one owed its existence unambiguously to the direct initiative of the political leadership, although political leadership played a part, alongside the agency itself, in initiating two other decrees. The Criminal Checks Decree required that those participating in Corporation for Community and National Service voluntary programmes, such as volunteers to befriend elderly people (the Senior Companion Program), or older people who act as 'foster grandparents' to young people, undergo background checks in the relevant state criminal registry and the National Sex Offender Public Registry. As an official put it:

> We were looking at all of this in view of recent happenings involving sex predators. Our inspector general [a political appointee] engaged us in a conversation and said that he was unhappy that a lot of our programs were not complying with the provisions. [ECP: How did he know?] The inspector general audited the programs—the office goes out and looks at what is going on—it is a big office with lots of investigators. The inspector general raised this as an issue.

In the second case where the intervention of the political appointee heading the organization was critical, the impact was rather indirect. The Federal Communication Commission's (FCC) Katrina Decree gave effect to some of the recommendations of the Independent Panel Reviewing the Impact of Hurricane Katrina on Communications Networks published in 2006 (available http://www.fcc.gov/pshs/advisory/hkip). The Panel was initiated by the FCC chairman, Kevin J. Martin, a political appointee. However, the Katrina Decree reinforced what was being decided in the agency and did not constitute a major departure imposed from the top. Among other things the decree placed obligations on communication providers to report when communications networks were damaged during emergencies. But the decree was close to what was being planned within the FCC already. As an official put it:

> Commission staff were already working on ways to streamline outage reporting. When the report came out recommending reforms, they dovetailed with what the bureau wanted. The report recognized that it was already being worked on and they more or less agreed that we should continue doing it. The panel had recommended a voluntary process. The overall theme was voluntary. When the order came out it simply acknowledged what we already do.

Moreover, the decree also contained provisions not directly included in the report's recommendations.

In the third case where the political leadership can claim a significant role in agenda setting, the decree introducing changes to slaughterhouse rules in the wake of BSE ('mad cow disease') outbreaks, the political executive's press announcement that the USDA would tighten up decrees was a crucial stimulus to develop the decree. As an official put it:

> The issue was so high profile with the discovery of BSE cases that at the secretary of agriculture level, Anne Veneman came out and made a press statement [in December 2003 when a case of BSE was discovered in Washington State] about what we would do. Then we started working on it.

However, in the BSE case the officials involved pointed out that the USDA's Food Safety and Inspection Service (FSIS) had already started work on the issue before the intervention of the Secretary of Agriculture. There had been a 'think piece' written nearly two years before the Washington State BSE case by the FSIS that had outlined proposals later contained in the rule, such as prohibiting 'downer' or 'non-ambulatory' cattle from being slaughtered (on the reasoning that if they cannot stand up, animals are more likely to be infected with BSE) and banning the use of stunning devices that cause parts of the brain to splatter and contaminate the carcass (see FSIS 2002). As the official put it: 'We were gearing up our work on it anyway because of the case earlier in Canada... we were looking at these things [measures] all the time.' In fact, one of the main points about the Secretary of Agriculture's initiative was that it indicated that there would be strong political support for a rule: 'The issue was, did we have the legal authority to require that these things are removed from the food chain? Then we found consensus and moved forward.'

Given the highly pluralistic nature of US politics, and the opportunities that the formal procedures of rule-making offer organized interests to intervene in the process, much that might in other countries pass with little or no challenge is in the US controversial. This feature of the US system will be elaborated on below. Nevertheless, our examination of the circumstances producing our ten rules showed a significant role for the agency as the initiator of the rule—in five of the ten cases the rule was something that the agency started more or less on its own, in a sixth case the agency used the opportunity of a GAO investigation to secure support for something it had been wanting for a while. In two further cases the agency could respond to issues raised by its political leadership with measures they had already been planning and in the ninth case the rule-making was started in response to the report of another federal agency. Only in one case (Criminal Checks) did the intervention of a political executive seem to be the exclusive cause of the decree in the sense that there were no plans by the agency to regulate in this area. Nevertheless, the BSE case highlights the importance of political executive support in securing the passage of controversial decrees.

Bureaucrats in agencies can think of lots of things they would like to happen, but in the US system the distance between a twinkle in an official's eye and an agency decree[3] is in general much further than in any of the five other jurisdictions. In order to explain this, and the position of political executives in the development of decrees, we first need to set out a little more about the process of rule-making that limits bureaucratic discretion.

THE PLURALISTIC PROCESS OF DEVELOPING RULES

If you talk to any bureaucrats involved in developing rules, they will invariably make reference to the APA. This act, along with the many amendments and additions, governs how executive agencies can make rules. The principle is quite simple: there are statutory safeguards which prevent decrees from being issued without offering the opportunity for those interested to scrutinize and comment on what is being proposed. The pluralism extends to offering not only interest groups the ability to participate in the policy process, but also other parts of the bureaucracy, or even other people or parts of the same agency (West 1988).

One can list all the major stages that decrees can pass through, though not all have to pass through every one, as will be discussed below. If it is a 'significant' rule it will need to go through a lengthy and elaborate process of

---

[3] I.e. excluding Council regulations in the EU.

consultation. Although not required by the APA (though individual statutes under which decrees are issued may require them) the agency's intention to regulate and its thinking about an issue can be set out in an advance notice of proposed rulemaking (ANPR). Thus the Salmon Decree was the subject of an ANPR in September 2003. The APA specifies that rules are usually the subject of a 'notice of proposed rulemaking' (NPRM). In this stage the agency's thinking about a particular issue can be set out. The Lithium Decree, for example, was the subject of an NPRM published in the Federal Register in 2002 (RSPA 2002) which sets out the problems that lithium batteries pose, the proposals the agency intends to develop to deal with them, and giving ten weeks for interested parties to contact the agency.[4] The next stage is to develop a 'proposed rule' which sets out the precise wording of the rule and (where there has been a NPRM) will contain a summary of all the comments received at the NPRM stage and how the agency is addressing them, or, if they are not being addressed, why not. But before a 'significant' or 'major' proposed rule is published it is subject, according to the Paperwork Reduction Act of 1980 and Executive Order 12866,[5] to review by the Office of Information and Regulatory Affairs (OIRA) within the Office Management and Budget (OMB). The 'final rule' will also contain discussion of how any comments have or have not been addressed and also needs to have been examined by OIRA (see GAO 2003). Before they take effect, all rules must be submitted to Congress for examination, according to the 1996 Congressional Review Act, and Congress may pass a disapproval resolution. However, since we are only concerned with the production of the rule, since Congress made no direct contribution to any of our cases, and since only one disapproval resolution had ever been enacted up until 2008, it is not covered in this chapter.

The significance of a decree is a matter for OIRA to decide, usually on the proposal of the office of general counsel (the general legal affairs section) in the relevant agency or department. The general rubric is that a 'major' or 'economically significant' rule requiring OMB approval is one that would have

> an annual effect on the economy of $100 million or more, or adversely affect in a material way the economy; a sector of the economy; productivity; competition; jobs; the environment; public health or safety; or state, local, or tribal governments or communities. Create a serious inconsistency or otherwise interfere with an action taken or planned by another agency. Materially alter the budgetary impact of entitlements, grants, user fees, or loan programs, or the

---

[4] For a discussion of the impact of public notice and comment, see West 2004.
[5] Earlier versions of this executive order include Reagan's EO 12291, which covered all rules. The Bush administration continued using the Clinton Executive Order 12866 (which limited coverage to 'significant' rules), albeit in amended form. Amendments included elimination of the role of the vice president in regulatory review and strengthening the role of political appointees within the department or agency in the rule-making process.

rights and obligations of recipients of those programs; or raise novel legal or policy issues arising out of legal mandates, [or] the President's priorities... (OMB 2001)

The OMB also examines decrees for the kinds of information collection and paperwork burdens the decree puts on public and private organizations. However, the basic assumption behind OMB involvement is as a check and balance. As one decree writer put it:

> [T]he theory of the system of OMB scrutiny is that agencies that have a mission are on a mission, and they will regulate when regulation is not the best approach, since that agency's perspective is to make laws to do what they want to do. This may not be the best way to do things.

OMB can also seek to raise and resolve inter-agency disputes. One official pointed out:

> OMB is a referee and signal cop. If there is an argument between [our department] and [a related department] and we won't clear a rule, OMB won't let them publish the rule until it is resolved. It can be solved by consensus or OMB directive. Generally... OMB wants to see a consensus rather than directing a result.

Another official pointed to OMB almost as an additional form of quality control:

> Sometimes they [OMB] raise issues we don't expect to be issues. OMB is a useful check and balance. On this one they raised the X issue—we should have been prepared for that. We made a decision to put it in to see if it would fly—it wouldn't. They give you chapter and verse on why. I didn't disagree, well OK. It was not something we could bring into the final rule...

All those who with decrees going through OMB saw this stage of the process as an opportunity for the affected interest groups to try and change the decree. Because of the importance of this stage, rule writers feel they have to be scrupulous in paying attention to the comments they receive in the consultations (on the proposed rule or the NPRM), and the discussion of the reasons for the rule and how objections or suggestions have been treated is an extremely important part of the rule-writing process, as even a cursory glance at the Federal Register will confirm.[6] One of our decrees that should have been written by one office within one agency was, in fact, written by another specifically because of the need to have experience dealing with OMB:

> I drafted the proposed rule and finished the final rule. X's office had no experience of any of that. It had no experience of OMB... The rule had to cover the

---

[6] See West (2004) for a discussion of the limitations of public notice and comment in the development of rules.

comments, X had no experience of addressing comments. We had to provide simple final rules to address the comments.

One official described the opportunities this offered for interest groups in the rule for which he was responsible:

> OMB was well aware of [the reasons for the rule being opposed by several major corporations]. There are multiple chances these people get to make their case. OMB allowed those who wanted to be in on it to come in for a quasi hearing. We go and listen—we cannot participate. This gives them another shot—they state their position. This happened in between the draft and the final rule. There were five of the big companies... and they all bring in their counsel and they say the things they like and the things they didn't like. We went along and wrote away preparing for what may come later if we were challenged.

OMB, according to one respondent, 'killed' one proposed decree (an earlier version of the Lithium Decree). When the rule was submitted to OMB in 2003 it insisted that the PHMSA revisit the issue by taking greater account of the costs to business: 'After discussions with staff at the Small Business Administration, we are returning the final rule for your reconsideration' (OMB letter, 2 Aug. 2003). 'OMB might have had good reason', according to one official involved in aircraft security who wanted to see the rules in place, 'as there was no cost-benefit analysis'.

There are other procedures by which rules can come to be issued. Perhaps most important there is the interim rule procedure that allows a rule to come into effect straight away but is usually 'finalized' by subsequent development of a final rule, and there is the 'direct final' rule procedure that allows the publication of a final rule without any previous notice published in the Federal Register. This can be done in cases of decrees not deemed 'major' or 'of economic signifcance'. But they are all variations on the theme that almost anything of significance must be subjected to a process of review that prohibits the issue of a decree without having first offered the opportunity for the rule to be amended or blocked. In part that is why it generally takes longer to develop a decree. One of the decrees in the sample was started twelve years before the final decree was issued, and an interval of two or three years between the publication of an NPRM and the publication of a final rule is quite usual. Given the hurdles that controversial or significant decrees have to pass, the support of the political leadership to ensure that the decree goes through is essential, and securing political approval is an important part of the development of decrees.

HOW BUREAUCRATS DEVELOP DECREES

Before we look at the interplay between politicians and bureaucrats in the development of decrees, we can first outline briefly the process involved in putting a decree together. In contrast to the European countries (with the possible exception of Sweden), drawing up a decree was generally a collective and collegial activity, rather than the actions of one or two people. Certainly a small group within the agency was likely to be the main author of a decree. Yet when asked how the rule was actually drawn up, respondents tended to reply that 'a group' was constituted that could be composed of just people from the agency or, where other agencies were likely to be interested or affected, other agencies. They meet occasionally to iron out the issues in the proposed rule. When asked if this was a 'working group' respondents would reply that it was not quite as formal as that. One official described his group:

> I convened a working group in the HQ of all programs, grants and the inspector general—all who had an interest within the [agency]. We had numerous conference calls. We also consulted the departments that had an interest—Justice, the Attorney General for example.

And another:

> I was the primary author of the regulation. But I have a team. There is the Office of Public Health Science in the FSIS. I had a kind of working group and kind of went to people as I needed them. There was a basis of science studies, and we had to get the risk assessment people—they did the modelling to show what we are doing was effective. They were economists—we did an economic analysis so we had an economist, one from the inside [of the FSIS].

The use of deliberative groups also appears to be related to the need, at least for controversial or significant rules, to secure support from other agencies as well as the political leadership. As a key author of one such decree in the Department of Labor put it, when he was clear they had agreed what kind of rule to propose:

> We advised OMB, and we gave the heads up to folks in Homeland Security who were on the workgroup with us. The workgroup had people from Homeland Security, MB [Management and Budget], Labor and the Office of the Solicitor General. The workgroup conceptualized the notice of proposed rule making.... [ECP: Did you show it to the lawyers?] You see the guy who was in the room just as you came in? He is the head of litigation in the department. Those people look at it for legal vulnerabilities. They'll also be on working groups with us and review drafts. And we need lots of help to make it all read reasonably well.

And another:

> [ECP: Did you write the rule?] I used to write them all. Now I just get to tell people what to put in 'em.... Yes it is a collective—a team. There is not just one person there that does it. The product comes out of the office and goes up through the chain. If you're smart [as a rule writer] you'll brief people up the chain too. Bad rule-making is when people who have done the work fail to advise the management what the pros and cons are. They [senior management] can give pointers to smooth the waters if they are engaged. Bad rule-making happens

when management is not engaged. Management does not always want to be engaged either.

While this was the pattern for most rules with even the mildest degree of controversy, there was no workgroup for the entirely uncontroversial Privacy Act Decree, though even here there was very significant consultation within the office.

> [ECP: Was it straightforward?] I'll say it was straightforward as I've been doing these for 25 years. I know the procedures—having to take it through OMB and [such like]. [ECP: Did it take long to write this?] Not to draft rules like this, but to get the document checked for regulatory and legal tweaks can take months—close to a year... all cites [references to existing laws] have to be checked by someone to make sure they are correct.... I draft it and pass it on to M for review. M passes it on [to a legal department] to review it for legal aspects. Mostly they'll pick up typos—this... was a consolidation of existing systems [so there was not much else to pick up]. With Privacy Act system notices [like this rule] you usually get objections when a new system is being proposed—people raising questions about the reasons why people have access to this information.... This was a very boilerplate kind of rule. I might have needed to talk to M about substantive matters—which categories it is that are included [in the rule]. Yes we did have a few choices about categories. And I need to talk to the IT people about the way we maintain the records. And we need to talk to the security people to make sure we know how it is retrieved. We went from a paper to an automated system. I sent it to them before I sent it up.

GETTING POLITICAL SUPPORT

In the pluralist system of the United States it can be important to secure political support for a proposed rule to avoid the dilution of the measures the agency wants to see included in the final version of the rule, or even to avoid being forced to abandon the entire decree itself.[7] The importance of political support for agency objectives means that much attention needs to be devoted to getting support from the political leadership and, at least on one occasion in our sample, support from other institutions against opposition of political leadership.

For the Alien Substitution Decree, which sought to end 'alien substitution', the practice of applying for a green card for one person and subsequently changing the name on it, the opposition had always been very substantial.

---

[7] This research selected only final rules that were published in the Federal Register and therefore cannot say anything about decrees that fell at any of the hurdles that rules face, though several of the decrees examined were related to earlier rules which fell at these hurdles.

The Department of Labor had tried to regulate in this area before and the decree was overturned because a court found that the procedures for making the decree had not been properly followed (see *Kooritzky* v. *Reich* in the United States Court of Appeals for the District of Columbia Circuit 1994-03-18; Kooritzky was later jailed in 2002 for running a large immigration fraud based on alien substitution). As one official put it: 'Kooritzky realized he could make a fortune by overturning us on an APA violation and he made a heck of a lot of money through that.' The big IT firms who relied on skilled immigrant labour, and who used alien substitution in a legitimate way, were especially active in their opposition. The officials involved in writing the decree knew that there was little point in starting work on it until political support at the highest level within the administration was secured. Although the decree was foreshadowed in an earlier rule in 2004, political support was a major problem:

> You have to let the policy leadership people know it is contentious. This is big stuff, not just the Labor Secretary but he had the administration behind him. . . . It took us a while. . . . Resources are part of the decision to go ahead with this [are there people free who can work on this?], another is: are we on firm enough ground, is there policy support? It was not my final decision. It went on above me—it only holds true for this rule because of how it was. I report to the assistant secretary, a political appointee. At her level there were conversations—conversations at a policy level. . . . This was a big rule-making issue. . . . It got to a head and in 2006 we said we'd do something about it in a regulation. We were free enough and had time to do it. We had to do the necessary briefings with the policy people. We have a lot of people watching this area. The biggest feeder for this is the H-1B visa holder. They call it the 'IT visa' as all the big IT corporations use it to get people with talent. It's a high end visa. It is part of the recruitment and retention offer package to get people to stay here—and it brings in a huge bunch of talent that the employers count on. Bill Gates [Microsoft Corporation] opened up in Canada because he could not get enough visas. So we knew we'd get comments and provoke huge opposition, but we had the political will and support to face it. My job was to make sure we had support from the policy people and to start the process.

And the opposition was substantial and even personal, as the official recalls:

> The immigration lawyers association had a conference in May. I stood up to go to the podium [they had invited me to give a speech]. As I was on my way up, the man on the podium was calling for people to come forward as litigants for the rule we were writing. 'Anyone want to sue this guy?' What a way to introduce a guest speaker! That's lawyers for you.

The opposition intensified as soon as the notice of proposed rulemaking was published and especially after the draft rule was published.

> When we published the draft rule we got comments back, mainly 'you guys ought to be shot'. You have to wade though the stuff and deal with it [in the comments] or the chances of it being overturned and you being sued are high. It is an exceptionally legal environment.

The big IT companies used the OMB procedures to try and get the rule blocked, and right up until the end of the process those involved remained uncertain whether there was enough support to pass the OMB scrutiny without having to give way to the pressures for minimizing the impact of the rule.

> There were lots of comments on this recommending we change it. Most of the time the younger people [in the team] defer to the senior [in age] peoples' judgement. That's where our authority comes in. We know when we're outnumbered and know when we have to reduce or when we can increase what we are after. It helps to have grey hair doing this sort of thing—we're more savvy and experienced than the 21 year old kids who are more likely to fold.

The Salmon Decree was highly controversial, like much in the area of nature conservation. Here political support was not available in the Commerce Department, the part of government responsible for endangered species legislation at sea, as opposed to on land where the Department of the Interior was responsible. The protection of endangered species through the designation of their critical habitats had become something of a dead letter law, with the Bush administration being accused of deliberately dismantling the provisions of the Endangered Species Act to designate 'critical habitats' (*New York Times* 2002). A series of court cases required a reformulation of the way that critical habitats were designated.[8] A civil servant in the regional office of the National Marine Fisheries Service (an agency of the National Oceanic and Atmospheric Administration (NOAA), itself a bureau of the Department of Commerce) who realized that something had to be done took the unusual step, for European administrative systems at least, of seeking to engage the interest of the leadership of *a different* federal government department.

> [We] tried to get the leadership. We did not get decision making attention in the agency. So we went to Interior. Interior was providing the policy direction so that's where we went.

A court action taken by the Pacific Coast Federation of Fishermen's Associations and others (including some environmental protection groups), ordering that NOAA designate critical habitats, helped agency civil servants to get approval for a designation decree:

> We were sued by environmental interests who sued us for not having it [critical habitat designation] in place. We negotiated a schedule—a timeline we thought we could meet. We went to court with a settlement agreement and the court agreed and that bound the agency to the schedule. The court case helps funding and gets resources. When you have a court order it helps to make the rule-making

---

[8] For a discussion of the litigation, see the provisional rule in Department of Commerce (2004).

process go. Major landowners were opposed to it, for example, the Forest Service—those that manage forests—the Bureau of Land Management and some Indian tribes were opposed.

And even with a court order, it was not plain sailing with the Department of Commerce. A civil servant from the Northwest regional office explained:

> The draft rule took one and a half years to get published. I spent a lot of time in Washington.... Each step—each major decision point—we'd go back and give a presentation. Here's what we found, here are the decision points, here's what we recommend, is it OK to proceed? X was the only one from Commerce paying attention in the early stages.... The meetings were lively, oh yes. The Department of Interior's position was staked out: 'We hate critical habitat and it should be very narrow'.

Nevertheless:

> If you compare the proposed rule to the final you'll see that the key sticking point was how to use the exclusion authority [exclusion of some type of land from designation]. The Fish and Wildlife Service has a rule for bull trout [which]... excluded any land with a management plan in place—e.g. Forest Service land. The position was that the management plan provides protection so critical habitat designation does not benefit the species. That issue went to the Deputy Secretary of Commerce.

An external stimulus that is hard to resist, such as a court case, can help secure political support despite internal opposition within the administration, even opposition from its political leadership. Big events that change the political environment for decrees were also important in some of the cases. BSE outbreaks in Washington State allowed the FSIS a relatively clear path for the BSE Decree, Hurricane Katrina did the same for the FCC's provisions for disaster management, and media coverage of paedophilia cases helped the Criminal Checks Decree. In the case of the Lithium Decree the external impetus took the form of a video. The 1999 Los Angeles International Airport (LAX) fire that gave rise to the NTSB report (see above) was filmed, and this, according to one of the officials involved, was an important reason why the NTSB was interested in regulating the area. Moreover, the visual evidence was important in demonstrating that existing fire safety provisions in aircraft were unsuitable for dealing with lithium battery fires: the Halon fire suppression system did not, according to a report commissioned by the Federal Aviation Administration, suppress lithium fires. An official commented:

> Halon and its inability to cope with litihum fires was decisive. If we did not have that, we would not have had a chance. The FAA videotaped Halon not being able to deal with flames from a lithum battery fire and showed it to the NTSB. Showed them the flames not being impacted by Halon. Video has been very important in

all this, there was the video of LAX. If the whole thing was not videoed I wonder whether NTSB would have taken that much interest.

This view was endorsed in part by another civil servant who stressed the importance of 'the LAX incident—there was a video of it and it was a Keystone Cops type thing' as the fire services struggled to cope. Moreover, in a related but later episode, the question of whether there should be any decrees covering recharging laptop batteries in passenger aircraft was in part placed on the agenda by a dramatic video put on a popular website for video downloads: 'the PHMSA chief safety officer was motivated by the media especially when [videos of laptops exploding in airports and planes were put] on a YouTube-type website'.

With the State Department's changes to the Exchange Visitor rules, one might be hard pressed to see this as an issue generating much political opposition. However, as one of those involved in writing this decree explained, 'some view this...as an abuse of practice—taking jobs from Americans. Others will recognize it as part of developing our economy and culture.' Although within the State Department itself there were different views on this, the GAO report endorsed one particular view, and an official argued that this reflected the way the GAO was steered when it did its study:

> You can see when a conservative staff from GAO has been briefed by outreach-oriented 'let 1000 flowers bloom' types here, and you'll get a different outcome when a narrow conservative staff briefs a narrow conservative GAO team. A or B outcomes—you can see what is coming. That is how you can control the outcome—a manager would size up the GAO team and send the appropriate staff to do the briefing to get the outcome they wanted.

Whether or not this was an exaggeration, the GAO helped get the decree over its hurdles and issued. One of its authors generalized:

> Each policy has to have its 'cover' [thing that pushes it]. A year or two years ago we did a rule on criminal background checks for high school students. I wrote it and pushed it through the system in 20 days. That's quick. You can do it if you know how. Sponsors have to do a background check on host families. We had press articles and congressional letters that we were running an operation that made it possible for sexual predators to have people placed in their homes. That is a good example of how something can be done if there is a management will to do it. Coupled with the argument 'who will argue against that?'

Only two of our ten decrees did not rely on some such kind of 'cover' provided by external events to ensure political support for the rule. Both of these (Privacy Act and Community Connect Decrees) were not deemed 'significant' so they did not require scrutiny by OMB. Even officials developing the decrees that were not subjected to OMB scrutiny (the FCC Katrina Decree, the USAID Mentor Decree, and the CNCS Criminal Check Decree) felt they had to secure political endorsement of the proposals.

CONCLUSIONS

A European scholar might well be struck by the importance in the classical literature on US bureaucracy attached to the 'agency'. Selznick's (1949) *TVA and the Grass Roots* introduces the idea of 'agency ideology' to explain the behaviour of its management, Kaufman's (1960) *Forest Ranger* emphasizes the role of the Forestry Service in socializing its members into its norms and procedures, Downs's (1967) *Inside Bureaucracy* identifies an agency mission as central to defining the behaviour of some of the different types of bureaucrats he outlines, and Simon's (1945) *Administrative Behavior* gives significant weight to agency norms. This emphasis in the academic literature reflects the strong importance of the organizational subunit—bureau, agency, division, and such like—for the world of the federal bureaucrat in the United States. European scholars have always been aware that separate organizations—ministries or even units within ministries—often have distinctive approaches to policy problems and issues: officials within a department focusing on policing and prisons might be expected to favour different policies on drug abuse to those that might be generated by a department dealing with social workers. 'Where you stand depends on where you sit', as the popularization of the 'bureaucratic politics' model (Allison 1971) has it. The difference between the US and the European countries in this study might be one of degree, but it is nevertheless striking: in the US the agency is a strong lodestone which helps officials within it orient their behaviour.

One of the first signs that the agency is important is that in each interview the respondent was concerned to explain the history and status of the agency for which s/he worked. Thus, for example, when talking about the very modern task of providing broadband access to rural communities, an official in the Department of Agriculture began tracing the lineage of the agency through the 'great 1930s programs' of the Roosevelt era (including the 1936 Rural Electrification Act). And knowledge of history was even important for a newly created division in the State Department; we

> became the National Security Division, a new division. The first new division in 30 or 40 years. [Earlier we had been] . . . a free standing office in the Department of Justice. We were a creation of the Foreign Intelligence Surveillance Act of 1978 (following the Church and Pike committees of the 1970s [committees that sought to establish greater control over the intelligence services following scandals of the earlier 1970s]).

Such interest and pride in organizational lineage was somewhat rare in the other countries. The delimitation of the agency's responsibility—what interests it and what does not—is also shared by its officials. One official responsible for air safety pointed out that his agency was less concerned about the hazards posed by one material than another because the other material had a slower impact and posed a hazard to passengers after they left the plane, whereas his agency was concerned with hazards that could cause a crash in flight.

To point out that rules are proposed because they have emerged as desirable within the agency does not, of course, explain exactly where they came from. Some idea of the precise genesis of the rules has been offered here, but the common feature of the agency as the source is nevertheless important and distinctive. One reason it is distinctive is that it can pit the agency against the political leadership. However, since political support is so crucial in shaping what actually is issued, by selecting decrees that have actually been approved for this research we cannot find examples of initiatives started and then abandoned due to political leadership opposition. One recent example of this agency/leadership division could be found in the Fish and Wildlife Service where the deputy assistant secretary (a political appointee) responsible for Fish, Wildlife, and Parks 'repeatedly overruled agency scientists' recommendations on endangered species'. Public criticism of her tenure by officials from the service alleging 'improper political influence' helped undermine her position and contributed towards her resignation (*Washington Post* 2007).

The evidence of the decrees examined here suggests a significant role for politicians in their everyday bureaucratic production—less as agenda setters, if that is meant to mean initiating issues, and more as agenda selectors. Their support shapes what is likely to get through an extensive consultation process which offers multiple opportunities for blockage. Moreover, it will become apparent throughout this book that the decrees in the US context are significantly more likely to raise controversy than those found in the other jurisdictions. The number of decrees looked at in each jurisdiction, and the possibility of bias in selection either through the individual decrees chosen or even because what Europeans generally term 'secondary' or 'delegated' legislation (i.e. in US terminology administrative rules or regulations) has different functions in different systems (see e.g. Pünder 2009: 356-7) means one has to take this observation as rather tentative. The crowded interest group environment, the sheer size of the country, the number of distinct interest organizations it can sustain and the wider opportunities for local and business representation offered by the US political system (above all, the separation of powers) than generally found in European countries might be cited as reasons for finding that more issues are likely to raise significant controversy than in other countries.

However, the role of bureaucrats is also significant. The fact that the agency is a source of identity and that it has traditions, missions, and objectives that can be independent of the current executive political leadership can mean that its officials may play an important part not only in defining the range of issues that emerge to become the subject of decrees but also in shaping when they are presented to the political leadership, how they are framed to make them more acceptable, and also whether and what sort of 'cover' (the external feature that makes it politically acceptable to develop the decree) helps the decree reach the

Federal Register. We have, therefore, a somewhat different picture, when we look at the development of decrees, from the dominant picture of political leadership setting an agenda. In significant areas of policy, the agenda is set by the departmental officials who, like other actors in the policy process, also wait their chance for favourable political conditions to get a rule put through, in much the same way as the 'policy activists' waiting for 'windows of opportunity' in Kingdon's (2003) model.

ANNEX: DECREES INCLUDED IN CHAPTER 6

Reference	Agency	Short Name
72 FR 27904 Labor Certification for the Permanent Employment of Aliens in the United States; Reducing the Incentives and Opportunities for Fraud and Abuse and Enhancing Program Integrity	Employment and Training Administration (Department of Labor)	Alien Substitution
70 FR 52630 Endangered and Threatened Species; Designation of Critical Habitat for 12 Evolutionarily Significant Units of West Coast Salmon and Steelhead in Washington, Oregon, and Idaho	National Marine Fisheries Service (Department of Commerce)	Salmon
72 FR 48574 National Service Criminal History Checks	The Corporation for National and Community Service	Criminal Checks
72 FR 32540 Mentor-Protégé Program	USAID	Mentor
72 FR 38700 Prohibition of the Use of Specified Risk Materials for Human Food and Requirements for the Disposition of Non-Ambulatory Disabled Cattle; Prohibition of the Use of Certain Stunning Devices Used To Immobilize Cattle During Slaughter	Food Safety and Inspection Service (Department of Agriculture)	BSE
72 FR 52779 Community Connect Broadband Grant Program	Rural Utilities Service (Department of Agriculture)	Community Connect
72 FR 37655 Recommendations of the Independent Panel Reviewing the Impact of Hurricane Katrina on Communications Networks	Federal Communications Commission	Katrina
72 FR 33669 Exchange Visitor Program—Trainees and Interns	Office of Exchange Coordination and Designation (Department of State)	Exchange Visitor
72 FR 44930 Hazardous Materials; Transportation of Lithium Batteries	Pipeline and Hazardous Materials Safety Administration (Department of Transportation)	Lithium
72 FR 44382 Privacy Act of 1974; Implementation	National Security Division (Department of Justice)	Privacy Act

7

Regulated Bureaucratic Politics in the European Union

The European Union is often argued to be a 'bureaucrat's paradise' (Smith 2006). This often applies above all to the European Commission. Certainly many of its superficial characteristics are unlikely to give it great public appeal or attract much citizen affection. It is a large bureaucracy composed of impersonal sounding 'directorates general' housed mainly in an array of large and small anonymous public buildings, presided over by officials who bear the authoritarian-sounding name of 'commissioner' with decision-making procedures that seem to be governed by Byzantine rules and a myriad different committees and working groups. It even has its own Soviet-style institutional vocabulary, including 'comitology', 'derogations', and 'national action plans'. If one makes the dubious assumption that working in this environment appeals to bureaucrats, then that could be one reason why the EU could be described as a paradise. More commonly, the 'paradise' refers to the power of bureaucrats. It suggests a decision-making environment in which 'officials and civil servants are the central participants in the formulation of policies' (Jacobsson et al. 2001: 27). Bureaucrats are, however, central participants in the formulation of policies in many political systems.

The EU may be a bureaucrat's paradise in the sense that a lot of the basic policy-making work is conducted by hosts of officials from member states who participate in the main decision-making forums, above all in those that emerge around the committees and boards that shape Council and Commission decisions. The rail and air stations in Brussels are heavily populated with bureaucrats from member states on their way to and from meeting other bureaucrats from member states and EU officials. Yet in so far as it refers to the power to shape policy offered to European Commission bureaucrats themselves, the term 'paradise' is far less accurate. As Moravscik (2001) argues:

> The EU bureaucracy is in fact tiny, leaderless, tightly constrained by national governments, and almost devoid of the power to tax, spend, or coerce. Indeed, the EU lacks nearly every characteristic that grants a modern European state (let

alone the modern, *dirigiste* French state) its authority.... Sheer numbers would be unimportant, of course, if these Brussels bureaucrats were all-powerful, but executive power in the EU is so weak and diffuse that analysts cannot even agree where it resides, if anywhere.

Moravscik goes on to sustain the argument by pointing out that, for the big political issues, the Commission may enjoy 'some control over the legislative agenda', but he stresses the importance of member states and the growing power of the European Parliament. That the power of other institutions has increased since Moravscik wrote this might be taken to suggest that the power of the Commission bureaucracy has further decreased.

Others have argued that while the Commission as an institution might have limited powers, its bureaucracy might nevertheless be rather powerful. Four reasons for this argument stand out. First, the style of administration in the European Commission is to delegate power to lower level bureaucrats. Stevens and Stevens (2000: 175) point to interview material that suggests that 'relatively junior officials' are given responsibility for major policy tasks (see also Weiler 1999). Second, the kinds of issue the Commission has most responsibility for are highly technical and more likely to place the technical specialists of the Commission in a position of power. As Stevens and Stevens (2000: 223) suggest, Commission officials 'have no monopoly of agenda setting in such circumstances, but they have an important influence on it, and there is markedly more scope for them to define the problem and undertake the choice of solution'. As Marks *et al.* suggest, Commission officials are the 'hub of numerous highly specialised policy networks of technical experts designing detailed regulations' (1996: 355). Third, as Weiler (1999: 277) argues, the constraints on Commission decree-making, above all through comitology procedures, might be more apparent than real since the Commission 'has become, de facto, the dominant voice in comitology and could not care less about its formal lack of control; its viewpoint prevails in an overwhelming number of instances'. This point has even greater importance if Weiler (1999: 278) is correct in arguing that there is a strong danger that the decisions made in such forums are 'taking place at a level of public input and accountability which are not commensurate with the importance of such regulation': big political questions might be being handled in bureaucratic decision-making arenas associated with more routine matters of detail. Fourth, as Diamant (1957) argued in the case of Fourth Republic France, deadlock within political decision-making forums might increase the power of bureaucracy. With the fragmentation of decision-making in the European Union the possibilities for greater gridlock through the increasing power of the Council and Parliament might allow the Commission and in particular its bureaucracy to have greater power. Tsebelis and Garrett (2001: 383) argue that, although the 'discretionary space' open to the Commission might have declined since the late 1980s, the 'proliferation of secondary legislation in this period increased the number of issue areas in which the Commission could exercise its discretion'.

In this chapter I look at the experience of making seven decrees, three proposals for Council and/or Parliament regulations and four of the Commission's own regulations. The central question addressed in this chapter is whether, once we get down to examining the detailed work of putting together decrees and proposals for decrees, the constraints that contemporary scholarship highlights on the Commission as an institution apply in quite the same way, and in particular whether such constraints limit the scope for lower level bureaucrats in the Commission to shape policy. The four Commission regulations did not require the agreement of Council or the European Parliament. The Tariff Simplification Decree simplified and standardized a range of existing rules governing the import of some agricultural products (those covered by an import license regime) from outside the EU. Forest Focus set out the rules for administering a programme (no longer in existence) protecting forests from fire and pollution, and the Silkworm Decree tidied up the law on the EU's support for the silkworm industry. The Horse Medicines Decree set out the list of medicines that could be administered to horses that could end up as meat for human consumption.

The sample includes one decree that, although drafted by the Commission, had to be negotiated and approved in Council—the decree covering the quotas ('total allowable catches') of a range of fish that may be caught by the fishing fleets of each member state in specified sea areas. Two of the decrees in the sample involved officials from the Commission proposing measures that then had to be approved by the European Parliament and Council. The Marco Polo Decree provides support for 'intermodal transport', above all moving freight transport off roads and on to rail and sea and inland waterways. The Stability Instrument Decree recast the European Union's framework for intervening in conflicts and crises worldwide, mainly through financing short-term relief and longer-term prevention and rebuilding. For example, Africa and the Middle East have been significant foci of attention for the Stability Instrument.

THE PLAYERS

This book is concerned with bureaucratic decision-making processes, how they work, and the circumstances surrounding politicians' interventions in them. While EU propaganda is always keen to point out that there are fewer officials working in the EU than are employed in many municipal authorities in its member states, there are certainly many more politicians than can be found in most national governments. Two of the major decision-making institutions of the European Union consist of elected representatives. The Council lists 1,283 'representatives of the governments of the member states who regularly take part in Council meetings', of which nearly 800 are members of elected governments and the remainder are the permanent secretaries and state secretaries who attend Council meetings on their behalf. In addition there are the 785 Members of the European Parliament. In this chapter I am primarily concerned with the political executives of the Commission. Twenty-seven commissioners are nominated by elected governments, and though many commissioners may have direct experience of electoral politics, their democratic legitimacy in the EU is secondhand. This does not distinguish commissioners as unelected political executives from political executives in some other jurisdictions, notably the United States. A more significant difference is that those who appoint the commissioners are bound not to give commissioners 'any instructions' and commissioners are bound by the oath of office not to accept any if they do. In short, commissioners are supposed to act independently of the member states that appoint them. The method of appointment is political, their authority is not. Nevertheless, as the appointed sectoral heads of the Commission's administration, they have direct responsibility for what is done in the directorates general assigned to them.

The Commission is divided into thirty-three directorates general, each generally headed by a commissioner, though the correspondence between Commission portfolio and directorate general has only recently become so neat. The old Transport and Energy Directorate General (now DG Mobility and Transport), for example, until 2010 had two separate commissioners for energy and transport and the DG Budget still had two commissioners in summer 2011. Turning to the bureaucratic personnel, the highest rank of official below the commissioner is the director general responsible for the whole DG. Then come deputy directors general responsible for groups of directorates, and each directorate is headed by a director. Below the director is a head of unit and below that various degrees of administrator with titles that vary substantially: 'head of sector' and 'deputy head of unit' among the most senior to 'policy officer' or 'adviser', usually indicating less seniority. The rankings do not correspond neatly to pay grades, with some directors being on the same pay level as some directors general, so precise numbers cannot easily be given. However, in the administrative staff of the Commission (i.e. excluding ancillary, clerical, and support staff as well as staff of agencies and research centres) we can show the approximate numbers in the different pay bands and the ranks associated with them (Table 7.1).

Which of these bureaucratic positions are 'political' appointments? In principle, none are. The basis for appointment and promotion at all levels to the Commission below commissioner is 'merit'. However, 'merit' used to be moderated by a series of other considerations of which the most important was 'national balance'. To ensure that each member state has a reasonable

Table 7.1. Positions at the top of Commission Directorates General

Rank	Grade	N
Director-general	AD16	30
Director-general/director	AD15	243
Director/head of unit/expert	AD14	573
Head of unit/expert	AD13	458
Head of unit/head of sector/senior administrator	AD12–AD9	4,570
Other administrators	AD8–AD5	3,466

Source: Budget 2008 Annex PARTC (http://eur-lex.europa.eu/budget/data/P2008_VOL1/EN/nmc-grse-qAP2000182/index.html) and Staff Regulations of the European Union (http://ec.europa.eu/civil_service/docs/toc100_en.pdf).

number of its own nationals in the top jobs had long been a principle of EU personnel policy. There have never been formal quotas, but in the past, under the so-called 'national flags' system, some Commission posts were 'reserved' for different nationalities. After the late 1990s there was a substantial and successful effort at reform to make merit more important and nationality less (Kassim 2008) such that it is generally claimed that the 'national flags' system has ended, replaced by a competitive process of appointment. Of course, member states frequently try and exert any pressure they can to ensure that they get at least their 'fair share' of top positions within the Commission, and the degree to which they succeed is unknown (Egeberg 2004). In this sense the process surrounding senior appointments at the level of director and above is political. However, as Georgakakis (2010) points out, the increasing independence from direct political control of senior bureaucratic careers within the Commission has led to an increasing 'sociological gap' between commissioners and their senior officials.[1]

Commissioners also have their own private staffs—*cabinets*—which in principle can fill functions that include ensuring that the bureaucracy is responsive to commissioners' initiatives and wishes, although they are also involved in developing relations between the commissioners and other European institutions as well as the media and the public. Members of *cabinets* can also serve as proxies for commissioners in the conduct of relations between Commission directorates general. *Cabinets* are headed by a *chef de cabinet* and usually consist of around half a dozen members. Three members of the *cabinet* must be nationals of a country different to that of the commissioner. In truth, however, *cabinet* members played a small part in our European cases. This might have

---

[1] There is another type of official about which relatively little is known: the *experts nationaux detachés* (*ENDs*) ('seconded national experts') who can work within the Commission for periods between six months and four years. These are not, strictly speaking, Commission employees as they are paid by their employing institution (usually the civil service of a member state). For a discussion, see Trondal (2007). They come into one of the cases (the Forest Focus Decree).

been a result of the cases selected, though some of them have strong political resonance and might reasonably be expected to arouse political interest. However, in such cases the commissioners became directly involved. Or it might be a matter of the style of different commissioners. We know that *cabinet* members have been closely involved in some EU high politics issues, such as the development of the Delors agenda for closer integration (Ross 1995).

THE LIMITED ROLE OF BUREAUCRATS IN INITIATING DECREES

The Commission's central role in proposing legislation has been enshrined in the treaties that have governed the European Union since the days of the European Coal and Steel Community in the 1950s. In European lawmaking 'primary' legislation takes the form of a treaty negotiated between member states under condition of unanimity, as well as measures passed by the Commission, the Council, and the European Parliament that take the form of 'secondary' legislation: directives, regulations, decisions, and opinions. The Commission has the 'right of initiative' to propose measures of secondary legislation, some of which may be issued by the Commission on its own authority, others which are proposals on which the Council must decide and issue its own, and others which require, under 'co-decision', the agreement of Council and Parliament. For secondary legislation, the Commission has an important power to initiate that places it at the heart of decision-making in the European Union. It is therefore somewhat surprising that in the seven decrees examined in this research the role of Commission *bureaucrats* as initiators was highly limited.

Where the issues are political and raise substantial interest from European politicians and member states, we might expect bureaucrats to have a lesser role in agenda setting than in areas with lower political profiles. Thus we might expect that the decrees that require the approval of Council or Council and Parliament are generally among the more controversial as they require the approval of European and member state politicians. So the limited role in initiating legislation by Commission officials might be expected for the Council regulation on fish quotas, and the two decrees passed with the agreement of Council and Parliament under co-decision (the Stability Instrument and Marco Polo Decrees). The initiation of work on the Fish Quota Decree was simply a matter of routine, even if the proposed decree leads to one of the most intense intergovernmental conflicts in the EU's calendar. The volume of deep sea fish stocks that the fishing fleets of EU member states can catch are set every year, and when the old decree expires a new one has to be put in its place. The procedure is based on an annual cycle of commissioning scientific advice from the International Council for the Exploration of the Sea (ICES) which produces a report on the state of deep sea fish stocks—fish such as blue ling, roundnose grenadier, and orange roughy that have become more attractive with the decline in other shallow-water fish stocks.

To a large degree the initiative for the Marco Polo decree derived from timings and procedures set in earlier legislation and the role of Commission officials in initiating the legislation was largely confined to whether they started work on the proposals earlier or later to meet a fixed deadline. The Marco Polo initiative was taken several years earlier with the establishment of the original Marco Polo (Marco Polo I) programme following a Commission commitment, set out in the 2001 Transport White Paper, to develop a transport programme that seeks to reduce the volume of freight on roads and encourage the use of rail and water transport. The original Marco Polo I was a five-year programme that was due to expire in 2007. The legislation setting out Marco Polo I (Regulation (EC) No. 1382/2003 of the European Parliament and of the Council of 22 July 2003, preamble para. 13) was clear about what had to happen before Marco Polo I expired: 'the Commission should therefore evaluate the implementation of this Regulation. It should present, not later than 31 December 2006, an assessment report on the results of the Marco Polo Programme, accompanied if necessary by a proposal for the amendment of this Regulation.'

The Stability Instrument Decree was directly initiated by the Commission rather than drafted in response to commitments established by convention or law. It was proposed as a means of 'rationalizing' the foreign aid given by the European Union to crisis-hit regions of the world. Responses to crisis previously required the use of up to seven separate EU funding schemes (see Dewaele and Gourlay 2005). The basic idea behind the proposal was to simplify funding, making it more flexible and responsive to policy priorities. As we will see below, others, above all in the Council and the European Parliament, saw this also as a Commission grab for power. Its origins were less the initiative of one commissioner and more, as one of the officials working on it described it, as the

> confluence of different processes. It started with the Peace Group. A group chaired by Pascal Lamy [Commissioner for Trade 1999–2004]. It was an internal reflection group on external relations and their insight was that there should be a policy framework—there was insufficient link between the different funding instruments and policy.... This discussion may or may not have gone somewhere except for the seven year negotiation on 'financial perspectives'. This was about sorting out the headline political priorities for the next seven years.... The services were developing their thoughts. Things were going up and down the hierarchy and things were being whittled down that way.

> ... There was no master plan or overall strategy. There was a general shared idea—that there should be fewer instruments and they should be policy related and not sectoral.

Moreover it was not clear there was going to be a decree on the matter, and certainly not one of the scope and ambition reflected in the Commission's proposal for a Stability Instrument, until a commissioner indicated there should be.

> There were substantive discussions and discussions of scale. But then the instruction came down from Patten that he wanted a big instrument. That is why we put it all in there and a lot was stripped out in the negotiation. The notion that it was to have crisis management was controversial to other DGs. That was a problem of constituency. But Patten was clear—there was to be crisis management. We were to respond to crises by amalgamating the different instruments. It was also something new. We were after money for a crisis response. While in the past you go to Parliament for money to deal with an emergency on a contingency basis, this time the money was to be in the [Commission's] main funding.

Of the four Commission regulations—decrees that do not need Parliament and/or Council approval—three were effectively elaborations of decisions taken earlier. The Silkworm Decree was a 'codification' of existing law. In 2001 the Commission proposed (in a communication dated 21.11.01 COM 645 final) that the *acquis communautaire* be codified—all the laws that had been passed in particular policy areas should be brought together in single documents. The idea, according to the communication, was to 'allow citizens and the business sector, in both the EU and the Candidate Countries seeking membership to benefit from a more accessible and transparent legislative framework'. The initiative had progressed more slowly than had been expected, and was relaunched in 2006. The intention was that legal officials from the Commission's Legal Service (and there are eight officials in the relevant group of whom five are directly engaged on codification) should identify bodies of legislation for codification, put them in a single law, and have them adopted through an advanced approval procedure. One of the conditions of codification is that the law must be preserved in its existing form, with no additions, subtractions, or amendments. This meant also that any inconsistency or vagueness in the existing legislation must be preserved in the codified version, a procedure known as 'consolidating the doubt' in English law drafting, a procedure that has mercifully been abandoned (see Kent 1979: 30). One might well wonder why a short decree, only changed marginally since its creation in 1973, needed to be codified. Part of the answer is that any law likely to be changed in the near future cannot be codified, and it was not uncommon for DGs to ask for particular laws not to be codified as there were plans to change them which would make any codification a waste of time. Officials in DGs can block codification, as one official complained:

When we had our text ready for adoption by the Commission [codifying two safety regulations]—right at the final stage—at the end of last year we discovered a proposition was being submitted to legislate both directives. None of us was informed, even though we'd been discussing this with them for years. [On another occasion, this time to do with an agricultural product] . . . I had codified the texts consulting their lawyers regularly. I went two times to the [relevant comitology] Committee . . . On both occasions I could not get it adopted. They raised linguistic points and they generally opposed the text as there was a policy proposal about to be developed so they said no implementing regulations should be codified.

The Silkworm Decree was chosen in part because it was simple and could be codified. An official involved explained one of the dangers of codifying even a rather obscure law—officials would be reminded of what the law actually was and decide that it was about time it should be changed.

The Horse Medicines Decree permitted the use of certain medicines on horses that could end up as meat for human consumption, and this was set out in the Veterinary Directive from which it arose (2001/82/EC and the amending decree of March 2004/726). According to an official involved 'we knew that we would have to amend the law. It was there in the proposal to Parliament (under the co-decision procedure), it was one of our original proposals, so we knew we had to do something for this.' There was little chance of any commitment falling into obscurity as 'horses have a strong lobby—the horse lobby is specially strong from the UK and Ireland and to a lesser extent Germany. There is not such a strong lobby in the south of Europe.' The precise origins of the Forest Focus Decree were less clear as they were written by a detached national expert who, according to a former colleague, 'left around 2004 and went back to the German Ministry of the Environment'. Nevertheless, the decree itself followed a European Court of Justice order requiring that the parent decree (Regulation (EC) No. 2152/2003 of the European Parliament and of the Council concerning monitoring of forests and environmental interactions in the Community) be rewritten under co-decision: 'all legislation on Forest Focus had to be changed so it was done under another article in the treaty'.

Perhaps the greatest degree of bureaucratic initiative of all the decrees came in the decree that, after the Silkworm codification, changed least. The Tariff Simplification Decree sought to standardize the import quota rules across a range of agricultural products. There were a variety of considerations that led to such a simplification. There was a general push towards simplification, of which the silkworm codification was part, within the Commission in general and within DG Agriculture in particular. 'Beef had something like twelve regulations and that made things complicated. In house we knew this was needed' said one of the officials involved. In addition a 2000 Court of Auditors report recommended simplification and the Commission had been committed to meet its recommendations (see European Commission 2004: 5). There was an additional information technology impetus, as another official put it: 'we are also introducing IT tools [to manage quotas]. Sometimes the side effects of IT is that you get the need for simpler or clearer rules—for the management of the quotas more than supervision.' The level at which this decree was initiated was 'quite low down, certainly not at director general or higher level, but at the level of the head of unit'.

As an initiator of decrees the role of the bureaucracy of the European Commission appears limited from the cases we have examined here. In six of the seven the initiative for making the decree appears to come from elsewhere—from a routine (Fish Quotas), from a commitment made in an earlier legislative process (Horse Medicines and Marco Polo), from a court decision (Forest Focus), from commissioners (Stability Instrument), and a cross-institutional strategy to simplify legislation (Silkworm). In the seventh (Tariff Simplification) the officials initiated the proposal, though they were responding to a variety of stimuli both external and internal to the Commission. Moreover, the initiative was for a tidying up—making some changes to the management of import quotas—rather than a significant development or extension of policy.

SUPERVISED DEVELOPMENT

One of the striking features of the development of European Union decrees in our sample is not only the degree to which it is supervised, but the variety of bodies within whose constraints those who develop decrees must work. This to some extent makes the question of the 'political' supervision of bureaucratic activity more complicated as there are other institutions that could be described as 'political' involved in the development of decrees. For the Council/Parliament decrees, the approval by them brings the possibility of intervention from elected Members of the European Parliament as well as executive leaders from national governments or their representatives. For Commission decrees, certainly those that require approval by the comitology committees, such committees are sometimes even assumed to form an indirect form of Council control over the Commission bureaucracy through such committees acting as intermediaries 'supervising' the role of the Commission (see Héritier and Moury 2008: 30). However, for the purposes of this study our concern with political control is with the politician involvement from the political executive within the Commission—i.e. the commissioners and their *cabinets*—as it is the commissioner in whose name the officials within the Commission work.

Two of the decrees were developed on the basis of scientific and technical advice from outside the Commission—the Fish Quotas and Horse Medicines

Decrees. While in both cases the Commission officials interpreting the advice were technically trained, one indeed was formerly a member of the body offering the scientific advice, the degree of discretion officials exercised about what should be put in the proposed decree varied significantly between the two.

The Fish Quotas Decree was based on advice on fish stock levels regularly commissioned from the International Council for the Exploration of the Sea (ICES). The ICES, founded in 1902 and with twenty member countries, provides through its working groups scientific advice to national governments and international bodies on the marine environment of the North Atlantic (see ICES 2001). Officials in DG Fisheries then have to decide how they turn the invariably dire warnings of diminishing fish stocks into a proposal for Council regulation. As one put it:

> The advice is exactly that, advice, not telling us how we use it. And it is advice on fish stocks and it is not their [ICES] task to offer political choices. We have to consider how long we should take to reduce fishing and what is feasible. . . . So the Commission proposal is not the same as the scientific advice. We are always criticized for staying too close to the scientific advice when we make our proposals. We don't think of the 'socio-economic issues'; that's the words the politicians that want to criticize us use.

The basic choices to be made are whether to stick to the scientific advice and offer a set of proposals that directly reflects the estimated fish stocks, or moderate the proposals to reflect the demand from many member states and fishing interests within them for fishing quotas higher than the scientific advice suggests. This choice is made with the certain knowledge that, once the proposal is placed before Council, member states with significant fishing fleets will oppose the more stringent limits suggested by the science, with the result that the scientific advice is diluted.

The decision on which strategy to pursue—following the scientific advice closely or seeking a proposal that has a greater chance of being accepted by Council—is that of the commissioner, not of an official. As one official put it, the narrow range of the responsibility of commissioners means that they become closely involved in highly detailed work in this particular DG.

> This is a small DG. We have a commissioner for fisheries for the first time with this new Commission. Before that we had an agriculture and fisheries commissioner. The reason was not that someone thought we needed someone especially for fish but because we have so many member states. They have to find a role for the commissioner. So that brings with it a private office and a *cabinet*. The previous commissioner had one member of the *cabinet* responsible for fisheries. This changes the relationship with the political level. He has a lighter portfolio so his people get into the detail. I should say that this is a general problem of the Commission, not a matter of style of an individual commissioner.

The strategies followed by different commissioners have varied as between those sticking to the scientific advice and those trying to tailor the advice to what Council might be more likely to accept. One official pointed that the DG had produced an unofficial scorecard that indicated that the strategy the commissioner pursued made little difference to the end result.

> [You] can analyse the distance between the scientific advice and the measure that the process produces [after Council has decided on quotas]. We took a look at this recently over the last four or five years and the deviation, one can say, between the scientific advice and the final decision is 40 per cent, that is to say the advice asks for a 60 per cent reduction in quotas and they get 20 per cent.

This result was irrespective of whether the commissioner concerned stuck closely to the scientific advice (as one commissioner did) or tried to modify it to produce something closer to what is likely to be accepted (as did the other in the small sample).

The scientific advice for the Horse Medicines Decree came from a different source: the Committee for Medicinal Products for Veterinary Use (CVMP), a committee responsible for preparing the opinion of the European Medicines Agency largely comprised of officials from national government organizations involved in veterinary medicine regulation. At issue was what precise medicines should be on the list of substances that could be given to horses that could end up for human consumption. The Council and Parliament Regulation ((EC) No. 726/2004) that allowed the Commission to draw up this list specified it could only be compiled on the basis of a 'harmonized scientific evaluation carried out by the European Medicines Agency'. The role of the CVMP is to establish the 'maximum residue limits' of veterinary medicinal products permissible in food produced by or from animals for human consumption. The CVMP set up a small *ad hoc* sub-group and produced the list that the official writing the decree incorporated directly into it. For the official who wrote most of the legislation (and this official had taken over responsibility from a detached national expert who had since left), deciding what should be in the legislation was not an entirely straightforward reproduction of the CVMP list. The official concerned felt the need to do an 'unofficial consultation' with other parts of the Commission and described how it went:

> I got in touch with DG Sanco [Health and Consumer Affairs] and the [Commission] Legal Service unofficially... The Legal Service said that the legal form for this should be a regulation as it would have immediate effect and did not need transposition. DG Sanco got their scientific people to ask us to give the list back to CVMP in order to respond to some of the questions they had. They wanted more structures and more indicators. They wanted a whole lot of other things that I refused. [*ECP: How was it possible for you to refuse what they asked for?*] This is a sensitive issue. A lot depends on the personalities working there. You sometimes

get people who like to listen to the grass growing and assess anything as a huge risk and will not let anything through that poses the slightest risk at all. I'm a pragmatist. I can see different sides and try and put them together. If someone in another DG does not have the experience you have to try and find a way forward through diplomacy—compromise and persuasion... We had to give [the list] back to the CVMP to see if they agreed with us or the consumer people [in DG Sanco], and they just expanded the justification for why things were on the list.

While external consultation with associations and member states will be discussed below, the compilation of the list itself involved consultation between the EMEA (European Medicines Agency) and the Federation of European Veterinarians (FVE) and the European Association for Veterinary, Pharmacology and Toxicology (EAVPT) (see EMEA 2004: 2). More generally one official involved pointed out:

> We had close contacts with the associations, we met on lots of occasions and we sent them drafts. And anyway, they were involved in the technical side through the EMEA. We did this whole regulation for the veterinarians, so it would have been nonsense to have kept them out of it.

In both cases the bureaucrats involved in writing the legislation sought the advice of scientific experts. They also had a role in specifying what kind of advice should be provided in the form of the detailed questions posed (in Horse Medicines) or of commissioning the scientific research report (in Fish Quotas). Moreover the officials in the teams receiving the advice and producing the decrees were themselves scientifically trained experts in the areas covered by the advice. Yet these things did not give the bureaucrats any special power to shape the eventual decisions. The main decisions on how this advice was to be used were not taken by the bureaucrats in the Commission, but by others, and these decisions were in turn shaped by the inter-institutional and intergovernmental processes that characterize decision-making in the European Union.

Senior-level supervision was, as has been discussed, particularly apparent in the development of the of Fish Quotas Decree. One key reason for this is that the decree was both controversial in that it raised issues on which member states had differing interests and perspectives and another is that the decree had formally to be approved by the Council. Such approval generally requires negotiation between the Commission and Council and, as we will see later, securing approval brings with it the involvement of the most senior levels of the Commission. For these reasons we might expect the development of the two other regulations (in addition to Fish Quotas) requiring Parliament and/ or Council approval, the Marco Polo and the Stability Instrument Decrees, to be closely managed by senior levels during the initial stages at which a Commission proposal, in the form of a Commission Document, is published. A Commission Document (COMDOC) is a formal publication of a proposal, set out in the *Official Journal of the EU*, the place where all EU laws, among other things, are published, and is given a formal status and number as a Commission Document which forms the basis for negotiations with the institutions whose approval has to be given for the proposal to become law.

It would be misleading to suggest that the process of producing a Commission Document in the three cases was top–down, in the sense that every decision of substance was settled by the top and the lower levels had merely to fill in the details. Rather the deliberation that went on in our three cases was better described as a dialogue between the lower and upper levels of the bureaucracy with ample opportunities for the senior levels to shape the Commission proposal at all stages.

The early stages of developing the Stability Instrument involved, as an official describes it, a range of discussions

> going on within the Commission, at commissioner level.... Although I want to stress that it was not even at this stage a top–down process. Discussions were going on in both directions at the same time. The services were developing their thoughts. Things were going up and down the hierarchy and things were being whittled down that way.

Once the general strategy of developing these ideas through proposals for reformed sets of instruments had been settled, the job of drafting the proposals was handled by

> a small working group of interested people. We were working to a timetable set by the commissioners. We had to get the whole package in by a certain date as it was linked to the negotiations on the financial perspective. We're asking for more money and it is more convincing if we know what we want to do with the money.

All legislation and proposals to be submitted to the College of Commissioners must, according to the Commission Rules of Procedure (c2000/3614 Article 21) be submitted to other directorates general as part of the 'interservice consultation', to enable other parts of the Commission to be aware of the intention to legislate. While we will discuss this aspect further in the next section, the inter-service consultation in this case was not left until the working group had done its work. In the case of the Stability Instrument, which covered the activities of several DGs, consultation between RELEX (the External Relations DG) and other DGs was, as one person involved put it, 'constant ... in the drafting process'.

The Marco Polo Decree differed from the other two Commission proposals for Council or Council/Parliament regulations insofar as the relevant senior levels of the Commission involved in developing some of the key features of the decree were the director and the director general. The commissioner himself appeared to be largely uninvolved; it was at the level of the director and director general that such decisions were taken. For example, the question of the relationship between the Marco Polo programme and other initiatives was a central question of the scope of the programme. As one official below the level of head of unit suggested, this was not a matter in which the commissioner intervened:

> Since TEN-T [the wider Trans-European Network] is developing slowly, the approach is that they have to select projects in a transparent way. The decisions had not been taken, but Marco Polo was starting. We had to ask whether we linked the two of them and wait till Motorways of the Sea had been settled before we start Marco Polo.... This was a big discussion. I am the programme manager not a policy person. I have contact with all the people.... I am supporting policy. We have a person in charge of policy for Motorways of the Sea. He wanted to stop Marco Polo till TEN-T had developed. The head of unit agreed with the policy officer. But the director was more in favour of Marco Polo with Motorways of the Sea and the DG agreed with the director.... I was in the middle of all this. You have two different approaches. I was in the middle. I have no policy role. But the decision was taken in the hierarchy.

The officials put this absence of commissioner involvement down to rather different things. One argued that it was a function of the fact that Marco Polo was the revision of an existing decree.

> The *cabinet* of the commissioner tends to have more influence when it is developing a new proposal, they tend to say things, than when we are implementing things. When we are giving birth to a regulation we have to take them into account.

Another put it down to the style of the individual commissioner:

> The role of the commisioner depends on personality and circumstances. We have a French commissioner, but he nearly always receives everything when it is done. Nearly all the decision we take go through.

Nevertheless, in the four decrees that did not require the consent of Parliament and/or Council, senior Commission involvement was far less marked than in the co-decision decree proposals. We have already seen that the Horse Medicines Decree was developed by the relevant official—at a rank below that of head of unit—drafting the proposal under the supervision of the relevant comitology committee. Of the other three in this category only the Tariff Simplification Decree left any significant discretion to officials with limited direct supervision from either very senior levels (director or above) within the Commission or from organizations outside the relevant DG (DG AGRI). The object of the exercise was to simplify and standardize an array of import quota regimes. Preparation of the document involved the officials, two or so rungs below the head of unit, developing the text of a decree but acting on the direct guidance of the head of unit.

> We really discussed this together with the head of unit before getting down to it. In fact we had to discuss whether in fact we needed a horizontal regulation [i.e. a rule covering a range of schemes rather than a series of sector-specific rules]. I had a different opinion—he [the head of unit] pushed for horizontal and that is what we did. Everything done by way of talking to the head of unit was done in meetings or email. He discussed options and he did check the wording of a few particular sentences. It did not go up higher [with one exception].... The commissioner and *cabinet* were certainly not involved. This was nothing new, so there was nothing in terms of new policy for them to get involved in.

The officials developing the decree approached their work by looking at existing rules.

> What we did was to compile a huge list of regulations and analyse the different models they reflected. We picked up things repeated frequently. We learned from things like the best way to calculate the coefficient and how to beat fraud. We looked at the common elements.

They consulted within DG AGRI as they were writing.

> The way we went about consulting internally with other units was not drafting it and sending it out. If we found we were looking at something like the cereals regulation we would get in touch with cereals to ask them about it and then talk to others about what we were thinking of doing. It was done a lot by phone calls and emails: 'We're drafting this article this way, what do you think?'.

The senior levels became involved once, on a set of issues associated with fraud: 'some units had different views so we had to take it up the hierarchy', in this case to the director general.

The Tariff Simplification Decree offers an example of a straightforward form of delegation: letting lower levels of the bureaucracy get on with the job, with senior levels only involved above all for conflict resolution, formal approval, and, when asked, guidance, even though there were few substantive changes to existing policy. The Forest Focus Decree, another Commission-only decree, was similar in that it changed little and it was also produced in a similar way: 'one person did the draft. It then got passed up the hierarchy.' This is a form of delegation not found in the co-decision decrees, where the senior levels were more closely involved in framing the content of the decrees, or in the Commission's own Horse Medicines Decree where the content was based on the advice of a scientific committee. The straightforward form of delegation is found in two of the other Commission-only regulations. The Silkworm Decree was simply a matter of a member of the Legal Service sitting down and writing a consolidated version of a short decree that had only been lightly amended. In the consolidation process there were no changes to the law, not even to anomalies or inconsistencies. The official from the Commission's Legal Service described the work:

Well, one as simple as the silkworm might take half a day just to write, though you have to go and present and discuss your draft. Some that have been modified thirty or so times take longer. And when there are serious inconsistencies in the text it takes longer. [ECP: *And when you see an inconsistency in the law, do you have to resolve it?*] I wish I could say that we did, but there are times where you keep the ambiguity in the codified text and leave the ambiguity in the legislation.

The discussion of the draft within the DG involves the member of the Legal Service meeting the officials of the relevant DG (essentially part of the legitimation of the decree and discussed further below): the drafting involved the member of the Legal Service working on his own. As an official from the DG put it 'We did not choose to codify this. The Legal Service presented us with the codification when it was done.' While the officials in the DG might try and use the consolidation process to bring about a change in the law, it will be resisted, as it was in this case. The Forest Focus Decree was similarly developed with little discretion among the officials drafting it. The revisions it made to existing provisions were to some degree a formality as they filled an ECJ mandate requiring that the regulations be recast under a different paragraph of the Treaty of Rome. Its most novel feature, a long annex, was, according to one official involved, 'a copy-and-paste job from the UN manual on forest monitoring'.

The process of drafting a decree appears to offer relatively little discretion to lower grade officials. In the development of Commission proposals for Parliament and/or Council Regulations in this study the role of the commissioners was strong. In the Commission-only decrees the role of bureaucrats at head of unit level and below was generally much stronger, but in areas where the issues were quite limited—Forest Focus, Silkworm, and Tariff Simplification all for different reasons consisted largely of replicating existing decrees although, Silkworms aside, the drafting process did bring about modest changes to existing decrees. In the Commission-only decree that marked the largest change from the status quo—the Horse Medicines Decree—senior officials were also not involved. However, the content of this decree was circumscribed by the scientific advisers from the member states. In developing decrees the room for manœuvre for Commission officials appears rather limited.

LEGITIMATION

All Commission regulations and proposals for Council or Council/Parliament Regulations have to go through internal Commission deliberation. Once a directorate general has produced a draft regulation or proposal, it has to be subjected to an *inter-service consultation*: a formal process according to which every directorate general with an interest in the issue is consulted. As the Commissions's Rules of Procedure (article 21) put it:

Before submitting a document to the Commission, the department responsible shall, in sufficient time, consult other departments which are associated or concerned by virtue of their powers or responsibilities or the nature of the subject, and shall inform the secretariat-general where it is not consulted. The Legal Service shall be consulted on all drafts or proposals for legal instruments and on all documents which may have legal implications. The directorates-general responsible for the budget, personnel and administration shall be consulted on all documents which may have implications concerning the budget and finances or personnel and administration respectively. The directorate-general responsible for financial control shall likewise be consulted, as need be.

Most important in the inter-service consultations for our decrees was the Legal Service. Aside from the Commission regulation effectively drafted by the Legal Service (the Silkworm Decree) the Legal Service forced significant changes in all three other Commission regulations. It prohibited the development of the shorter Forest Focus Decree initially proposed, it forced changes to the Horse Medicines and Tariff Simplification Decrees. As one official describes it 'the things we got from the Legal Service were about general principles of Community law. Checking that the penalties are not disproportionate and fit what we are doing here.'

For Commission-only decrees the approval of the commissioner appeared entirely unproblematic in all four cases; in the Silkworm Decree it was not necessary and in the other three the commissioners nodded them through *after* they had comitology and parliamentary approval. As was found in the case of the Horse Medicines Decree, Commission-only decrees have to be approved through comitology *committees* (for a discussion see Rhinard 2002). The Commission (2007) lists 258 'Comitology Committees assisting the European Commission' (for a discussion of how they work, see Manuela Alfé et al. 2007). These committees go under a variety of names, but they are for the most part made up of experts in a particular policy area from civil services and other public bodies in EU member states and their opinion is sought, either on an advisory or statutory basis for proposed Commission decrees. Since the 2006 reforms of the comitology process, the powers of the Council and Parliament have extended to give them a greater role in the approval of some decrees. However, few Commission decrees, and none in our sample, have so far involved a challenge from the Council or Parliament after consideration by the comitology committees (see Christiansen and Vaccari 2006). Three of the four Commission-only decrees had to pass comitology procedures. The Silkworm Decree went through a separate procedure as the changes it introduced were strictly formal and not substantive. In the Forest Focus and Tariff Simplification Decrees the procedure was unproblematic as the officials, after presenting the case to the relevant committees, simply did not hear any objection within the specified time limit.

For two of the three Commission decrees that required comitology approval, the process was painless: with Forest Focus and Tariff Simplification the officials hoped that after presenting it to the Committee (it was in both cases a director and a desk officer who presented the proposal to the committee) they would not hear any objection within the specified time. Their wishes came true. For the Horse Medicines Decree it was a little more complicated since the comitology process allowed the official writing the decree to fend off attempts by one member state to seek to develop a list of medicines on the basis of criteria other than those set out by the relevant directive it was seeking to implement.

> We had the meeting of the standing committee... The [member state's] comments came up. I had all my comments with me and could give good answers to the question [they raised]. And I could even offer that I had asked the committee again to confirm [that I was right] and they had said 'yes'. I could show that I took it seriously etc. The proposal was agreed to unanimously in the standing committee, even the representatives from the member state agreed. And without amendment.

After comitology approval the Horse Medicines Decree went for thirty-day approval in Parliament and then approval through the Commission. The Commission procedure consisted of gathering together all the comments received in internal consultations as the regulation was being developed and how they had been responded to, entering it on a standard form, and 'passing it up the hierarchy', eventually to the College of Commissioners. The official was called in to explain to a member of her commissioner's *cabinet* what she had done and why and after that it was 'approved on the nod'. In the other two cases, Forest Focus and Tariff Simplification, Commission approval and acquiring the commissioner's signature were formalities.

Legitimation is significantly more problematic with proposals for Parliament and/or Council Regulations proposed by the Commission. For the Fish Quotas Decree (i.e. a Council Regulation) the first stage of the procedure of securing Council approval is the deliberation by the Permanent Representatives of the Member States (COREPER). As Bostock (2002: 231) suggests, COREPER's 'role is... limited in cases where ministers decide that they wish personally to deal with dossiers at a high level of detail' and so most of the action takes place in the meetings of Council. Bostock goes on to describe the fisheries negotiations as the main example of such a case—a view endorsed by a senior official involved in developing the fisheries decree who complained:

> The problem is that decisions are taken based on short-term perspectives... Even ministers in Council discuss numbers, when they should not... They should deal with the political principles.... As I see it, it should be a fairly technical task to translate what the principles are into numbers.... Of course the political level

should decide. But in the December Council it becomes a matter of ministers bringing back the numbers of fish above the levels suggested by the Commission and you get the press releases 'we have managed to get more fish for our fisheries than the Commission said we should have'.

The formalities of presentation of the Commission's proposals to COREPER is handled by senior officials, at levels of head of unit and above. The policy officials become involved as auxiliaries in the frantic and usually fierce negotiations going on till the early hours of the morning in December of each year, covering quotas and other fisheries issues. As one described it:

> There will be the Commission team and the member states will have their own people and sometimes Commission services. The [Fisheries] Commissioner is given one big room for his officials.... In the round of negotiations with the member states we work together with the commissioner and with the *cabinet* team. There is no strict rule about how many people go along, it depends on how big the regulation is, or how sensitive it is... You go along to these things and you have to stay on your guard. Every member state comes along with different interests and you have to be awake to think about what they might want and know how to respond. The Deep Sea Regulation was not that bad, we were three days and we weren't there till late at night, which is just as well as you are not that bright after one o'clock.

The Stability Instrument and the Marco Polo Decrees required more or less protracted negotiation between the Commission, Parliament, and Council. For the Stability Instrument the negotiations involved a range of constitutional-legal technicalities affecting the powers of the different European institutions in the field of emergency aid (discussed in Bartelt 2008). For the Marco Polo Decree the issues involved above all the criteria of eligibility for applying for funding. In both cases the negotiations involved the GRI (Groupe des relations interinstitutionelles)—a specialized arrangement within the Commission for dealing with such matters. One of its functions is to advise on negotiating strategy, tactics, and formalities. Another is to establish where ground can be given and not given in negotiations with other EU institutions. Formally GRI, composed of members of all ministerial *cabinets* charged with responsibility for inter-institutional affairs, met once a week. The Secretariat of GRI, located within the Secretariat of the Commission, handles much of its work. One of its central functions is to broker a whole Commission view in such inter-institutional negotiations. As one official from the GRI Secretariat put it:

> Where the question affects other DGs or strategic issues or creates problems with other institutions, we get involved. Any changes in the packet that would involve the budget DG or the Legal Service. The preparatory work will have involved consultation with a whole range of DGs. Everything that goes to a plenary meeting goes to GRI before it goes to the plenary and it has to have the backing of the whole College [of Commissioners]. Even the simplest negotiation will be validated by the whole Commission. It has to be endorsed in the same way.

For the Commission officials involved in the Stability Instrument Decree it was a difficult set of negotiations with Council and Parliament and they had to work within the constraints of the broad commissioner/*cabinet* level priorities. 'You ended up with negotiations with the Council and dealing with negotiations in Council and then with Parliament—yes on two fronts. And then there was the home front in the Commission, and that was not easy either.' There was, as an official involved said, some scope for officials to work things out at sub-*cabinet* level as regards cross-Commission ('inter-service') negotiations, and a limited scope for negotiation with other institutions by interpreting and representing the lines GRI will take.

> I can go some way in this without GRI. I can speak without the GRI and say what we can give, and I can say that here are probably the red lines as far as GRI are concerned and I can even identify different lines to GRI.

In terms of *tactics* one official involved in gaining support for the Stability Instrument, which proved to be a contentious piece of legislation, felt he could range freely in trying to help it through: 'I was pretty independent in how I went about lobbying. Nobody was at all bothered about that.' However his independence in handling the *substance* of the negotiations was far more limited. As he added, 'I had the COMDOC and that was agreed so I knew what the aim was, any big changes from that needed GRI [approval]'. Similarly with the Marco Polo Decree, the scope for independent action or discretion in the negotiation was limited by the GRI arrangement as well as the requirement that anything of significance had to be agreed at *cabinet* level. On the fact that he had to give ground on one of the issues under negotiation, the official commented:

> How did I know I could give in? I discussed mainly with my director—he has a good awareness of what will be acceptable and what we can take, and he agrees on the amendment, and he has to take it to the DG and eventually to the *cabinet*.

In both Marco Polo and the Stability Instrument, the Presidency of the Council was crucial in brokering an agreement.

CONCLUSIONS

The notion that the bureaucrats of Brussels are powerful has been primarily the stuff of popular criticism of the EU, of bureaucracy, or of both. Scholarly evaluations of the role of the Commission have been more circumspect and have tended to emphasize the constraints on the Commission as a whole as a decision-maker in the fragmented system of authority of the European Union. Nevertheless there are a range of perfectly valid reasons to believe that the officials working within the Commission have significant policy-making power: they deal in technical policy areas that might operate under the radar of the political concerns of the Parliament and Council, the controls on Commission decision-making power are not as strong as they look on paper, there is said to be a culture of delegation of important functions to lower level officials, and frequent political deadlocks might enhance bureaucratic power.

The evidence in this chapter does not support this argument. Commission officials working on two of the three proposals that had to go through inter-institutional processes of co-decision tended to develop them under the close direction of their commissioners. With the third, the Marco Polo Decree, the commissioner remained largely uninvolved in the development of the proposals, but the legitimation process brought close involvement of the Council and the Presidency, as well as Parliament, in shaping its key features. So even this decree was developed with significant political direction, although not immediately that of the commissioner. If the Commission is supposed to be a 'bureaucrat's paradise' because officials are free to develop policy proposals on their own and make sure they become law by using the Commission's power of initiative, then the decrees requiring Parliament and/or Council approval in this study suggest it is not.

For somewhat different reasons bureaucrats writing the Commission's own decrees did not have substantial autonomy. In one decree (Silkworm) the content was specified by the terms under which it was developed: no changes were allowed to existing legislation by the special codification procedure employed to produce it. In two decrees (Forest Focus and Tariff Simplification) the officials were substantially constrained by the existing decrees in the area and could make little substantive change to them and what limited changes they proposed had to be submitted to the comitology committee. In the decree where significant new decisions were taken (Horse Medicines) the process was constrained by existing laws setting out the criteria for deciding what should be included in the regulation, by the procedural requirement to accept the recommendations of an expert committee, and by the comitology process.

The view of European Commission bureaucratic power from the perspective of decree-making confirms the views of those who have tended to suggest a limited power for Commission bureaucrats. On closer inspection, the two big powers, of agenda setting and making decrees in its own name, seem to bestow remarkably little scope for independent action on its own bureaucrats. As Larsson and Trondal (2006: 23) suggest, 'most of the initiatives' in this respect 'are the result of some kind of external pressure from domestic governments, single initiatives from MEPs, the consequence of existing *acquis* or programme obligations, obligations emanating from international treaties and so on'. In its own decree-making 'the Commission and the comitology committees stay very well within the boundaries that the legislator has assigned to them (Larsson and Schaefer 2006: 547). Commission officials are thus highly regulated in their approach to decree-making.

ANNEX: DECREES INCLUDED IN CHAPTER 7

Name	DG	Short Name
Commission Regulation (EC) No 1301/2006 of 31 August 2006 laying down common rules for the administration of import tariff quotas for agricultural products managed by a system of import licences	Agriculture and Rural Development (AGRI)	Tariff Simplification
Commission Regulation (Ec) No 1737/2006 of 7 November 2006 laying down detailed rules for the implementation of Regulation (EC) No 2152/2003 of the European Parliament and of the Council concerning monitoring of forests and environmental interactions in the Community	Environment (ENV)	Forest Focus
Commission Regulation (EC) No 1744/2006 of 24 November 2006 on detailed rules for aid in respect of silkworm	Agriculture and Rural Development (AGRI)	Silkworm
Commission Regulation (EC) No 1950/2006 of 13 December 2006 establishing, in accordance with Directive 2001/82/EC of the European Parliament and of the Council on the Community code relating to veterinary medicinal products, a list of substances essential for the treatment of equidae	Enterprise and Industry (ENTR)	Horse Medicines
Council Regulation (EC) No 41/2006 of 21 December 2006 fixing for 2007 the fishing opportunities and associated conditions for certain fish stocks and groups of fish stocks, applicable in Community waters and, for Community vessels, in waters where catch limitations are required	Fisheries (FISH)	Fish Quotas
Regulation (EC) No 1692/2006 of the European Parliament and of the Council of 24 October 2006 establishing the second 'Marco Polo' programme for the granting of Community financial assistance to improve the environmental performance of the freight transport system (Marco Polo II) and repealing Regulation (EC) No 1382/2003	Energy and Transport (TREN)	Marco Polo
Regulation (EC) No 1905/2006 of the European Parliament and of the Council of 18 December 2006 establishing a financing instrument for development cooperation	External Relations (RELEX)	Stability Instrument

8

Bureaucrats, Politicians, Choice, and Motivation

This investigation has brought us familiarity with some strange and exotic, as well as a number of distinctly prosaic, episodes in politico-administrative policy-making. So far the argument has been along the lines that a small sample of decrees in any one jurisdiction helps illuminate processes of decision-making, generally poorly understood in most jurisdictions, and can offer a fresh perspective on patterns of policy-making within it. Such illumination was an important objective of the research, but the main purpose was to try to answer the questions arising from the apparent likelihood that political executives could only become involved in a tiny portion of the deliberations that produce policies in their names: when do politicians get involved in policy-making, what happens when they do, and what happens when they stay out of policy-making? The purpose of this chapter is to stand back and look at the body of evidence supplied by our fifty-two decrees and answer these questions.

The questions are addressed in the order they were posed, starting with the nature of political involvement in decree-making. It goes on to look at what might explain such patterns before discussing briefly the bureaucratic reaction to political interventions. The chapter then moves to the topic of bureaucratic choice in making policy where political direction is largely absent and explores both the constraints on choice and the problematic nature of bureaucratic discretion. I then go on to explore the implications of the findings for our understanding of bureaucratic roles in policy-making, above all their motivations, and draw some conclusions about the relationship between bureaucracy and democracy.

THE SPORADIC INVOLVEMENT OF POLITICIANS

Varieties of Involvement

Since it was the basic starting point of this research that political executives could not play a large part in the everyday process of policy-making, we

Choice and Motivation 147

should not be surprised to find that their involvement in the kinds of policy decisions surrounding decree-making is indeed sporadic in the sense that it was seldom constant. It would be misleading to regard decree-making within the executive as some kind of continuous process of bargaining between politicians and bureaucrats.

We can develop this argument further by distinguishing between different kinds of involvement by politicians. Involvement varies, as has been suggested in the structure of the individual chapters, according to the *stage in the policy process* at which it is found. In some cases politicians and their auxiliaries can become involved as agenda setters by initiating bureaucratic work on the decree, they can be participants in developing the decree, and they can be significant in securing legitimation for it once it has been developed. Involvement also varies by *intensity*. In some cases politicians and their auxiliaries were *actively* involved in the sense that they made positive decisions that helped shape the decree. In other cases the role of the politician was largely *passive*—approving what is being done in their name.

Politicians and their auxiliaries—their advisers and political appointees—played an active part in the initiation of decrees just over one-third of the time (in eighteen out of fifty-two cases, Table 8.1—the assessments on which these and other calculations and tables are based are set out in the Annex at the end of this chapter). Yet before devoting significant effort to developing a decree, civil servants simply informed politicians and/or auxiliaries that work was starting on it (thirteen cases). In twenty-one of our fifty-two decrees politicians were not even directly involved in this minimal passive way in its birth.

Moving on to policy development, many decisions taken or faced by civil servants were referred upwards during the process of developing the decree. In the development of decrees active political involvement was slightly higher (twenty-one cases), although a significant proportion (fifteen out of fifty-two cases) of interventions in policy development were passive—approving, acquiescing in, or offering support for what was being proposed. It is not surprising that the stage at which the politicians or their auxiliaries are almost always involved (forty-nine out of fifty-two cases) in some way is in the legitimation of decrees. It is common, though not invariably a constitutional requirement, that decrees are signed by ministers or senior appointed officials and thus at a minimum some passive political involvement is almost guaranteed. Active involvement by politicians can be found in nine cases—where the

Table 8.1. Involvement in the decrees by the political level

	Not Involved	Passive Involvement	Active Involvement
Initiation	21	13	18
Development	16	15	21
Legitimation	3	39	10

support of politicians was needed to ensure that the decree passed through procedural hurdles such as parliamentary, judicial, or executive approval. Two French *arrêtés* and one US decree signed by career officials account for the three decrees in which political leadership was not involved at all in legitimation. If we exclude the final legitimation stage of decree-making on the ground that in most cases it is less significant for the eventual shape of the decree,[1] in fifteen cases there was no evidence of the decree having been put to a politician or an auxiliary at some stage before it was sent for a formal signature.

The fact that politicians or their auxiliaries are involved actively in the development of twenty-one out of our fifty-two decrees (40 per cent) is, if anything, much higher than one might have expected. This figure, however, probably exaggerates somewhat the involvement of politicians and their auxiliaries. If we look at the types of interventions by politicians, they were not invariably 'strategic' or sustained. For example, while the minister gave a clear steer about what he wanted to see in the UK Fire Services Decree, his concern was largely limited to ensuring that the decree addressed ethnic minority recruitment and this issue formed a small part of a much larger decree. In five other decrees the active involvement by politicians was similarly limited. Thus active and sustained political involvement, even though it might fall short of fully or extensively supervising how a decree was developed, could be found in at most fifteen cases.

We cannot assume that, with sixteen cases of active and sustained involvement in developing decrees, the other thirty-six decrees were developed effectively by bureaucrats or processes in which bureaucrats played a significant part. Many decrees involved virtually no policy deliberation at all. The German decree fixing the amounts of money to be given to *Länder* as part of the intergovernmental fiscal equalization arrangement, was essentially a formality which involved almost no policy deliberation, the policy deliberation having been completed years before in negotiations about fiscal equalization formulae (Renzsch 2010). Eight of the fifty-two decrees fell into this category. These contrast with decrees which involved some policy deliberation, as narrow as whether to allow a slightly higher sugar content to be added in Champagne production or as broad as what precisely the catch limits should be for European fisheries.

Patterns of Bureaucrat–Politician Interaction

If we define political involvement as sustained and active political involvement, in the development of a decree such that major contours of the decree

---

[1] The major exception here is with the three EU decrees issued under the authority of the Council and Parliament.

were directly shaped by expressed politician priorities, and acknowledge that some decrees involve no appreciable policy deliberation, we can distinguish between four types of decree-making process. The classification of decrees is approximate as they tend not to correspond neatly to one form of the four policy-making patterns. Decrees vary in length. Some can be quite lengthy and do a range of different things. Even in the most politically contentious of decrees in which ministers become closely and continuously involved, there are parts that attract less attention and there are also consequential parts which are little more than formalities. Nevertheless, one can broadly divide the fifty-two decrees into groupings broadly on the basis of whether such politician involvement in key aspects of developing the decree was sustained rather than sporadic or passive, and whether significant policy choices can be found in any of the various components of the decree.

Directed bureaucratic policy-making (fifteen decrees) is found when politicians and auxiliaries become directly and actively involved in developing key aspects of a decree and where the decree makes some changes to existing policy. An example of this kind would be the French Casinos Decree, involving as a key issue the introduction of the Texas Hold 'Em poker game into French casinos and a range of changes in regulations for running casinos that addressed key issues of principle and substance affecting casino owners and employees. Here, as can be seen from Chapter 2, the development of the decree soon was taken over by the Minister of the Interior (later President of the Republic), Nicolas Sarkozy. The role of the bureaucrats in developing this decree became one of offering advice and technical assistance (such as framing the decree in a form that is consistent with French law), but on the key issues they followed the instructions of the political leadership in the form of the minister and his *cabinet* and top officials.[2]

Undirected bureaucratic policy-making (twenty-nine decrees) refers to the pattern found when civil servants are largely left with at best indirect instructions about how a decree should be developed, or no instructions at all. The development of the German Ship Safety Decree, discussed in Chapter 4, was bureaucrat-led and the bureaucrats made significant choices in a range of key areas connected with the decree. These choices might be passed on to politicians or their auxiliaries for approval, but this type of policy-making refers to decrees where the bureaucrats have significant initiative in shaping the main contours of the decree. In the Ship Safety Decree provisions the Transport Ministry civil servant took it on herself to develop the relaxation of the zero

---

[2] The category includes one EU decree (Horse Medicines) not strictly under direct political supervision but under that of a scientific committee made up of specialists from member states. The process involved, of referring any decisions to an external body, was similar to that found in politician-directed policy-making.

tolerance limit for ships' captains in the knowledge that the minister would be very likely to accept it.

Consequential policy-making (eight decrees) involves the bureaucracy in putting together decrees where the initiative rests with bureaucrats but they (and indeed the politicians they serve) have little or no discretion in shaping the decree. An example of this kind of decree is the EU Silkworm Decree that simply brought two existing decrees into one in the process of simplification of the corpus of legislation. Nothing at all was changed by this decree. Indeed under the formal rules governing the simplified decree-making process employed, no detectable change to existing provisions could legitimately be made. Where the decisions on the decrees are constrained entirely by previous decisions or by the decision of other bodies, the role of bureaucrats is different from their role in the other two forms (although, as will be discussed below, it is not necessarily insignificant). That this consequential group is smaller than the first two reflects the non-randomness of the selection of decrees for the study. When selecting decrees for inclusion in the study the huge number of decrees that appeared to be effectively formalities and involved little or no policy deliberation were intentionally omitted. That eight were nevertheless included indicates how hard it is to tell what a decree is about in advance of looking in detail into how it was made.

We will not be elaborating much on the role of bureaucrats in decrees developed under consequential policy-making, on the ground that by definition these decrees involve little or no policy deliberation since they are the direct result of earlier decisions, or are so strongly constrained by them, such that bureaucratic and/or political choices are excluded from their production. It is, however, important to point out that part of the activity of developing consequential decrees might involve making sure that the decree *remains consequential*. That is to say, to make sure that the routine decree does not smuggle in a policy change. In most cases all involved in making consequential decrees understand that trying to use the consequential decree-making process to make changes in policy is illegitimate and sometimes unlawful. In one of the consequential EU decrees, however, there were pressures to go beyond existing policy. Some individual member states tried to use the opportunity provided by the Silkworm Decree to make changes to policy and had to be rebuffed. Protecting the legislative process from being used to make changes beyond the legal scope of the legislation is also a feature of non-consequential decrees. For example, some member states tried to incorporate policy changes outside the scope of the EU directive in the Horse Medicines Decree and the civil servant concerned drew it to the attention of the comitology committee which defeated the ploy.

A fourth pattern of policy-making, where there is active politician involvement but no policy deliberation, is logically possible and we have an example of a decree that comes close to this. The French Rhine Transport Decree was negotiated internationally by officials from the Transport Ministry where the decree was actually written. It had to be later issued as a separate decree by the Foreign Ministry and signed by the Foreign Minister. This might be termed a *ceremonial* pattern of policy-making. However, the original Transport Ministry decree was not ceremonial and so it has not been included as such here and I discuss only the three types of policy-making found in the fifty-two decrees.

UNDERSTANDING POLITICIAN INVOLVEMENT

Cues for Involvement

As discussed in the introduction, much of the literature on delegation places emphasis on controversy, specifically some form of explicit or latent disagreement between politicians and civil servants, as a cue to politician involvement. Politicians are prompted to intervene either directly after they identify things they do not like in routine monitoring of the bureaucracy ('police patrols') or indirectly after procedural devices have alerted interest groups to proposals the groups do not like, which leads them to raise the alarm with politicians who might then decide to intervene ('fire alarms'). As we will see below, there is certainly a link between controversy and political involvement. However, fire alarms, police patrols, and the related 'deck stacking' hypothesis do not account for the *process* by which politicians and their auxiliaries become involved.

If we take all fifty-two decrees, in no case did politician involvement follow an interest group, or any other outside body, blowing the whistle or raising the alarm about what bureaucrats were planning. In all cases of directed policy-making the involvement of the politicians or their auxiliaries came either from the very start—especially in the cases where the political level was also involved in initiating the policy as, for example, with the French Casinos Decree or the US Criminal Checks Decree—or the decree-making process had not progressed very far before politicians became involved. For both fire alarms and police patrols the suggestion is that bureaucrats are caught *in flagrante delicto* by a politician or auxiliary monitoring the work of bureaucracy or by interest groups raising their concerns. In general with decrees developed under both directed and undirected policy-making, it was the bureaucrats themselves that passed the issues up to the political level. To continue with metaphors connected with policing: the civil servants 'grassed themselves up' to the political levels. In making decrees, whether directed or undirected, career officials generally informed their superiors: in controversial cases to make sure of political support and in non-controversial cases as a matter of courtesy and procedural propriety. The exceptions could be found in cases where the political level was deemed to know about the matter anyway—most importantly in the UK where decrees implementing primary legislation were considered to have been approved at the same time as the broad strategy of developing the primary legislation from which the decrees were derived.

In fact, bureaucrats interviewed placed great importance on obeying procedural norms and rules, at least the most significant ones, and political approval features significantly among such norms and rules. The broad contours of the procedures to be observed in undirected policy-making are broadly similar across all jurisdictions where it was found. Initially comes political approval to begin work on a decree. Explicit approval—sending up a formal request to start work on a proposal—tends to be reserved for the more controversial or politically visible decrees; in many cases the approval is deemed to have been given already, above all in cases where there is little or no choice but to issue a decree (e.g. implementing European Union legislation). Internal bureaucratic consultation, whether inter- or just intra-ministerial/agency, is required in all but the most consequential of decrees. The principle of hierarchy is the most common means of resolving conflicts that emerge from such consultations: disagreements between two or more units or subunits within an organization get pushed up to a senior level for arbitration or decision. Inter-ministerial (or inter-agency) conflicts or disagreements follow a similar pattern in that they are pushed upwards for resolution. Those that are not agreed at the bureaucratic level between civil servants of equal rank get pushed upwards and can reach the level of bilateral or multilateral ministerial or even *cabinet* negotiations, as with the French Farmers Decree.

External consultation of some form, whether informally talking to outside interests or a staged internet or write-in public consultation, is common to all but the consequential decrees, and political approval or acquiescence is often sought again at this stage too; not least because the ministry or agency is 'going public' on its proposals and the political leadership needs to approve this. There are different kinds of approval of legal form designed to ensure that the form of the decree and its content do not violate principles of constitutionality or legality, ranging from judicial approval by the Conseil d'État, approval by Justice Ministry (Germany), or a committee within the legislature (UK). The norms governing which particular decrees are subjected to this are highly variable, and politicians can be brought in to the process again if such approval is problematic. Final political approval may take the form of the decree being signed off by an individual minister, a full agreement from the collective Cabinet, and/or the more elaborate procedures governing co-decision between different parts of government including the comitology and co-decision procedures of the EU and ratification by the *Bundesrat* in Germany. All in all, informing politicians is part of the bureaucratic policy-making routine.

This bureaucratic routine of informing the top does not dispense entirely with the 'fire alarm' argument. Informing politicians early on might be taken as indirect support for the fire alarm notion: that bureaucrats secure the necessary political support early. Even so, the argument would go, it is the procedure of securing OMB approval in the US that causes them to seek such support. Knowing that the alarm will go off anyway, bureaucrats raise it themselves. It is even possible to see this mechanism in action from bureaucrats' accounts of the process of decree-making. In the US Broadband Decree, for instance, the civil servants wanted to keep the changes to the decrees small so that it need not go through the full comment procedure: 'Originally we would try and do [something different] but [the department's legal advisers] said that was too much of a change. We'd need to send that out for comment. [And] we took [their] advice...'

The central difficulty with regarding bureaucratic self-disclosure as supporting the 'fire alarm' argument is that it confuses a specific set of rules with a general condition of hierarchical life in a bureaucracy. It is a basic norm that superiors should be kept informed when something is done in their name and another that bureaucrats must be able to legitimize their actions. In the US these norms were not the creation of the US Administrative Procedure Act of 1946. Gellhorn (1986: 232) for example argued the Act itself 'was declaratory of what had already become the general, though not yet universal, patterns of good behavior; nudging the laggards did no harm, though my own guess is that changes for the better were of small dimensions'. Moreover in other jurisdictions, such as France and the UK, informing the political level appeared to be even more remotely related to the formal procedures of external political control than in the US. In the UK, for example, those decrees that required parliamentary approval by an affirmative vote were no more likely to be drawn to the attention of ministers than those that were not, and French decrees were no more likely to be raised with a member of the ministerial *cabinet* or the minister because they were *décrets en Conseil d'État* (French decrees that had to be referred to the judicial Conseil d'État) rather than other forms of decree. Internal norms rather than the impact of external scrutiny or outside interests caused issues to be brought to the attention of politicians or their auxiliaries in the decrees examined here.

Politicians' Disposition

Another argument links the technical character of the issue at stake with the level of politician involvement: the technical or scientific nature of an issue is commonly thought to make it less likely that an inexpert politician will interfere (see Schattschneider 1960). The argument is certainly a powerful one that relates to a wider set of propositions about political conflict management and public involvement in political debates. However, on the basis of the fifty-two decrees we have no firm reason to believe that scientific or technical issues and language excludes politicians as a whole from intervening in policy-making processes. Of the thirteen decrees which appeared to have significant scientific or technical content, three involved directed, nine undirected policy-making, and one was in the consequential category. Moreover, it is quite possible for politicians to become closely involved in technical matters. Perhaps the clearest example of this comes from the EU Fish Quotas Decree where the dominance of expert scientific evidence does not prevent political involvement by the commissioner and his *cabinet* or even, somewhat outside the scope of this research, the members of the Council who make the biennial negotiation around fish stocks among the most politically contentious issues discussed in the European Union. Indeed, as discussed in Chapter 7, one of the scientists involved in this decree complained that politicians were *too involved* in the technical issues and too little concerned with the broad direction of fisheries policy.

Knowing the level or nature of interest group involvement does not appear to have a particularly strong impact on whether politicians became involved in directed policy-making. Most of the decrees, forty of the fifty-two, involved some interest group consultation. Those that did not included three directed, one undirected, and seven consequential decrees. Politician involvement may indeed, as in the case of the French Casinos Decree, be associated with interest group lobbying for a policy. In another French case, the Farmers Decree, politician involvement had the effect of *excluding groups* from the process of policy-making as the higher levels of the politico-administrative system could make their decision without negotiating with them. In a Swedish directed case, the Rescue Services Agency Decree, politicians became involved although no outside interests voiced any preferences about the policy. Conversely, there are plenty of examples of undirected decrees that were at the centre of controversies between groups, including the contentious US Lithium Decree in the US and the Alcohol Disorder Zones Decree in the UK.

Disposition does, however, appear to be more closely related to the propensity for politicians or their auxiliaries to become involved when one considers the political importance of the decree. While definitions of whether something is 'minor' or not are highly subjective, we have already established that some decrees are consequential—effectively formalities that put in legal form decisions that have been made elsewhere or tidy up the law. Yet on the other had there are politically major decrees, such as the French Osteopaths Decree, that brought demonstrators out on to the streets of Paris, or the reform of the green card process that pitched the legal might of major US electronics corporations among others against the federal government in the Alien Substitution Decree.

Eight of our decrees, the consequential decrees, can be classed as 'truly minor'. At the other extreme, a further fifteen could be classified as 'truly major' since they address issues that are politically significant (such as the minimization of exposure to BSE in the US) or sensitive (such as modifying the UK Labour Party manifesto promise to introduce home information packs for house buyers). The remaining twenty-nine fall in between these two: these are decrees with a discernible intended impact on the interests and behaviour of individuals and organizations but they are politically neither sensitive nor of truly major significance. We may call these of 'moderate significance'. In this category I would include decrees that affected BBC and ITV use of bandwidth to broadcast TV programmes in the UK, the German Ship Safety provisions, and the EU Horse Medicines Decree determining which medicines can be given to horses that enter the food chain. They involved appreciable changes, but their significance was primarily to a relatively small group and did not become linked to wider public societal conflicts.

Unsurprisingly, politicians are less likely to become involved in the truly minor decrees. However, aside from this, the significance of the decree does not make such a clear difference to the pattern of policy-making that might be expected to produce it. There is a clear tendency for the truly major decrees to be developed under directed policy-making: of the fifteen truly major decrees, ten were so developed, but five were developed under undirected policy-making. The figures look more supportive to the 'importance matters' argument if we consider that twenty-three of the twenty-nine undirected decrees were of moderate significance (compared to five of the fifteen directed) and only five of the twenty-four undirected decrees involved truly major issues (compared to ten of the fifteen directed). If one were to guess the style of policy-making from the significance of the issue at stake, one would be right in forty out of fifty-two cases (77 per cent) or, if one prefers to exclude the consequential decrees on the ground that they are by definition minor, thirty-three out of forty-four cases (75 per cent).

Institutional Capacity

If we consider the exceptions to this expectation that the political level becomes involved on truly major issues we get an indication that there are features related to the politico-administrative system as a whole that might affect the forms of policy-making by which issues are handled. Three of the five 'moderate importance' decrees which were handled by directed policy-making (i.e. where politicians were involved when one might have expected them not to be) were from Sweden, and three of the five 'major significance' decrees handled by undirected policy-making (i.e. where politicians were not involved when one might expect them to be) were from the UK.

Table 8.2. Patterns of policy-making by jurisdiction

	Consequential	Undirected	Directed
Germany	2	4	0
EU	3	1	3
France	0	7	3
Sweden	1	0	6
UK	1	11	0
US	1	6	3
TOTAL	8	29	15

Table 8.2 gives the breakdown of the incidence of the three policy-making patterns found in each country. It is perfectly possible that with such a small sample in each country the fact that there are no directed decrees in Germany is simply bad luck—with six decrees the chance of missing one such decree is reasonably high. This point has to be considered a possibility. However, there is a range of features characteristic of each country, noticeable in the material gathered for the body of decrees in our sample, that might explain why some forms of policy-making are more likely than others. The small number of cases prevents one from reading too much into any breakdowns of the different numbers, but if we look at the figures along with the content of the chapters the evidence suggests that the politico-administrative systems of different countries probably shape the role of politicians and bureaucrats by encouraging some forms of policy-making and discouraging others. This is most obviously the case in Sweden (Table 8.2) where six of the seven decrees were brought in with the close involvement of state secretaries, advisers, and (less frequently) ministers. In a small Swedish ministry headed by a political state secretary and housing several political advisers it is not difficult for politicians and their appointees to drive policy agendas, even on issues that in many other jurisdictions might be left entirely to bureaucrats.

The importance of the broader politico-administrative structure is further suggested by the fact that three of the four directed policy-making group of decrees in the European Union sample were proposals for decrees to be made by the Parliament and/or Council under co-decision that involved member state consultation. Since these involved significant bargaining with member states, the higher leadership (though, as with the Marco Polo Decree, not always the commissioner) within the Commission tended to become closely involved. Of the Commission's own decrees, which needed no other approval or approval of comitology committees, three of the four fell into the consequential category where no significant policy-making discretion was exercised by the civil servants involved. The fourth, the Horse Medicines Decree, was closely supervised by an 'expert' panel and comitology committee so that, although by the criteria used to classify our decrees it was 'undirected' by the Commission political leadership, it had the characteristics of a decree made under 'directed' policy-making, where civil servants alone make fewer choices about the content of the decree and work to turn the decisions of others into law.

Of those decrees where significant policy choices were to be made, politician involvement was least in Germany and the UK where such decrees were handled under undirected policy-making—i.e. main contours of the decree were effectively constructed by bureaucrats albeit with the approval of politicians. The reasons for the absence of direct politician involvement in policy-making in these two countries might be, extrapolating from the discussion in Chapters 3 and 4, rather different. The lack of decrees under directed policy-making in Germany might reflect two distinctive features of the German system. First, there are arrangements to ensure that a range of key political issues is settled outside the decree-writing process. This clearly covered the consequential Fiscal Equalization Decree, as key political decisions were taken after a process of intergovernmental bargaining years before. But such separation of political negotiation from rule writing can also be found in undirected decrees in Germany. Some of the more contentious points of policy (but certainly not all of them) were covered in the process of developing the *Eckpunktpapiere* governing the Noise Maps and Milk Quotas Decrees, albeit with federal bureaucrats playing an influential role in them.

If the lack of directed decrees in Germany reflects the fact that major political conflicts surrounding the decrees tend to be dealt with in separate political arenas (i.e. the political direction comes *before* the process of decree-making), the absence of directed policy-making in the UK is more likely to reflect a general reluctance among politicians to get directly and actively involved in the activity of rule-making as well as the importance that UK civil servants place on ensuring that what they are proposing conforms with political expectations before they invite politicians to become involved at each stage in the process (Page 2001; Page and Jenkins 2005). The UK pattern of civil servants inviting ministers to exercise authority contrasts very strongly with the French pattern in which a politico-bureaucratic leadership structure in the form of the *cabinet* allows politically connected bureaucrats to identify which of the issues being worked on in their part of the ministry are politically sensitive, take them out of the hands of the ordinary ministerial bureaucrats and handle them themselves. In the French system the procedure for routine checking with the *cabinet* on anything sensitive allows the higher politico-administrative structure to take the issues it selects out of the hands of the routine administrative policy-making level and handle them for itself, as happened with the decrees covering Farmers, Casinos, and Osteopaths. Nevertheless, some sensitive issues (such as Bird Flu) among other decrees described above of 'moderate importance' that involved policy discretion were handled at the administrative level under undirected policy-making.

The US pattern is similar to the French in that it is the only other country in the sample with a spread across all three patterns of policy-making (while the EU Horse Medicines Decree must be classified as 'undirected' it was effectively directed, see above). In two of the decrees developed under directed policy-making the political level took a major interest from the start even though the issues, albeit related to sensitive questions, were not divisive political issues—criminal history checks for volunteers in a range of voluntary organizations and technical aspects of telecommunications in disasters (following lessons learnt from Hurricane Katrina). In a third the political level pushed forward an already well-established bureaucratic impetus (to make a range of changes to cattle slaughtering procedures in the wake of BSE).

Again, while the number of decrees in the sample is small, they nevertheless suggest that bureaucratic responses to direction might also display some significant national differences around the general proposition that the major issues tend to be the ones that attract political attention. In general civil servants developing decrees make every effort fully to follow the express wishes of those giving direction. In this sense the notion that bureaucrats 'shirk' or otherwise subvert the clear and expressed wish of political leaders is based on an entirely misleading view of the nature of how public bureaucracies work. However, acting on directions does not necessarily mean an inability of bureaucrats to shape policies. With the French cases, once the issues had passed from the administrative to the higher politico-administrative level, the role of the middle-level bureaucrats tended to cease as their superiors took them forward. In Sweden too, the extensive intervention of political advisers, ministers, and appointed officials gave bureaucrats relatively little to do on their own by way of making or shaping policy decisions. In the European Union and the United States, directed policy-making involved significant further input from the bureaucrats writing the decrees. Direction meant close involvement and significant steering of bureaucratic work, but not the removal of much of the deliberation from the administrative level as in France and Sweden. Civil servants in the EU and the US made significant contributions to the policy work even under direction.

Politics as Trumps

What happens when politicians get involved, whether in directed decrees or the less intensive intervention in otherwise undirected decrees? They generally get their way: civil servants make every effort to follow the express wishes of their political leaders. The only time in the study this proved difficult was where the prevailing political preferences clashed directly with a court mandate (in the US Salmon Decree). However, generally politicians get their way and this can happen through a variety of mechanisms.

a) when political executives or auxiliaries put items on the bureaucratic agenda, suggesting items that would not have been the subject of a decree were it not for their intervention (e.g. the Swedish Free Year Decree);

b) when the political level effectively takes over the lead in developing or negotiating the legitimation of a decree and shaping it according to their preferences (e.g. the French Osteopaths Decree);

c) by ensuring that the decree does what they want it to do by instructing bureaucrats on part or all of its content (e.g. the UK Fire Services Decree); or

d) by making decisions on proposals passed on to them by bureaucrats (e.g. the German Noise Maps Decree).

The first two mechanisms conform to general expectations about political leadership in bureaucratic systems and refer to directed policy-making processes. The fourth less so since it places the initiative, as well as the structure of the choices to be made, in the hands of the civil servants and affords politicians a sometimes limited role and thus is characteristic of undirected policy-making. The third can belong to either directed or undirected policy-making depending on the extent to which they give direction: whether their directions shape much of the decree or just limited parts of it. There is no evidence in the fifty-two decrees of bureaucrats using either the timing of the approach to the politician or auxiliary, or skewing the question put to the political level, either to 'bounce' politicians into a decision or to remove any effective choice from them. So, a popular conspiracy theory is not validated.

MAKING POLICY WITHOUT POLITICAL DIRECTION

Shirking and Subordination

Given that political direction can be generally characterized as sporadic—relatively infrequent and limited in scope—one would expect the corresponding scope for bureaucratic decision-making to be substantial. As discussed in Chapter 1, a significant literature on bureaucratic motivations suggests that a range of characteristics—self-interest, socially acquired values, professional values, or agency values—might lead bureaucrats to act or propose action in ways that conflict with what politicians want or might be expected to want. In the language of the public choice approach (though the claim is by no means limited to this approach), bureaucrats 'shirk'.

One problem of the 'shirking' hypothesis, in so far as it suggests that bureaucrats act on the basis of individual self-regarding motivations, is that the evidence to support it is so sparse one must doubt whether such motivations are at all significant (Brehm and Gates 1997). Moreover, if one takes the notion that bureaucratic values are derived from past socialization (see Sowa and Selden 2003) or different varieties of self-interest (Niskanen 1971), including status gratification (Dunleavy 1993), the evidence in earlier chapters suggests it might be hard to link many of the issues bureaucrats deal with to such personal motivations. For example, it is hard to see what the bureaucrat concerned stood to gain materially, in status terms or through the satisfaction of some wishes acquired through socialization, from setting the population size of towns that have to produce a noise map at 200,000 rather than 150,000 in the German Noise Maps Decree. It is unlikely that many bureaucrats will have developed as children or young adults particularly strong preferences about most of the things they deal with prior to doing the job they do—views on designing milk quotas, assessing the liability of pharmaceutical companies to damages claims in times of civil emergency, or eligibility for mesothelioma payments, for example. Moreover, it is hard to know exactly how one might explore the impact of such motivations. Psychological investigation might help here. However, the necessary experimental design is not only likely to be extremely hard to conduct, it might also be difficult to control effectively for the great variety of influences and constraints that would be expected to shape decision-making. To say such explanations are difficult to handle or investigate is not, however, to dismiss them. It is possible, however, to say that there is little available evidence to justify giving them any significant weight in explaining the choices bureaucrats make in putting together the decrees examined in this analysis.

A Plurality of Constraints

A wider problem with the 'when the cat's away' argument as applied to bureaucratic activity is that, once one examines what helps explain the choices made by bureaucrats in the absence of direct political control, a whole range of additional constraints on their behaviour becomes apparent. We can classify them in two broad groups on the basis of how the bureaucrats concerned tended to account for the form and structure of the decree in the interviews.

The first group arises from *conformity with precedent*. Precedent imposes a powerful constraint not because bureaucrats are instinctively conservative or even risk-averse. Rather, decrees, like many other kinds of policy instruments, have to conform to existing patterns of policy and policy intervention. Many decrees add to or amend a legal framework. Indeed, this is how many of them have any effect at all. The relationship with existing laws often means that there are limits to what can be proposed without fundamentally changing these legal frameworks—a task not usually achievable by a decree. The constraints of existing policies is particularly clearly seen in the case of a codified legal system such as that found in France, where decrees generally consist of small changes to voluminous legal codes. A French civil servant explained: 'Decrees all change codes. They are not free standing.' Thus, if you want to reduce your payments to farmers by altering the age at which farmers are eligible for transfer payments under the *agriculteurs en difficulté* scheme you have to amend the *Code rural* and the way you do that is by *décret*. The constraints of legal frameworks are not simply the province of codified Roman law legal systems: pre-existing legislation sets up frameworks which specify what actions can be taken to change a regime. Thus, for instance, in the United States the series of incidents involving lithium polymer batteries generated debate within the federal government (above all, the two main agencies involved in airline safety) about how the *existing* Hazardous Materials (HAZMAT) rules should be amended and the range of actions was significantly defined by the existing regime.

The second group of constraints arises from *avoiding potential vetoes*. Procedural norms not only constitute cues for political involvement (see above); negotiating them requires bureaucrats to anticipate potential opposition or sticking points as they frame their proposals. Where the approval of politicians is required (and as has been discussed, reference to a politician or auxiliary for approval is universal for any decree) bureaucrats devote significant attention to anticipating their likely reactions. Moreover, decrees that have implications for other departments or agencies generally have to secure some kind of agreement with them. Similarly where it is necessary to secure the approval of a supervisory body, whether a dedicated specialized scrutinizer of legislative proposals (such as the French AFSSA or an EU comitology committee), a body exploring the legality or constitutionality of the decree (such as the Conseil d'État or the UK parliamentary scrutiny committees), bureaucrats seek to frame proposals in such a way as they will pass through them.

Table 8.3 presents some of the major constraints that tended to be found in the accounts that civil servants gave of the shape and timing of each of the undirected decrees. The first two columns indicate the constraints of domestic and European law. Since decrees are generally understood to be 'subordinate' legislation, it is hardly surprising that the constraints of what is contained in parent and related domestic law played a significant role in the accounts given of twenty-seven out of twenty-nine decrees. In the two exceptions (the UK Energy Billing and the French Rhine Transport Decrees) the constraints of international law (an EU directive and an international agreement respectively) were so strong that existing domestic legislation appeared to play little significant role. International law (mainly European Union law) played a significant role in shaping fourteen out of the twenty-nine decrees. The third column indicates the constraints imposed by the reactions, largely anticipated,

Table 8.3. Sources of constraint under undirected policy-making

Country	Decree	Conformity with Precedent		Avoiding Potential Vetoes		Supervisory Bodies[i]
		Domestic Law	International/ EU Law	Political Leadership	Interagency Bargaining	
D	Noise Maps	x	x	-	x	Bundesrat/Länder
D	Milk Quotas	x	x	-	-	Bundesrat/Länder
D	Civil Emergencies	x	x	-	x	Bundesrat/Länder
D	Ship Safety	x[ii]	x	x	x	Bundesrat/Länder
EU	Horse medicines	x[ii]	-	-	-	CVMP/comitology committee
F	Bird Flu	x	x	-	x	AFSSA
F	Soups	x	x	-	x	AFSSA/Conseil d'État
F	Rhine	-	x	-	x	Central Commission for Navigation on the Rhine[iii]
F	Cosmetics	x	x	-	x	AFSSAPS
F	Housing	x	-	-	x	Conseil superieur des HLM/Conseil d'État
F	Handicap	x	-	-	x	Ad hoc working parties on reform/Conseil national des personnes handicappées/Conseil d'État
F	Champagne	x	-	-	-	Comité national des vins et eaux-de-vie/Organisme de défense et de gestion du vin de Champagne
UK	Home Information Pack (HIP)	x	-	x	x	Two ad hoc groups/Merits Committee
UK	Fire Services	x	x	x	-	Business and Community Safety Forum/Merits Committee
UK	Mesothelioma	x	x	x	-	Parliament (affirmative resolution required)

	Case				Body
UK	Alcohol Disorder Zones	x	-	-	JCSI/Merits Committee
UK	Police Best Value	x	-	x	Merits Committee
UK	Mental Capacity	x	x	x	Mental Health Bill Implementation Advisory Group
UK	Energy Billing	-	x	x	Better Regulation Unit
UK	Animal Mutilations	x	x	-	Parliament (affirmative resolution required)
UK	TV Multiplex	x	-	x	Ofcom
UK	Casinos	x	x	-	Parliament (affirmative resolution required)
UK	Criminal Justice	x	-	x	Ad hoc group
US	Salmon	x	-	x	OMB
US	Labour Certification	x	-	x	OMB
US	Lithium	x	x	x	National Transportation Safety Board/OMB
US	Exchange Visitor	x	-	x	Government Accountability Office
US	Community Broadband	x	x	-	OMB
US	Mentor	x	-	x	OMB

i. Abbreviations and acronyms explained in adjacent text.
ii. EU law is classed as 'domestic' in this case.
iii. An international regulatory body.

of politicians (those decrees reflecting active and sustained intervention by politicians are classified as being passed under directed policy-making, and thus not included in Table 8.3). In fourteen of the twenty-nine accounts of directed policy-making the anticipated reaction of the politician plays a significant role. Ten of these are from the UK cases. Interagency bargaining (which includes inter-ministerial bargaining but not intra-ministerial discussion or negotiation) was found in nineteen cases.

The last column includes a diverse range of bodies, generally specific to the jurisdiction in question, which have either veto powers over legislation or a significant advisory role that would be difficult to circumvent. Thus the role of the *Länder* through the need for *Bundesrat* approval of legislation was apparent in all four German undirected decrees in Table 8.3; a statutory advisory body (Committee for Medicinal Products for Veterinary Use) and a comitology committee (Standing Committee on Veterinary Medicinal Products) supervised the production of the EU Horse Medicines Decree; the French tradition of 'expert' and representative supervisory bodies meant that French civil servants' accounts referred to bodies such as the Agence française de sécurité sanitaire des aliments (AFSSA), the Agence française de sécurité sanitaire des produits de santé (AFSSAPS), the advisory Conseil supérieur des HLM and Conseil national des personnes handicappées and the statutory Organisme de défense et de gestion du vin de Champagne. Of the seven French decrees in Table 8.3 the Conseil d'État appeared to play a significant role in three. In the UK cases parliamentary approval (an affirmative resolution in Parliament) for the decree was a significant part of the story in three cases, and the parliamentary bodies (the Merits Committee and Joint Committee on Statutory Instruments, JCSI) in another three. In addition, one UK decree was significantly shaped by Ofcom, the independent regulator and competition authority for the UK communications industries, and two others by *ad hoc* but formally constituted advisory groups (such as the Business and Community Safety Forum). In the United States the Office of Management and Budget played a significant part in five of the six accounts, the Government Accountability Office which audits accounts and increasingly performance made recommendations which played a part in the Exchange Visitor Decree and the Lithium Decree was in part a response to the report by the National Transportation Safety Board.

Of course, to say that an institution or law played a significant role in an account given by a bureaucrat of how a decree was put together does not necessarily imply enormous constraint and the elimination of any bureaucratic choices. It does, however, suggest that bureaucrats, when they describe what they do, are thinking of a range of constraints within which they do their work and develop a decree. It is not possible to classify the undirected decrees in terms of the 'discretion' that they offer the bureaucrats that write them, in part because we have no clear metric of assessing discretion, in part because any assessment would involve a counter-factual argument about what would have happened if apparent constraints had been ignored, and in part because discretion is often a matter of perception: those on the receiving end of a decree might be expected to be generally more likely than those who write them to think that it could have been written differently or not at all.

However, one can say that in many cases the choices of the bureaucrats writing the decrees appeared to be severely constrained. For example, the official writing the Horse Medicines Decree was applying Directive 2001/82/EC on the Community code relating to veterinary medicinal products and in particular a recent amending decree made under it (Regulation (EC) No. 726/2004 of 31 March 2004 laying down Community procedures for the authorization and supervision of medicinal products for human and veterinary use). Writing the decree essentially meant getting a list of medicines from the Committee for Medicinal Products for Veterinary Use (described on its website as a thirty-four-strong body of experts, 'nominated by the Member States, in consultation with the [European Medicine] Agency's Management Board'), sending the list out for public consultation, consulting within the Commission units in other Commission DGs, and getting the final list approved by the Standing Committee on Veterinary Medicinal Products, the comitology committee whose approval is required for a proposed decree to come into effect. If one adds up all the constraints listed in Table 8.3, no decree is accounted for with fewer than three constraints. It is thus clear that once one discounts sustained and active political control, a whole range of other constraints help shape bureaucratic activity, such that the notion that the absence of political constraint means that bureaucrats shape decisions according to their own preferences is inaccurate and fanciful.

Subordination and Discretion

Bureaucrats involved in shaping policy, especially but not only where political direction is unclear or absent, tended to emphasize when accounting for their actions the constraints to which they respond and generally do not claim that they have a particularly wide scope for shaping policy. This is hardly surprising since it is the essence of a bureaucratic career that it is a career of *service*. This does not suggest that bureaucrats have or should have any kind of unique or rare selfless moral dedication to serve others. Rather it is the nature of the job that they are generally subordinate, whether to other bureaucrats, politicians, or regulatory and supervisory institutions. If one wants to be promoted on merit one has to conform to expectations about what kind of behaviour is deemed to be meritorious. One could see this as reflecting a form of self-interest, but by this token there is nothing that is not self-interest and the notion loses all meaning. In public bureaucracies, conformity with procedural norms, following political guidance, and observing constitutional and legal constraints are basic components of conceptions of merit; non-observance would require some special justification. This is not to say that acting as a subordinate is all there is to being a bureaucrat, but any creativity and initiative has to observe the constraints imposed by subordination. Indeed, Max Weber (1972: 632) makes subordination the defining characteristic of a bureaucratic as opposed to a political career. One of the consequences as regards relations between bureaucrats and politicians of this subordination has been discussed already: the general observance of procedural norms that involve bureaucrats bringing issues to the attention of politicians.

A second consequence of the subordinate character of bureaucracy is the way in which conflicts with, or opposition to, political leadership are handled. A strategy of 'sabotage', one device that public choice theories assume to result from bureaucrats opposing politicians, insofar as it means deliberately ignoring or undermining the instructions of a politician, is unlikely to be prevalent not only because of the predisposition of bureaucrats to observe rules but also because such actions are likely to require active conspiracy rather than individual recalcitrance. While none of the decrees examined here involved anything approaching 'sabotage', it seems likely that such collective action would be difficult to organize, sustain, and hide from administrative or political superiors where such heavy normative emphasis is placed on compliance.

However, this is not to say that the policy work of bureaucrats does not bring them into conflict or potential conflict with political masters. As discussed above, the most common response to disagreements with politicians is to give the politicians what they want. In five cases, however, we can see evidence of a distinctive bureaucratic approach to handling disagreements or potential disagreements with politicians, *mobilizing force majeure*: using a third party within the structure of the state to persuade politicians to change their minds. In one of the US cases (the Salmon Decree) it was the courts which eventually led a reluctant political leadership to accept what bureaucrats within the Commerce Department felt it should do, and in another (the Exchange Visitor Decree) a Government Accountability Office report helped civil servants in the State Department give priority to a revision they had long wanted. In the UK Home Information Packs Decree the civil servants dealt with the anticipated political reluctance to delay introducing part of the scheme (a party election manifesto commitment) by commissioning the Deputy Chief Executive of the Land Registry, a 150-year-old agency responsible for the legal registration of land and the transfer of property, to point out the difficulties that would arise from putting it into force prematurely. In two French decrees (Soups and Bird Flu) the recommendations of the AFSSA neutralized the nervousness among politicians and auxiliaries that the proposed measures generated.

A third consequence of the subordinate character of bureaucracy is that it becomes difficult to talk of 'bureaucratic discretion' as a sort of space where bureaucrats are given, by design or negligence, the opportunity to act without instruction or constraint, as the 'hole at the centre of a doughnut' (Jowell 1973)—a space where the rules allow bureaucrats to decide more or less what they like. Where the written rules do not tell bureaucrats what to do, a range of generalized rules, norms, and expectations not only prevents them from doing as they please, but makes the whole notion of 'doing as they please' problematic. To take a hypothetical example, a bureaucrat might feel it is desirable, for whatever reason, to abolish a particular regulatory scheme and is perfectly free to suggest it, but if it has no chance of gaining political approval, all the civil servant stands to achieve is the prospect of being regarded as someone without any political sensitivity. Bureaucrats might thus be expected to limit their actions to what is acceptable for someone in their subordinate position and what is feasible given the wider constraints within which they operate.

THE NATURE OF BUREAUCRATIC INTENTIONS

If it is correct to argue that bureaucrats writing decrees and doing 'policy work' (Page and Jenkins 2005) do not have programmatic intentions in the same way that a party or interest group has policy intentions, and that the notion that they are motivated by self-interest or socialization is implausible, we are left with the open question of what it is that motivates bureaucrats. We know from our case study materials that they influence the shape of the decrees they write. Much political science understanding of influence and power is based upon intentionality—A has power over B insofar as A gets B to do things that B would not otherwise do (Dahl 1969). Yet without conventional interest-based or socialization-based theories of motivation, how can we characterize the nature of bureaucratic influence? In a nutshell: what are the goals that bureaucrats pursue when they shape policy?

Their objectives and the resulting influence of bureaucrats on the process of policy-making come from the character of their jobs as subordinates. Bureaucrats are given responsibility for a particular patch of public policy. In its most basic form, success as a bureaucrat in dealing with your patch means essentially making sure that no awkward political, legal, or financial irregularities or embarrassments arise in it, that the policy runs reasonably well, and that, where they exist, politicians' wishes for the patch are accommodated as best they can be. This goal tends to produce three types of activity which shape bureaucratic interventions in the policy process as far as decree-making is concerned.

Routinization

First, bureaucrats *routinize* public policy. Once a policy change has been accepted by a department or agency, irrespective of where it comes from, whether it is a party election commitment or an initiative proposed by groups or even by civil servants themselves, it has to conform to procedural and formal norms in order to become a set of legitimate policy provisions. Bureaucrats take proposals through deliberative procedures—these vary from system to system but include, among other things, intra- and inter-organizational negotiation in government, consultation with interests, approval by relevant supervisory bodies, and votes in legislatures. In order to get things to pass through these procedures they must make calculations about the strength of any political support they have from their own political leadership and whether this is enough to take the proposal through unchanged or whether they have to amend proposals in order to get them through. Routinization also requires developing the substance of the proposed policy as a set of measures that conforms to an existing body of measures in the same or similar policy area, or at least does not create awkward incompatibilities or inconsistencies.

In both forms of routinization, procedural and substantive, bureaucrats are not simply automatically translating existing 'constraints' into public policy but making judgements about how policy should be shaped to meet them. It was not, for example, automatic that the *only* solution to the problem of developing a policy on the air transport of hazardous lithium batteries in the face of industry opposition to further regulation was the curious compromise of the US Lithium Decree. It was possible that something harsher might have got through and would have gone further to satisfying the National Transportation Safety Board whose negative report on a fire at Los Angeles International Airport created the need to make a decree in the first place. In developing the proposals that ended up in the EU Fish Quota Decree, the civil servants used the existing regulatory regime (the Total Allowable Catch system) to respond to scientific advice on fish stock depletion as set out in the directives governing European fisheries. They might conceivably have proposed more radical changes to the regime. The civil servants developing the UK Fire Services Decree who set less mandatory performance targets for firefighting services could conceivably have done the reverse—they could have stuck with the more directive regime of the previous years, but instead they chose a different way of developing performance indicators for the service.

Bureaucrats typically make decisions about how to routinize policy, and it is often assumed that such decisions are conservative or biased towards the status quo, especially when helping to make policy under directed policymaking (see e.g. Aberbach *et al.* 1981: 256). This is frequently the case. Altering incrementally existing statutory provisions to accommodate a policy change is a parsimonious way of making a policy, and the kind of 'consensus mongering' that results from procedurally mandated consultation might be expected to be likely to lead often to agreement on limited change. But it is not invariably conservative. The French Soups Decree deregulated soup production partly on the ground that this was consistent with changes introduced elsewhere in the food industry in France. The process of consultation on the UK Animal Mutilations Decree, which set out to regulate the conditions under which one surgical procedure was allowed (the laproscopic insemination of sheep), itself produced a wider set of changes to the law, covering procedures such as trimming birds' beaks, than civil servants originally anticipated.

Regularization

Second, bureaucrats *regularize* policy. Regularization refers to the activity of amending or altering policy when there is a perceived technical problem that means the law is either incomplete or deficient: there is something awry in the patch that needs straightening. Regularization is often behind consequential decrees. The change from one regime for administering the environmental protection scheme 'Forest Focus' in the EU led to the development of a new decree; and the extension of existing privacy provisions to a new database led to the US Privacy Act Decree. Much of the initiative behind decrees implementing EU legislation can be explained not as a result of any direct instruction to implement, but as a regularization of the law as civil servants see that the law in their patch is deficient and government could be open to formal infraction procedures were they not to act. Here as elsewhere, regularization can also be behind the introduction of decrees making significant policy changes. Perhaps the most significant such decree in our sample was the US Salmon Decree which reflected concerns among civil servants responsible for portions of the Endangered Species Act of 1973, confirmed by court decisions, that the law was not being properly implemented. Regularization also played a significant role in the development of the French Osteopaths decree. The law as constructed anticipated the development of a framework for regulating osteopathy as a profession and this led to the process of recasting the law surrounding the practice of osteopathy and the training of osteopaths. Moreover, within this law the decree in our sample reflected the regularization of the position of osteopaths who happened to be stuck in a no-man's-land between the old and the new regulatory regimes. The whole reform of the parts of the mental health care regime that led to the UK Mental Capacity Decree arose from the identification of gaps in the existing regime, and the deficiency was even given a name, the 'Bournewood Gap', after the name of the hospital in which an incident led to a critical European Court of Human Rights case.

Regularization is not necessarily an automatic process. In some cases where the irregularity or problems are obvious or immediate, such as where a court has identified it, the pressures for regularization are strong. Moreover, the perception of irregularities may also require significant bureaucratic judgements, judgements over whether the 'time is right' to make the changes (e.g. the EU Horse Medicines Decree, so a civil servant involved explained, might have been introduced earlier but the director general wanted to wait until after the 2004 enlargement of the European Union to start work on it) as well as whether to remedy it at all. The method for analysing decree-making did not look at the possibilities for decrees that were not developed. Large parts of primary legislation in the UK lie on the statute books 'uncommenced'—i.e. not brought into force by implementing and commencing decrees—and judgements about regularization can be expected to be reflected in what is *not* the subject of a decree.

Policy Adjustment

A third activity is *policy adjustment*. It refers to the desire to make things work better or respond to known or coming problems in the patch. In some cases this can be very similar to some forms of regularization, but the difference between the two lies essentially in whether the proposed remedies are conceived as a means of resolving some problem, or filling some lacuna, in the existing arrangements as currently conceived (regularization) or whether what is being proposed is designed as an improvement of existing arrangements (policy adjustment). Thus, for example, the US Alien Substitution Decree changed significantly the conditions of the green card scheme for immigration in order to combat the increasingly visible signs of immigration fraud and was an example of adjustment; the US Salmon Decree involved regularization as it reflected an application of the existing statutory principles which had not been implemented.

Adjustment refers to the ability of civil servants to propose changes to the arrangements in their patch to achieve what they would judge to be improvements, and this of necessity also requires bureaucratic judgements. Thus the civil servant writing the German Ship Safety Decree perceived the existing rules on ships captains being prohibited from drinking any alcohol while at sea as problematic and believed she saw a way to improve it, just as the French civil servant writing the Bird Flu Decree thought the regulations on the movement of birds could be changed to allow pigeon racing. Adjustment not only shapes the judgements of bureaucrats as they develop policy under directed and undirected policy-making, it also helps to account for the agenda-setting role of the bureaucracy. Thus, for example, the changes produced by the US Exchange Visitor Decree had been proposed by civil servants running the scheme within the State Department and taken up by the Government Accountability Office as a recommendation which they were happy to draft and the civil servants proposing the changes to immigration policy under the US Alien Substitution Decree had to ensure that they first had political support before they could start drafting it.

The fact that some changes are considered as 'improvements' raises the question of how proposals are evaluated. On what grounds do bureaucrats evaluate whether a policy adjustment needs to be made and whether what they are proposing is an improvement? The specific rationalizations behind bureaucratic initiatives reflect a range of considerations specific to the case in hand. However the evidence from the preceding chapters does suggest that bureaucrats in the different jurisdictions tend to emphasize rather distinctive bases, in particular a distinctive *locus standi*, from which proposals for policy adjustment as well as regularization are evaluated. For the German and the American civil servants interviewed, the *locus standi* was that of themselves or their organization as experienced administrators of the relevant programmes. While not all civil servants had served for a long time looking after the particular patch, many had; moreover in the German and American cases they could call on the accumulated experience of the *Ressort* or agency.

For the French and European civil servants the *locus standi* was significantly provided by external sources of expertise—the advisory or scientific 'expert' group or, in the French case, the 'specialist' interest group. Of course in the EU case the specialist expertise was often mandated through rules that require consultation of specialist expert groups (as with the Fishing Quota Decree) or through comitology procedures. While it is also frequently mandatory to consult similar advisory and expert groups in France, significant French bureaucratic initiatives resulted from civil servants identifying interest group recommendations (the Bird Flu and Soups Decrees reflected interest group pressure) as legitimate candidates for improving their patch.

In Sweden and the UK the *locus standi* is somewhat harder to identify as bureaucratic initiative in proposing decrees was limited (Sweden) or predominantly involved regularization and adjustment (UK). However, in the UK the anticipated perspective of the minister appears to play a significant role in the decree-making initiatives that emerged from the bureaucracy, as with the need to avoid the embarrassment of the policy mess that would have resulted had not the House Information Pack (HIP) decree been passed. There were simply not enough qualified professionals to produce HIPs in the way the original legislation required, so the introduction of this part of the HIP scheme had to be delayed. Similarly, in the Police Best Value decree civil servants approached the task of changing the framework for judging the 'efficiency' of police forces in part through assessing how ministerial views on the subject had changed in favour of reducing the number of performance indicators.

CONCLUSIONS

President de Gaulle's Christmas card to me might not have been written by him personally, but it was produced by a set of procedures and routines over which he presided. Other politicians might not have replied, indeed Ludwig Erhard and Mao Tse-tung did not. De Gaulle's response could have reflected some direct volition—a specific instruction from the president to his civil servants that Christmas cards should be responded to. It may have been the product of a routine—that French politicians generally make arrangements for replying to correspondence in this way—that his civil servants interpreted without even asking him. Or it may have been something in between. Similarly, with decrees many things apart from direct involvement can link politician to government action. Shaping policy-making, and in particular shaping bureaucratic actions, is not necessarily a contact sport.

A wide range of bureaucratic routines and norms push issues to the attention of political leaders, even though the attention required from them is often minimal. All the decrees in this study reflected in some form the most powerful norm steering bureaucratic issues to the attention of political leadership: the notion that any significant choices be approved by it. Some decrees appear to manage to avoid this requirement entirely, but only because the choices they reflect are believed to have been taken earlier and already legitimized. In many cases the political leadership simply acknowledges and acquiesces in what is put in front of them or makes marginal suggestions, although in a significant number of cases it offers active and sustained guidance on what is to be done.

In all three circumstances, the fact that political leadership legitimizes bureaucratic actions is more than a democratic fiction. It underpins the whole operation of the bureaucracy. If a bureaucrat were to develop a decree without deemed or actual political authorization it would be likely to be construed less as an affront to democracy than as incompetence, as anything vaguely controversial is likely to be brought to politicians' attention anyway at some stage and anything uncontroversial is unlikely to be held up by them. One could construe this as a sort of 'fire alarm'. However, the idea that employees seek authorization for actions they take in the name of the organization for which they work, and avoid actions that are unlikely to be authorized, is such a basic feature of organizational life that the metaphor adds little to our understanding of it.

Nevertheless, the procedures for ensuring that this norm of approval is observed are somewhat variable: in Germany the formal preparation of the *Vorlage* and its progress through the politico-administrative system are set out in a gemeinsame Geschäftsordnung; in France the *cabinet* system means that the representatives of the ministry's political leadership have routine contacts with bureaucrats working on policy; and in Britain and the United States the internal procedures are generally less formalized. Moreover, the arrangements for the involvement of the political leadership are also highly variable, from the pattern found in Sweden, where a relatively large group of political auxiliaries can take a highly active role in shaping what bureaucrats do, to the more sporadic 'hands off' pattern found in the United Kingdom.

Even taking into account the variability of political intervention in bureaucratic processes, and with the possible exception of the Swedish decrees in the study, bureaucrats nevertheless have a significant role to play in shaping decrees. Their role is generally variable and they usually have a good idea very early on whether they are dealing with policy issues in which considerable political interest is likely to be shown or whether they will be largely left to get on with developing the decree themselves—whether the issue is likely to be a case of directed, undirected, or consequential policy-making—but can switch even if things change. Once one strips away the constraints imposed by any political leadership on how bureaucrats go about drafting decrees, one finds a range of other constraints: constraints above all derived from the legal, constitutional, and organizational environment in which decrees are being developed. Bureaucratic judgements about what should be done become so intricately bound up with what can be done within the confines of this environment that the suggestion that there exists a realm of bureaucratic discretion, where bureaucrats can shape policies according to their own preferences, is at best pointing to a set of considerations that marginally affect what bureaucrats do. Bureaucrats have to exercise judgements. The evidence suggests that bureaucrats in different systems, in the exercise of these judgements, are more likely to be influenced by different features of their working environment: interest groups in France, specified sources of expertise and authority in the European Commission, the accumulated experience of the *Ressort* or agency in Germany and the US, and by interpretations of ministerial will in the UK.

How much confidence can one have in conclusions drawn from a handful of decrees when in some of our jurisdictions thousands of them are passed each year? We simply do not know for certain whether a different sample would have led to different conclusions, but it is very likely that a large random sample of all decrees would have produced a picture suggesting preponderance of consequential policy-making in countries such as France and the UK where decrees are routinely used for essentially formal purposes that would elsewhere be filled by an agency or ministerial decision or announcement. Can a few selected decrees offer a reliable guide to what goes on within bureaucracies? In some respects one can have greater confidence about the generalizability of some of the findings than others. The principles of the operation of major institutions, such as the Conseil d'État or the gemeinsame Geschäftsordnung, are unlikely to vary substantially from one decree to another. Some of the discussion, such as the analysis of how often politicians intervene in the policy process earlier in this chapter, has offered estimates of scale and frequency based on the sample. But these should not be taken as population estimates from a sample, rather as indications that the phenomena and events to which the numbers refer are not rare or unique.

The kinds of statements for which the evidence can only be at best suggestive are those that concern the patterns of bureaucratic behaviour in individual jurisdictions. Whether the preponderance of interest group initiated legislation is truly distinctive for France or whether there are in reality plenty of examples of decrees developed under directed policy-making in Germany which the sample simply missed, are examples of issues that cannot be determined with any confidence with such a small sample. While the evidence base for such arguments in this book is a larger number of case studies than usually used in cross-national comparisons, it still does not make up the size of sample from which reliable population estimates could be drawn. Nevertheless, limited though it may be, the methodology allows for the development of plausible assessments of the everyday operation of different bureaucratic systems based on empirical evidence rather than on conjecture, the use of empirical indicators only indirectly and tenuously related to the phenomena they are supposed to refer, or other methods of making theoretical bricks without empirical straw.

Do any of the findings make any difference to what actually happens? Are some ways of making decrees better than others? One thing that has been omitted is any evaluation of the quality of the work done on decrees. It would certainly make a neat conclusion to a comparative study to be able to show that a particular feature leads to good decrees and good government and another to bad. While one might imagine that some features of decree production are more likely to result in better decrees—say the 'expertise' of the bureaucrats producing them—the simple fact is that we do not know this to be the case. It is not just that a study of this kind cannot expect to perform an evaluation of each of the decrees examined, or even that a convincing assessment of the individual contribution of a decree to the success or otherwise of broader policy objectives for which the decree is a small part is probably beyond reach, but also that political science is generally very bad at reaching a clear definition about what is successful and what unsuccessful in policy terms (McConnell 2010).

Nevertheless, the evidence does suggest that bureaucrats might be better able to make a distinctive contribution to policy-making in some jurisdictions than others. Routinization and regularization appear to be rather generalized skills of a bureaucrat. Although the legal training and indeed the place of law in the administrative process vary substantially, the ability to understand how one might put together a decree that sets your patch in order is a largely transferable skill and one could detect no appreciable difference between jurisdictions in the ability of bureaucrats to exercise it. The most creative contribution of bureaucrats is that which brings the experience of bureaucrats as a group that actually manages and/or delivers public policies to bear on the deliberative problem-solving process of policy design—the policy adjustment role of bureaucrats. While bureaucrats from all jurisdictions were involved to some degree in policy adjustment, it was primarily in the United States and Germany, where agencies and *Ressorts* served as repositories of past experience and where lengthy service in a particular position or sector is not uncommon, that the *locus standi* from which policy adjustment appears to be developed is that of bureaucratic experience. Rather than holding up a mirror to political elites by concentrating on anticipating their wishes or selectively transmitting the proposals of interest groups, one might expect the contribution of such bureaucratic expertise to problem-solving to be valuable not necessarily because it is 'right', but because it brings a valuable perspective to the process of policy-making that otherwise is lost.

Where do these findings stand in relation to the optimism or pessimism about bureaucracy and democratic political control discussed in the first chapter? On the one hand they fall into the optimists' camp. The idea that bureaucrats use their position to shape policy as they wish away from the gaze, if not control, of politicians finds no supporting evidence. In fact a range of general procedures, bureaucratic norms, and institutional arrangements specific to individual systems ensure that politicians have a chance to intervene in even the tiniest issues of public policy should they wish. Moreover, they intervene more often than one might expect, even though such intervention remains sporadic and bureaucrats generally do as they are told. On the pessimistic side, little is lost from Weber's picture of modern bureaucratic society if we consider that the bureaucrats themselves do not have that much independent power. A host of constraints built up by past bureaucratic and political decisions, legal forms, and institutional structures narrow the scope for political choices. Bureaucrats as well as politicians are caught up in Weber's 'iron cage of bondage'.

ANNEX TO CHAPTER 8: CLASSIFICATION OF MAJOR PROPERTIES OF DECREES

Name	Country	Political involvement Initiation	Political involvement Development	Political involvement Legitimation	Significance	Scientific	Form of Policy-Making
Employee Insurance	D	Not involved	Passive	Passive	Minor	No	Consequential
Fiscal Equalization	D	Not involved	Passive	Passive	Minor	Yes	Consequential
Noise Maps	D	Active	Active[i]	Passive	Moderate	Yes	Undirected
Milk Quotas	D	Passive	Passive	Passive	Moderate	No	Undirected
Civil Emergencies	D	Not involved	Not involved	Passive	Moderate	No	Undirected
Ship Safety	D	Not involved	Not involved	Passive	Moderate	No	Undirected
Forest Focus	EU	Not involved	Not involved	Passive	Minor	No	Consequential
Tariff Simplification	EU	Not involved	Not involved	Not involved	Minor	No	Consequential
Silkworm	EU	Not involved	Not involved	Not involved	Minor	No	Consequential
Stability Instrument	EU	Active	Active	Active	Major	No	Directed
Fish Quotas	EU	Not involved	Active	Active	Major	Yes	Directed
Marco Polo	EU	Active	Active	Passive	Major	No	Directed
Horse Medicines	EU	Not involved	Not involved	Passive	Moderate	Yes	Undirected
Casinos	F	Active	Active	Active	Major	No	Directed
Osteopaths	F	Active	Active	Active	Major	Yes	Directed
Farmers	F	Passive	Active	Active	Major	No	Directed
Bird Flu	F	Not involved	Passive	Active	Moderate	Yes	Undirected
Soups	F	Not involved	Not involved	Passive	Moderate	Yes	Undirected
Rhine	F	Not involved	Not involved	Passive	Moderate	Yes	Undirected
Cosmetics	F	Not involved	Not involved	Passive	Moderate	Yes	Undirected
Housing	F	Not involved	Not involved	Passive	Moderate	No	Undirected
Handicap	F	Not involved	Not involved	Passive	Moderate	Yes	Undirected
Champagne	F	Not involved	Not involved	Not involved	Moderate	No	Undirected
Rescue Services	S	Passive	Active	Passive	Moderate	No	Consequential
Agency Unemployed Graduates	S	Active	Active	Passive	Moderate	No	Directed

Case	Country							
Women's Organizations	S	Active	Active	Active	Active	Major	No	Directed
Free Year	S	Active	Active	Active	Passive	Moderate	No	Directed
Public Employment	S	Active	Active	Active	Passive	Moderate	No	Directed
Farm Payments	S	Active	Active	Active	Passive	Major	No	Directed
Electrical Goods	S	Active	Active	Active	Passive	Major	No	Directed
Offender Management	UK	Not involved	Not involved	Not involved	Passive	Minor	No	Consequential
Criminal Justice	UK	Passive	Passive	Passive	Passive	Minor	No	Undirected
Home Information (HIP)	UK	Active	Passive	Passive	Active	Major	No	Undirected
Fire Services	UK	Passive	Passive	Active[i]	Passive	Moderate	No	Undirected
Mesothelioma	UK	Active	Active	Passive	Passive	Major	No	Undirected
Alcohol Disorder Zones	UK	Active	Active	Passive	Passive	Moderate	No	Undirected
Police Best Value	UK	Passive	Passive	Passive	Passive	Moderate	No	Undirected
Mental Capacity	UK	Passive	Passive	Passive	Passive	Moderate	No	Undirected
Energy Billing	UK	Passive	Passive	Passive	Passive	Moderate	No	Undirected
Animal Mutilation	UK	Passive	Passive	Passive	Passive	Major	No	Undirected
TV Multiplex	UK	Passive	Passive	Passive	Passive	Moderate	No	Undirected
Casinos	UK	Not involved	Not involved	Not involved	Passive	Moderate	No	Undirected
Privacy Act	US	Not involved	Not involved	Not involved	Passive	Minor	No	Consequential
Katrina	US	Active	Active	Active	Passive	Moderate	No	Directed
BSE	US	Active	Active	Active	Passive	Major	Yes	Directed
Criminal Checks	US	Active	Active	Active	Passive	Moderate	No	Directed
Salmon	US	Active	Active[i]	Active[i]	Active	Major	Yes	Undirected
Alien Substitution	US	Passive	Passive	Active[i]	Active	Major	No	Undirected
Lithium	US	Passive	Active[i]	Active[i]	Passive	Moderate	Yes	Undirected
Exchange Visitor	US	Not involved	Passive	Passive	Passive	Moderate	No	Undirected
Community Connect	US	Passive	Not involved	Not involved	Passive	Moderate	No	Undirected
Mentor	US	Not involved	Passive	Passive	Passive	Moderate	No	Undirected

i. Not sustained (see text).

References

Aberbach, J. D., Putnam, R. D., and Rockman, B. A. (1981) *Bureaucrats and Politicians in Western Democracies* (Cambridge, Mass.: Harvard University Press).

Allen, C. K. (1956) *Law and Orders: An Inquiry into the Nature and Scope of Delegated Legislation and Executive Powers in English Law* (London: Stevens & Sons Ltd).

Allison, G. (1971) *Essence of Decision: Explaining the Cuban Missile Crisis* (Boston: Little Brown).

Anton, T. J. (1969) 'Policy-Making and Political Culture in Sweden', *Scandinavian Political Studies*, 4: 88–102.

——(1980) *Administered Politics: Elite Political Culture in Sweden* (The Hague: Martinus Nijhoff).

Arrow, K. J. (1964) 'Research in Management Controls: A Critical Synthesis', in C. Bonini, R. Jaediche, and H. Wagner (eds), *Management Controls: New Directions in Basic Research* (New York: McGraw-Hill).

Arter, D. (1999) *Scandinavian Politics Today* (Manchester: Manchester University Press).

——(2006) *Democracy in Scandinavia: Consensual, Majoritarian or Mixed?* (Manchester: Manchester University Press).

Balla, S. J. (1998) 'Administrative Procedures and Political Control of the Bureaucracy', *American Political Science Review*, 92/3 (Sept.): 663–73.

Ballmann, A., Epstein, D., and O'Halloran, S. (2002) 'Delegation, Comitology, and the Separation of Powers in the European Union', *International Organization*, 56/3: 551–74.

Barkow, R. E. (2010) 'Insulating Agencies: Avoiding Capture through Institutional Design', *Texas Law Review*, 89/1: 15–79.

Bartelt, S. (2008) 'The Institutional Interplay Regarding the New Architecture for the EC's External Assistance', *European Law Journal*, 14/5: 655–79.

Baumgartner, F. R. (1989) *Conflict and Rhetoric in French Policymaking*. Pittsburgh, Pa.: University of Pittsburgh Press.

——and Jones, B. D. (1993) *Agendas and Instability in American Politics* (Chicago: Chicago University Press).

Bendor, J., Taylor, S., and Van Gaalen, R. (1987) 'Stacking the Deck: Bureaucratic Missions and Policy Design', *American Political Science Review*, 81/3: 873–96.

Benn, T. (1980) *The Case for a Constitutional Civil Service* (London: Institute for Workers' Control).

Bergeal, C. (2004) *Rédiger un texte normatif* (Paris: Berger-Levrault).

Bergh, A., and Erlingsson, G. (2009) 'Liberalization without Retrenchment: Understanding the Consensus on Swedish Welfare State Reforms', *Scandinavian Political Studies*, 32/1: 71–93.

Berman, G., Broadbridge, S., Gillie, C., Peck, M., Strickland, P., Ward, P., and White, E. (2005) *The Violent Crime Reduction Bill*, Research paper 05/49 (London: House of Commons Library).

Bostock, D. (2002) 'COREPER Revisited', *Journal of Common Market Studies*, 40/2: 215–34.

Boyne, G. A. (1986) 'Socio-economic Conditions, Central Policies and Local Authority Staffing Levels', *Public Administration*, 64/1: 69–82.

Branigin, W. (1998) 'Visa Program, High-Tech Workers Exploited, Critics Say', *Washington Post* (26 July), A1.

Brehm, J., and Gates, S. (1997) *Working, Shirking, and Sabotage* (Ann Arbor, Mich.: Michigan University Press).

Bundesministerium des Innern (2000) *Moderner Staat—Moderne Verwaltung Gemeinsame Geschäftsordnung der Bundesministerien* (Berlin: Bundesministerium des Innern).

Butler, D., Adonis, A., and Travers, T. (1994) *Failure in British Government: The Politics of the Poll Tax* (Oxford: Oxford University Press).

Cairney, P. (2009) 'The "British Policy Style" and Mental Health: Beyond the Headlines', *Journal of Social Policy*, 38/4: 671–88.

Christiansen, T., and Vaccari1, B. (2006) *The 2006 Reform of Comitology: Problem Solved or Dispute Postponed?* EIPASCOPE 2006/3 (Maastricht: European Institute of Public Administration).

Codex (2001) *Codex Standard for Bouillons and Consommés* (CODEX STAN 117-1981, Rev. 2-2001): www.codexalimentarius.net/download/standards/286/CXS_117e.pdf

Cole, A. (2008) *Governing and Governance in France* (Cambridge: Cambridge University Press).

Colebatch, H., Hoppe, R., and Noordegraaf, M. (eds) (2010) *Working for Policy* (Amsterdam: Amsterdam University Press).

Council of Europe (2002) *Assessing Disability in Europe: Similarities and Differences Report Drawn up by the Working Group on the Assessment of Person-Related Criteria for Allowances and Personal Assistance for People with Disabilities* (Strasbourg: Council of Europe Publishing).

Crick, B. (1964) *In Defence of Politics* (Harmondsworth: Penguin).

Crozier, M. (1964) *The Bureaucratic Phenomenon* (London: Tavistock).

—— (1979) *On ne change pas la société par décret* (Paris: Grasset).

Dahl, R. A. (1969) 'The Concept of Power', in R. Bell, D. V. Edwards, and R. H. Wagner (eds), *Political Power: A Reader in Theory and Research* (New York: Free Press).

DCMS/Home Office/ODPM (2005) 'Drinking Responsibly: The Government's Proposals', Jan.: http://www.homeoffice.gov.uk/docs4/consult_alcohol.html

Department of Commerce (2004) *National Oceanic and Atmospheric Endangered and Threatened Species; Designation of Critical Habitat for 13 Evolutionarily Significant Units of Pacific Salmon (Oncorhynchus spp.) and Steelhead (O. mykiss) in Washington, Oregon, and Idaho; Proposed Rule*, 14 Dec., 50 CFR Part 226 (Washington, DC: Department of Commerce).

Department of Transportation (Research and Special Programs Administration) (2002) *Hazardous Materials; Transportation of Lithium Batteries Notice of Proposed Rulemaking*, 2 Apr., 49 CFR Parts 171, 172, 173, and 175 (Washington, DC: Department of Transportation).

Derlien, H.-U. (2003) 'Mandarins or Managers? The Bureaucratic Elite in Bonn, 1970 to 1987 and Beyond', *Governance*, 16/3: 401–28.

—— (2005) 'German Public Administration: Weberian despite "Modernization"', in K. K. Tummala (ed.), *Comparative Bureaucratic Systems* (Boulder, Colo.: Lexington Books).

de Tocqueville, A. (1945) *Democracy in America* (New York: Alfred A. Knopf).

Dewaele, A., and Gourlay, C. (2005) 'The Stability Instrument: Defining the Commission's Role in Crisis Response', *European Security Review*, 25 (ISIS Europe): 8–12.

Diamant, A. (1957) 'The French Administrative System: The Republic Passes But the Administration Remains', in William J. Siffin (ed.), *Toward the Comparative Study of Administration* (Bloomington, Ind.: Indiana University Press).

Downs, A. (1967) *Inside Bureaucracy* (Boston: Little Brown).

Dunleavy, P. J. (1993) *Democracy, Bureaucracy, and Public Choice* (Hemel Hempstead: Harvester Wheatsheaf).

Dyson, K. (1982) 'West Germany: The Search for a Rationalist Consensus', in J. Richardson (ed.), *Policy Styles in Western Europe* (London: Allen & Unwin).

—— (2010) *The State Tradition in Western Europe* (Colchester: European Consortium for Political Science Research Books).

Egeberg, M. (2004) *Organising Institutional Autonomy in a Political Context: Enduring Tensions in the European Commission's Development*, ARENA Working Paper Series WP 02/04 (Oslo: Centre for European Studies).

Ehrman, H. (1961) 'French Bureaucracy and Organized Interests', *Administrative Science Quarterly*, 5/4: 534–55.

Eichbaum, C., and Shaw, R. (eds) (2010) *Partisan Appointees and Public Servants: An International Analysis of the Role of the Political Advisor* (Cheltenham: Edward Elgar).

Elder, N. C. M. (1970) *Government in Sweden: The Executive at Work* (Oxford: Pergamon).

—— and Page, E. C. (2000) 'Accountability and Control in Next Steps Agencies', in R. A. W. Rhodes (ed.), *Transforming British Government* (Houndmills: Palgrave Macmillan).

EMEA (2004) *CVMP Proposal for a List of Substances Essential for the Treatment of Equidae* (EMEA/CVMP/720/04-FINAL) (London: European Medicines Agency).

Eriksson, L.-E., Lemne, M., and Pålsson, I. (1999) *Demokrati på remiss*, Demokratiutredningens skrift nr 30, Statens Offentliga Utredningar 1999: 144 (Stockholm: Regeringskansliet)

Eschenburg, T. (1955) *Herrschaft der Verbände?* (Stuttgart: Deutsche Verlags-Anstalt).

European Commission (2001) *European Transport Policy for 2010: Time to Decide* (Luxembourg: Office for Official Publications of the European Union).

—— (2004) *Final Report from the Commission to the Council and the European Parliament on the Simplification of the Common Market Organisation in Fruit and Vegetables*, 10.8.2004 COM (2004) 549 (Brussels: European Commission).

—— (2007) *Comitology Committees Assisting the European Commission* (Brussels: Commission of the European Union): http://ec.europa.eu/transparency/regcomitology/include/comitology_committees_EN.pdf

Eymeri-Douzans, J.-M. (2008) 'Les Cabinets ministériels', *Regards sur l'Actualité,* 339 (Mar.): 63–74.
—— (2012) 'France: No Rewards But Privileges', in B. G. Peters and M. Brans (eds), *Rewards of High Public Office* (London: Routledge).
Finer, H. (1937) *The British Civil Service* (London: Fabian Society).
FSIS (Food Safety and Inspection Service of the US Department of Agriculture) (2002) *Food Safety and Inspection Service Current Thinking on Measures that Could Be Implemented to Minimize Human Exposure to Materials that Could Potentially Contain the Bovine Spongiform Encephalopathy Agent* (Washington, DC: FSIS: http://www.fsis.usda.gov/oa/topics/bse_thinking.htm accessed Jan. 2008).
GAO (2003) *Report to Congressional Requesters September 2003* (Washington, DC: General Accounting Office).
Gay, O (2010) *Special Advisers,* Standard Note: SN/PC/03813b (London: House of Commons Library).
Gellhorn, W. (1986) 'The Administrative Procedure Act: The Beginnings', *Virginia Law Review,* 72/2: 219–33.
Georgakakis, D. (2010) 'Tensions within Eurocracy? A Socio-Morphological View', *French Politics,* 8/2: 116–44 (doi:10.1057/fp.2010.9).
Geuijen, K., and t'Hart, P. (2010) 'Flying Blind in Brussels: How National Officials do European Business without Political Steering', in H. Colebatch, R. Hoppe, and M. Noordegraaf (eds), *Working for Policy* (Amsterdam: Amsterdam University Press).
Goetz, K. H. (1999) 'Senior Officials in the German Federal Administration: Institutional Change and Positional Differentiation', in E. C. Page and V. Wright (eds), *Bureaucratic Elites in Western European States: A Comparative Analysis of Top Officials in Eleven Countries* (Oxford: Oxford University Press).
—— (2006) 'German Officials and the Federal Policy Process: The Decline of Sectional Leadership', in E. C. Page and V. Wright (eds), *The Changing Role of the Civil Service in Comparative Perspective* (Basingstoke: Palgrave).
Greer, S. L., and Jarman, H. (2010) 'What Whitehall? Definitions, Demographics and the Changing Civil Service', *Public Policy and Administration,* 25/3: 251–70.
Grémion, P. (1976) *Le pouvoir périphérique* (Paris: Le Seuil).
Hayward, J. E. S. (1973) *The One and Indivisible French Republic* (London: Weidenfeld & Nicolson).
—— (1983) *Governing France: The One and Indivisible Republic* (London: Weidenfeld & Nicolson).
—— (1984) 'Pressure Groups and Pressured Groups in Franco-British Perspective', in D. Kavanagh and G. Peele (eds), *Comparative Government and Politics: Essays in Honour of S. E. Finer* (London: Heinemann).
—— (2010) 'De la collusion au désengagement: Le fin de l'opposition entre centralisation et decentralisation', in Philippe Urfalino and Martha Zuber (eds), *Intelligences de la France: Onze essais sur la politique et la culture* (Paris: Presses de Sciences Po).
Heclo, H. (1977) *A Government of Strangers* (Washington, DC: Brookings).
—— and Madsen, H. (1987) *Policy and Politics in Sweden: Principled Pragmatism* (Philadelphia, Pa.: Temple University Press).

Heritier, A., and Moury, C. (2008) *The European Parliament and Delegation to Comitology* (Lisbon: CIES Working Paper, 39/2008: http://repositorio-iul.iscte.pt/bitstream/10071/716/1/CIES-WP40_Moury_.pdf).
Hewart (Lord Hewart of Bury) (1929) *The New Despotism* (London: Benn).
Hockerts, H.-G. (1980) *Sozialpolitische Entscheidungen im Nachkriegsdeutschland* (Stuttgart: Clett-Cotta).
Hood, C. C., and Lodge, M. (2006) *The Politics of Public Service: Bargains Reward, Competency, Loyalty—and Blame* (Oxford: Oxford University Press).
——Huby, M., and Dunsire, A. (1984) 'Bureaucrats and Budgeting Benefits: How do British Central Government Departments Measure up?', *Journal of Public Policy*, 4/3: 163–79.
Horn, M. J. (1995) *The Political Economy of Public Administration* (Cambridge: Cambridge University Press).
Huber, J., and Shipan, C. (2002) *Deliberate Discretion: Institutional Foundations of Bureaucratic Autonomy in Modern Democracies* (Cambridge: Cambridge University Press).
ICES (International Council for the Exploration of the Sea) (2001) *The ICES Strategic Plan* (Copenhagen: ICES).
Jacobsson, B., Lægreid, P., and Pedersen, O. K. (2001) 'Transforming States: Continuity and Change in the Europeanisation of the Nordic Central Governments', *Score Rapportserie*, 2001/4 (Stockholm: SCORE/Stockholm School of Economics).
Jary, G. (2008) *Joining the Civil Service* (London: National School for Government).
JCSI (Joint Committee on Statutory Instruments) (2008) *Eighth Report of Session 2007–08, HL Paper 47; HC 38-viii* (London: HMSO).
Jobert, B., and Muller, P. (1987) *L'état en action: Politiques publiques et corporatismes* (Paris: Presses Universitaires de France).
Johnson, N. (1978) 'Law as the Articulation of the State in Western Germany: A German Tradition Seen from a British Perspective', *West European Politics*, 1/2: 177–92.
Jordan, A. G. (1982) 'The British Policy Style or the Logic of Negotiation', in A. G. Jordan and J. Richardson (eds), *Policy Styles in Western Europe* (London: George Allen & Unwin).
——and Maloney, M. (2001) 'Britain: Change and Continuity within the New Realities of British Politics', in C. Thomas (ed.), *Political Parties and Interest Groups: Shaping Democratic Governance* (Boulder, Colo.: Lynne Rienner).
Jordan, G., and Maloney, W. (2007) *Democracy and Interest Groups* (London: Palgrave Macmillan).
Jowell, J. (1973) 'The Legal Control of Administrative Discretion', *Public Law*, 18: 178–220.
Kassim, H. (2008) '"Mission Impossible", But Mission Accomplished: The Kinnock Reforms and the European Commission', *Journal of European Public Policy*, 15/5: 648–68.
Katz, R. S., and Mair, P. (1995) 'Changing Models of Party Organization and Party Democracy: The Emergence of the Cartel Party', *Party Politics*, 1/1: 5–31.
Kaufman, H. (1960) *The Forest Ranger: A Study in Administrative Behavior* (Baltimore, MD: Johns Hopkins University Press).

——(1981a) *The Administrative Behavior of Federal Bureau Chiefs* (Washington, DC: Brookings).
——(1981b) 'Fear of Bureaucracy: A Raging Pandemic', *Public Administration Review*, 41/1: 1–9.
Kent, H. (1979) *In on the Act: Memoirs of a Lawmaker* (London: Macmillan).
Kerwin, C. M. (1999) *Rulemaking: How Government Agencies Write Law and Make Policy*, 2nd edn (Washington, DC: CQ Press).
——Furlong, S., and West, W. (2010) 'Interest Groups, Rulemaking, and American Bureaucracy', in R. F. Durant (ed.), *The Oxford Handbook of American Bureaucracy* (Oxford: Oxford University Press).
Kingdon, J. W. (2003) *Agendas, Alternatives and Public Policies*, 2nd edn (New York: Longman).
Kingsley, J. D. (1944) *Representative Bureaucracy* (Yellow Springs, Oh.: Antioch Press).
Knill, Christoph (2001) *The Europeanization of National Administrations: Patterns of Institutional Change and Persistence* (Cambridge: Cambridge University Press).
Krause, G. A. (2010) 'Legislative Delegation of Authority to Bureaucratic Agencies', in R. F. Durant (ed.), *The Oxford Handbook of American Bureaucracy* (Oxford: Oxford University Press).
Laffin, M. (1998) 'The Professions in the Contemporary Public Sector', in M. Laffin (ed.), *Beyond Bureaucracy? The Professions in the Contemporary Public Sector* (Aldershot: Ashgate).
Laird, F. (1990) 'Technocracy Revisited: Knowledge, Power and the Crisis in Energy Decision Making', *Organization and Environment*, 4/1: 49–61.
Larsson, T., and Bäck, H. (2008) *Governing and Governance in Sweden* (Lund: Studentlitteratur).
——and Schaefer, G. (2006) 'The Problem of Democratic Legitimacy in a Supranational Government', in H. Hofmann and A. Türk (eds), *EU Administrative Governance* (Cheltenham: Edward Elgar).
——and Trondal, J. (2006) 'Agenda Setting in the European Commission: How the European Commission Structure and Influence the EU Agenda', in H. C. H. Hofmann and A. H. Türk (eds), *EU Administrative Governance* (Cheltenham: Edward Elgar).
Light, P. C. (1995) *Thickening Government: Federal Hierarchy and the Diffusion of Accountability* (Washington, DC: Brookings).
Lindblom, C. E., and Cohen, D. K. (1979) *Usable Knowledge: Social Science and Social Problem Solving* (London: Yale University Press).
Lowi, T. J. (1964) 'American Business, Public Policy, Case Studies, and Political Theory', *World Politics*, 16/4: 677–715.
Lubbers, J. (2006) *A Guide to Federal Agency Rulemaking*, 4th edn (Washington, DC: American Bar Association).
McConnell, A. (2010) 'Policy Success, Policy Failure and Grey Areas In-Between', *Journal of Public Policy*, 30/3: 345–62.
McCubbins, M. D., and Schwartz, T. (1984) 'Congressional Oversight Overlooked: Police Patrols versus Fire Alarms', *American Journal of Political Science*, 28/1: 167–79.

McCubbins, M. D., Noll, R. G., and Weingast, B. R. (1987) 'Administrative Procedures as Instruments of Political Control', *Journal of Law, Economics, and Organization*, 3/2: 243–77.
Machiavelli, N. (1961) *The Prince* (Harmondsworth: Penguin).
Mann, H. (1952) *Der Untertan* (Berlin: Aufbau Verlag).
Manuela Alfé, M., Christiansen, T., and Piedrafita, S. (2007) 'The Role of Implementing Committees in the EU27', Paper for presentation in the ARENA seminar series, Oslo, 29 May.
Marier, P. (2005) 'Where did the Bureaucrats Go? Role and Influence of the Public Bureaucracy in the Swedish and French Pension Reform Debate', *Governance*, 18/4: 521–44.
Marks, G., Hooghe, L., and Blank, K. (1996) 'European Integration from the 1980s: Statecentric v. Multi-Level Governance', *Journal of Common Market Studies*, 34/3: 341–78.
Mayntz, R., and Scharpf, F. W. (1975) *Policy Making in the German Federal Bureaucracy* (The Hague: Elsevier).
——Andersen, M., Derlien, H.-U., Fiedler, J., Kussau, J., and Treiber, H. (1973) *Programmentwicklung in der Ministerialorganisation. Projektbericht der Projektgruppe Regierungs- und Verwaltungsreform* (Bonn, mimeo).
Mény, Y., and Thoenig, J.-C. (1989) *Politiques publiques* (Paris: Presses Universitaires de France).
Merits Committee (2008) *Joint Committee on Statutory Instruments Eighth Report of Session 2007–08*, HL Paper 47; HC 38-viii (London: HMSO).
Michels, R. (1962) *Political Parties* (New York: Free Press).
Moe, T. (1987) 'An Assessment of the Positive Theory of Congressional Dominance', *Legislative Studies Quarterly*, 12/4: 475–520.
Moravcsik, A. (2001) 'Despotism in Brussels: Misreading the European Union', *Foreign Affairs* (May/June): 114–23.
Müller, W. C. (2006) 'The Changing Role of Austrian Civil Service: The Impact of Politicisation, Public Sector Reform, and Europeanisation', in Edward C. Page and V. Wright (eds), *From the Active to the Enabling State: The Changing Role of Top Officials in European Nations* (Basingstoke: Palgrave).
National Audit Office (2006) 'The Delays in Administering the 2005 Single Payment Scheme in England' *HC 1631 Session 2005–6* (London: HMSO).
National School for Government (2010) 'What is the Civil Service' (Sunningdale: National School for Government, www.nationalschool.gov.uk/downloads/JTCSchapter2.pdf accessed July 2010).
New York Times (2002) 'U.S. Acts to Shrink Endangered Species Habitats', 20 Mar.
Niskanen, W. A. (1971) *Bureaucracy and Representative Government* (Chicago: Aldine Atherton).
NTSB (National Transportation Safety Board) (2008) *Docket No. SA-228, Exhibit No. 17c, NTSB Safety Recommendations Regarding Lithium Batteries and Response History* (Washington, DC: NTSB).
O'Connell, A. J. (2011). 'Qualifications: Law and Practice of Selecting Agency Leaders', Paper presented at the Northwestern Law 'Law and Political Economy Colloquium',

Chicago, Jan. (http://www.law.northwestern.edu/colloquium/politicaleconomy/documents/Spring2011_OConnell.pdf accessed Mar. 2011).
Office for Administrative Affairs (2010) *Facts and Figures: Swedish Government Offices Yearbook 2009* (Stockholm: Office for Administrative Affairs).
OMB (Office of Management and Budget) (2001) *OMB Regulatory Review: Principles and Procedures Memorandum for the President's Management Council Rulemaking OMB's Role in Reviews of Agencies' Draft Rules and the Transparency of Those Reviews* (Washington, DC: OMB).
Page, E. C. (1985) *Political Authority and Bureaucratic Power* (Brighton: Wheatsheaf).
—— (2001) *Governing by Numbers: Delegated Legislation and Everyday Policy Making* (Oxford: Hart Publishing).
—— (2003) 'The Civil Servant as Legislator: Law Making in British Administration', *Public Administration*, 81/4: 651–79.
—— (2006) 'The Origins of Policy', in M. Moran, M. Rein, and R. E. Goodin (eds), *Oxford Handbook of Public Policy* (Oxford: Oxford University Press).
—— (2009) 'Their Word is Law: Parliamentary Counsel and Creative Policy Analysis', *Public Law*, Oct.: 790–811.
—— and Jenkins, B. (2005) *Policy Bureaucracy: Government with a Cast of Thousands* (Oxford: Oxford University Press).
—— and Wright, V. (2006) 'Conclusions: The Demystification of High Bureaucratic Office', in Page and Wright (eds), *From the Active to the Enabling State: The Changing Role of Top Officials in European Nations* (Basingstoke: Palgrave).
Peters, B. G., and Pierre, J. (2004) *Politicization of the Civil Service in Comparative Perspective: The Quest for Control* (London: Routledge).
Pierre, J. (1995) 'Governing the Welfare State: Public Administration, the State and Society in Sweden', in J. Pierre (ed.), *Bureaucracy in the Modern State* (Aldershot: Edward Elgar).
—— (2004) 'Politicization of the Swedish Civil Service: A Necessary Evil—Or Just Evil?', in G. B. Peters and J. Pierre (eds), *Politicization of the Civil Service in Comparative Perspective: The Quest for Control* (London: Routledge).
Pollitt, C., and Talbot, C. (2003) *Unbundled Government: A Critical Analysis of the Global Trend to Agencies, Quangos and Contractualisation* (London: Routledge).
Premfors, R., and Sundström, G. (2007) *Regeringskansliet* (Malmö: Liber).
Pressman, J., and Wildavsky, A. W. (1973) *Implementation: How Great Expectations in Washington are Dashed in Oakland* (Berkeley, Calif.: University of California Press).
Public Administration Select Committee (2010a) *Outsiders and Insiders: External Appointments to the Senior Civil Service*, Seventh Report of Session 2009–10, HC241 (London: HMSO).
—— (2010b) *Outsiders and Insiders: External Appointments to the Senior Civil Service: Further Report with the Government Response to the Committee's Seventh Report of Session 2009–10*, Twelfth Report of Session 2009–10, Report and appendix, HC 500 (London: HMSO).
Pünder, H. (2009) 'Democratic Legitimation of Delegated Legislation: A Comparative View on the American, British and German Law', *International and Comparative Law Quarterly*, 58/2: 353–78.
Putnam, R. D. (1973) 'The Political Attitudes of Senior Civil Servants in Western Europe, a Preliminary Report', *British Journal of Political Science*, 3/3: 257–90.

Renzsch, W. (2010) 'Kontinuitäten und Diskontinuitäten in Entscheidungsprozessen über föderale Finanzbeziehungen oder: Die ewig Unvollendete', *Perspektiven der Wirtschaftspolitik*, 11/3: 288–306.

Rhinard, M. (2002) 'The Democratic Legitimacy of the European Union Committee System', *Governance*, 15/2: 185–210.

Rhodes, R. A. W. (2007) 'The Everyday Life of a Minister: A Confessional and Impressionist Tale', in R. A. W. Rhodes, P. t'Hart, and M. Noordegraaf (eds), *The Ethnography of Government Elites: Up Close and Personal* (Houndmills: Palgrave).

—— (2009) 'Frank Stacey Memorial Lecture 2008: Scenes from the Departmental Court', *Public Policy and Administration*, 24/4: 437–56.

—— (2011) *Everyday Life in British Government* (Oxford: Oxford University Press).

Ridley, F. F. (ed.) (1979) *Government and Administration in Western Europe* (Oxford: Martin Roberston).

Rose, R. (1977) *Managing Presidential Objectives* (London: Macmillan).

—— (1990) 'Inheritance Before Choice in Public Policy', *Journal of Theoretical Politics*, 2/3: 263–91.

Rose, N. and Miller, P. (1992) 'Political Power Beyond the State: Problematics of Government', *British Journal of Sociology*, 43/2: 173–205.

Ross, G. (1995) *Jacques Delors and European Integration* (Cambridge: Polity).

Rouban, L. (2007) 'Public Management and Politics: Senior Bureaucrats in France', *Public Administration*, 85/2: 473–501.

Ruin, O. (2000) 'Managing Coalition Governments: The Swedish Experience', *Parliamentary Affairs*, 53/4: 710–20.

Sager, F., and Rosser, C. (2009) 'Weber, Wilson, and Hegel: Theories of Modern Bureaucracy', *Public Administration Review*, 69/6: 1136–47.

Schattschneider, E. E. (1960) *The Semi Sovereign People: A Realist's View of Democracy in America* (Chicago: Chicago University Press).

Schmidt, V. A. (2006) *Democracy in Europe: The EU and National Polities* (Oxford: Oxford University Press).

Selznick, P. (1949) *TVA and the Grass Roots: A Study in the Sociology of Formal Organization* (Berkeley, Calif.: University of California Press).

Shapiro, S., and Guston, D. (2007) 'Procedural Control of the Bureaucracy, Peer Review, and Epistemic Drift', *Journal of Public Administration Research and Theory*, 17/4: 535–51.

Sharpe, L. J. (1976) 'Instrumental Participation and Urban Government', in J. A. G. Griffith (ed.), *From Policy to Administration* (London: Allen & Unwin).

Sherif, P. (1976) 'The Sociology of Public Bureaucracies: A Trend Report', *Current Sociology*, 24/2: 1–175.

Simon, H. A. (1945) *Administrative Behavior* (New York: Free Press).

Sklansky, D. (2002) *The Theory of Poker: A Professional Poker Player Teaches You How to Think Like One*, 4th edn (Las Vegas, Nev.: Two Plus Two).

Smith, A. (ed.) (2006) *Politics and the European Commission: Actors, Interdependence, Legitimacy* (London: Routledge).

SNFBP (Syndicat National des Fabricants de Bouillons et Potages) (2005) *Code de bonnes pratiques pour les soupes, bouillons et consommés* (Paris: SNFBP, Sept).

SOU (Statens Offentliga Utredningar) (2004) *Kvinnors organisering: Betänkande av Utredningen statligt stöd för kvinnors organisering*, SOU 2004: 59 (Stockholmn: Regeringskansliet).

Sowa, J. E., and Selden, S. C. (2003) 'Administrative Discretion and Active Representation: An Expansion of the Theory of Representative Bureaucracy', *Public Administration Review*, 63/6: 700–10.

Stevens, A., and Stevens, H. (2000) *Brussels Bureaucrats? The Administration of the European Union* (Houndmills: Palgrave).

Suleiman, E. N. (1975) *Politics, Power and Bureaucracy in France: The Administrative Elite* (Princeton: Princeton University Press).

Svara, J. H. (1998) 'The Politics–Administration Dichotomy Model as Aberration', *Public Administration Review*, 58/1: 51–8.

Talbot, C., and Johnson, C. (2007) 'Seasonal Cycles in Public Management: Disaggregation and Re-aggregation', *Public Money and Management*, 27(1): 53–60.

Teasdale, J. (2009) 'Statute Law Revision: Repeal, Consolidation or Something More', *European Journal of Law Reform*, 11/2: 157–212.

Thoenig, J.-C. (1987) *L'ère des technocrates* (Paris, L'Harmattan).

Tiessen, J., and van Stolk, J. C. (2007) *The Introduction of Single Farm Payments in Finland and Germany* (Santa Monica, Calif.: Rand Corporation for the National Audit Office).

Trondal, J. (2006) 'Governing at the Frontier of the European Commission: The Case of Seconded National Experts', *West European Politics*, 29/1: 147–60.

——(2007) *The Anatomy of Autonomy: Reassessing the Autonomy of the European Commission*, Working Paper, 4, Mar. (Oslo: University of Oslo ARENA Centre for European Studies).

Tsebelis, G., and Garrett, G. (2001) 'The Institutional Foundations of Intergovernmentalism and Supranationalism in the European Union', *International Organization*, 55/2: 357–90.

Ward, K. (2007) 'Casino Blues', *Environment and Planning A*, 39/7: 1534–9.

Washington Post (2002) 'Immigrant Fraud Case May Reach Beyond Virginia: Arlington Lawyer Accused of Filing Bogus Labor Forms', 31 July: B1.

——(2007) '7 Decisions of Species Revised. Fish and Wildlife Service Cites Possibility of Improper Influence', 28 Nov.: A3.

Weber, M. (1972) *Wirtschaft und Gesellschaft*, 5th edn (Tübingen: JCB Mohr).

Weiler, J. H. H. (1999) *The Constitution of Europe* (Cambridge: Cambridge University Press).

Weingast, B. R. (1984) 'The Congressional-Bureaucratic System: A Principal–Agent Perspective', *Public Choice*, 44/1: 147–91.

West, W. F. (1984) 'Administrative Discretion: The Pursuit of Rationality and Responsiveness', *American Journal of Political Science*, 28/2: 340–60.

——(1988) 'The Growth of Internal Conflict in Administrative Regulation', *Public Administration Review*, 48/4: 773–82.

——(1997) 'Searching for a Theory of Bureaucratic Structure', *Journal of Public Administration Research and Theory*, 7/4: 591–614.

——(2004) 'Formal Procedures, Informal Processes, Accountability, and Responsiveness in Bureaucratic Policy Making: An Institutional Policy Analysis', *Public Administration Review*, 64/1: 66–80.

Wille, A. (2010) 'The Politicization of the EU Commission: New Challenges, New Professionals?' Paper prepared for the 32nd EGPA Annual Conference, Toulouse, 8–10 Sept.

Wilson, J. Q. (1989) *Bureaucracy* (New York: Basic Books).

Wood, B. D., and Waterman, R. W. (1991) 'The Dynamics of Political Control of the Bureaucracy', *American Political Science Review*, 85/3: 801–28.

Index

Aberbach, Joel vi, 9, 13, 66, 168
Allison, Graham 16, 120
Anton, Tom 86, 97

Balla, Steven 8
Bureaucracy 1–18
  conflict resolution 12
  fear of 2
bureaucratic sabotage 14–15
bureaucrats
  belief systems 7, 16–17
  compliance with politician preferences 4
  discretion of 5, 9–10, 16, 146, 150, 156–7, 164–5, 167
  expertise 13, 171, 173–5
  motivations of 15–17, 159–75
  observation of procedural norms 152, 161, 165–6, 168
  policy adjustment role 170–2
  regularization role 169–70
  representative bureaucracy 15–16
  routinization role 168–9
  self-interest 15, 159–60, 165, 167
  socialization 15–16, 120, 160, 167
  subordination 166–7

Cairney, Paul 58
Cole, Alistair 26, 44–5
Crozier, Michel ix, 17, 26

decrees
  selection for study 20–1
  technical/scientific 21, 153–4, 176–7
  see also individual country entries
Derlien, Hans-Ulrich 84
Downs, Antony 12, 16, 120
Dyson, Kenneth 66, 169

Egeberg, Morten 127
Ehrman, Henry 45
European Court of Human Rights (ECHR) 51–2, 169
European Union
  bureaucrats' paradise 123–4, 143–4
  cabinets 18, 127–8, 132–3, 137–8, 141–3, 154
  civil service ranks and grades 126–7
  codification of laws 130–1
  College of Commissioners 136, 141

COMDOCs (Commission Documents) 135, 143
comitology 123–4, 131–2, 137, 140–1, 144, 150, 152, 156, 161–2, 164–5, 171
commissioners 123, 126–30, 132–4, 136–44, 154, 156
COREPER (Permanent Representatives of the Member States) 141–2
Council of the European Union 123–6, 128–30, 132–5, 137, 140–4, 154, 156
decrees
  development 132–9
  initiation 128–32
  legitimation 139–43
  selected decrees
    Fish Quotas 125, 128–129, 132–133, 135, 141–142, 145, 148, 154, 168, 171, 176
    Forest Focus 125, 127, 131, 132, 138, 139, 140, 141, 144, 145, 169, 176
    Horse Medicines 125, 131, 132, 133, 134, 135, 137, 138, 140, 141, 144, 145, 150, 155, 156, 158, 162, 164, 165, 170, 176
    Marco Polo 125, 128, 129, 132, 135, 136, 137, 142, 143, 144, 155, 156, 176
    Silkworm 125, 130–132, 138–139, 140, 144, 145, 150, 176
    Stability Instrument 125, 128–30, 132, 135–6, 142–3, 145, 176, 180
    Tariff Simplification 20, 125, 131–2, 137–41, 144–5, 176
detached national experts 127, 131, 134
EMEA (European Medicines Agency) 135
European Coal and Steel Community 128
European Parliament 124–6, 128–32, 137, 140–4
GRI (Groupe des relations interinstitutionelles) 142–3
interservice consultation 136
Legal Service of Commission 120, 134, 138–40, 142
national flags system 127
political appointments 126–7
political leadership 126–7
Presidency of the Council 143–4
RELEX (External relations DG) 136
Treaty of Rome 131, 139

everyday policy making vii–viii, 8–9, 11, 18–20, 23–5, 45, 54, 63–4, 67, 69, 86, 97, 98, 121, 146, 174
Eymeri-Douzans, Jean-Michel 27–8

Finer, Herman 47
fire alarm controls 5, 8, 12, 42, 151, 153, 172
forms of policy making
  ceremonial 151
  consequential 149–50, 152, 154–7, 169, 173, 176–7
  directed 149, 151, 154–9, 168, 170, 173, 174, 176–7
  undirected 149, 151–2, 154–9, 161–4, 170, 173–4, 176–7
France
  AFSSA (Agence française de sécurité sanitaire des aliments) 30, 36, 41, 161, 162, 164, 166
  AFSSAPS (Agence française de sécurité sanitaire des produits de santé) 36, 42, 162, 164
  bleu de Matignon 34, 36, 45
  cabinet 14, 18, 26–8, 34–5, 38–40, 42–3, 45, 48, 67, 149, 152–3, 157, 172
  civil service grades 27–8
  Conseil d'Etat 22–3, 31, 33–4, 36–7, 40–1, 43, 45, 152–3, 161–2, 164, 173
  conseiller technique 28, 34–5, 39, 45
  decrees
    development 33–42
    initiation 28–33
    legitimation 33–5, 36–7
    selected decrees
      Bird Flu 29, 30, 35–6, 41, 43, 157, 166, 170–1, 176
      Casinos 29–30, 36–8, 42–3, 45–6, 149, 151, 154, 157, 176
      Champagne 29, 32, 36, 41, 43–4, 46, 148, 162, 164, 176
      Cosmetics 29, 32, 36, 41–3, 46, 162, 176
      Farmers 29, 31–2, 36, 42, 46, 157, 161, 176
      Handicap 29, 32, 36–7, 41, 43, 46, 162, 176
      Housing 29, 32, 36, 40–1, 46, 162, 176
      Osteopaths 29, 31, 34, 36–7, 39–40, 42, 45–6, 154, 157, 159, 169, 176
      Rhine 29, 32, 35–6, 42–3, 46, 150–1, 161–2, 176
      Soups 29–30, 34, 36–7, 41, 43, 46, 162, 169, 171, 176
  decree types 7, 21, 28–9, 33–5
  'expert' bodies 30, 35–6, 41–5, 164, 171, 173
  grands corps 18, 27–8, 44
  hauts fonctionnaires 27–8

hierarchy in ministries 27–8
interest groups 26, 28–45, 59, 154, 171, 173–4
ni-ni, les 31, 39–40, 45
statism 43–4
trade unions 38–9, 44

Germany
  Bundeskanzleramt 70, 81
  Bundesrat 70, 78–9, 81–2, 152, 162, 164
  civil service ranks and grades 69
  classical bureaucrat 66, 83, 84
  decrees
    development 76–81
    initiation 72–6
    legitimation 81–3
  selected decrees
    Civil Emergencies 67, 73–4, 85, 160, 162, 176
    Employee Insurance 62, 67, 75–6, 85, 176
    Fiscal Equalization 67, 75–6, 85, 148, 157, 176
    Milk Quotas 67, 72, 74, 80–3, 85, 157, 160, 162, 176
    Noise Maps 67, 71–2, 76–8, 81–3, 85, 157, 159–60, 162, 176
    Ship Safety 67, 75–6, 85, 148, 157, 176
  Eckpunktpapier 77, 157
  Federführung 70–2, 76, 82–3
  gemeinsame Geschäftsordnung (GGO) 68–70, 72, 76–7, 80–3, 172–3
  Länder 13, 67–8, 70, 72, 74–5, 77–83, 148, 162, 164
  law, importance of 69–70
  Ministry of Justice approval 82–3
  ministry structures 68
  political craft 3, 66
  politische Beamte (political officials) 68–9, 76–7, 84
  Referat 69–83
  Ressort 71–2, 76, 78, 80–3, 171, 173, 175
  separation of politics from administration 83–4
  Staatssekretär 68–70, 78, 80
Goetz, Klaus 3, 66, 69
governmentality 17
Grémion, Pierre 44

Hayward, Jack x, 26, 44–5
Heclo, Hugh 14, 87, 93, 101–2
hierarchy, principle of 12, 152
Hood, Christopher 4, 9, 15, 18, 66, 68
Hooghe, Liesbet 124
Huber, John 13, 98

implementation 6

Index

Kassim, Hussein 127
Kaufman, Herbert 2, 9, 16–17, 120
Kerwin, Cornelius 11, 101
Kingdon, John 3, 6, 100, 122
Kingsley, J. Donald 47, 98
Krause, George 4, 8–10

Light, Paul 3, 7, 14
Lodge, Martin 4, 18, 66, 68

Marks, Gary 124
Mayntz, Renate 8, 69
Mény, Yves 44
methodology
   comparative 17–18
   decrees 18–22
   sample size 22–3, 156
Moravscik, Andrew 123–4
Müller, Wolfgang 14

Niskanen, William 15, 160

Peters, B. Guy viii, 3, 22
Pierre, Jon viii, 3, 88, 90
'police patrol' controls 5, 42, 151
politician involvement in decree making
   cues 11–12, 151–3
   disposition 12–13, 153–5
   frequency 146–8, 158–9
   institutional capacity 11, 14–15, 155–8
precedent, importance of 161–4
primary legislation 6, 19, 20, 152
principal-agent theory vii, viii, 5, 7–11
public choice approach 15–16, 24, 159, 166
Putnam, Robert 6, 9, 13, 66, 83, 168

representative bureaucracy 15–16
Rhodes, Roderick 4, 54–5, 63–4, 67
Rockman, Bert 6, 9, 13, 66, 168

Sarkozy, Nicolas 22, 32, 38, 39, 149
Scharpf, Fritz 8, 69
Schattschneider, Erwin 13, 153
Schmidt, Vivian 26, 43
scientific advice 30, 128–9, 132–6, 139, 149, 168, 171
Selznick, Philip 120
Shipan, Charles 13, 98
Simon, Herbert 17, 120
Suleiman, Ezra 13, 26, 29
Sweden
   advisers, political 87–8, 90–1, 93–8, 156, 158
   agencies in 5, 86, 89–90
   civil service ranks and grades 89
   decrees development 92–7
      initiation 90–2

   legitimation 92–3, 96–7
   selected decrees
      Electrical Goods 91, 97, 99, 177
      Free Year 90–1, 93–4, 98–9, 159, 176
      Public Employment 91, 95, 99, 176
      Rescue Services Agency 92, 96, 99, 154, 176
      Single Farm Payment 92, 94–5, 98–9, 177
      Unemployed Graduates 91, 95–6, 99, 176
      Women's Organizations 90, 96–7, 99, 176
   delning 93, 95–6
   gemensam beredning 93
   government as source of authority 87–9, 92
   political leadership in ministries 88
   remiss 97
   small size of ministries 88–9, 93, 98
   state secretary 88, 90, 92–3, 95–7, 156
   'Swedish Model' 86–7

technocracy 13
Thoenig, Jean-Claude 27, 44
Trondal, Jarle 127, 144

United Kingdom
   affirmative resolution 61–3, 153, 162–4
   anticipated reaction of ministers 4, 47–8, 55–8, 164, 166, 171
   civil servants, social background 47
   civil service grades and ranks 48–9
   conceptual divination 47–8, 56–8, 62
   consultation 58–60
   decrees
      development 52–61
      initiation 49–52
      legitimation 61–3
   selected decrees
      Alcohol Disorder Zones 50, 54–7, 60–2, 65, 154, 163, 177
      Animal Mutilations 50, 57–8, 61–2, 65, 163, 169, 177
      Casinos 50, 52–3, 65, 163, 177, 187
      Criminal Justice 50, 65, 163, 177
      Fire Services 51, 53, 65, 148, 159, 162, 168, 177
      HIP (Home Information Pack) 50, 55–7, 65, 162, 166, 171, 177
      Mental Capacity 51–2, 60–1, 65, 163, 171, 177
      Mesothelioma 50, 54–6, 63, 65, 160, 162, 176
      Offender Management 50, 52–3, 58, 165, 177

United Kingdom (*cont.*)
    Police Best Value 51, 54–5, 65, 163, 171, 177
    TV Multiplex 13, 51–2, 57–8, 61, 65, 163, 177
    Utilities Billing 50–1, 60, 65, 161, 163, 177
  guidance on decrees 49, 60, 64
  House of Lords 50, 61–2
  interdepartmental consultation 60–1
  Joint Committee on Statutory Instruments (JCSI) 61, 63, 163–4
  junior ministers 14, 48
  Merits Committee (House of Lords Committee on the Merits of Statutory Instruments) 61–3, 162–4
  Ofcom (Office of Communications) 51, 163, 164
  private office (of minister) 55, 62–3, 67
  Public Service Agreements 54–5
  special advisers (SpAds) 3, 48, 54, 63
  stakeholders 53, 57–9
  The Thick of It 47
  Yes, Minister 47
United States
  ANPR (Advance Notice of Proposed Rulemaking) 111
  agency, importance of 101, 105, 110, 112, 115, 120–1, 171
  APA (Administrative Procedure Act) 8, 100–1, 110–11
  civil service grades 103–4
  Congress, Houses of 3, 10–11, 101–2, 107–8, 111, 119
  courts 106, 116–18
  decrees
    development 105, 107, 119, 122, 163–4, 166, 170–1, 177
    initiation 7, 104, 107–8, 111, 113, 118–19, 122, 154, 161, 163–4, 168, 177
    legitimation 105, 107, 115, 119, 122, 169, 177
    selected decrees
      Alien Substitution 104–6, 115–16, 122, 154, 170–1, 177
      BSE (Bovine Spongiform Encephalopathy) 104, 109–10, 118, 122, 155, 158, 177
      Criminal Checks 104, 108, 118–19, 122, 177
      Exchange Visitor 105, 107, 119, 122, 163–4, 166, 170–1, 177
      Katrina 103–4, 108–9, 118–19, 122, 158, 177
      Lithium 7, 104, 107–8, 111, 113, 118–19, 122, 154, 161, 163–4, 168, 177
      Mentor 104–5, 107, 119, 122, 163
      Privacy Act 105, 107, 115, 119, 122, 169, 177
      Salmon 104, 106, 111, 117–18, 122, 158, 163, 166, 169–70, 177
    types of 110–11
  executive leadership positions 102–3
  Executive Order 12866 111
  GAO (Government Accountability Office) 100, 107, 119, 163–4, 166, 171
  Health Care Financing Administration 8
  'notice and comment' procedure 5, 8, 111–12
  NPRM (Notice of Proposed Rulemaking) 111–13
  OIRA (Office of Information and Regulatory Affairs) 102, 111
  OMB (Office of Management and Budget) 102, 111–14, 117, 119, 153, 164
  Paperwork Reduction Act 102, 111–12
  political appointees 3, 100–4, 108–9, 111, 116, 121

Weber, Max 2, 5, 8, 17, 47, 66, 84, 166, 175
Weiler, Joseph 124
West, William 8, 15, 101, 110–12
Wilson, James 18